Imperial Rome AD *193 to 284*

D1479245

The Edinburgh History of Ancient Rome
General Editor: J. S. Richardson

Early Rome to 290 BC: The Beginnings of the City and the Rise of the Republic
Guy Bradley

Rome and the Mediterranean 290 to 146 BC: The Imperial Republic
Nathan Rosenstein

The End of the Roman Republic 146 to 44 BC: Conquest and Crisis
Catherine Steel

Augustan Rome 44 BC to AD 14: The Restoration of the Republic and the Establishment of the Empire
J. S. Richardson

Imperial Rome AD 14 to 192: The First Two Centuries
Jonathan Edmondson

Imperial Rome AD 193 to 284: The Critical Century
Clifford Ando

Imperial Rome AD 284 to 363: The New Empire
Jill Harries

From Rome to Byzantium AD 363 to 565: The Transformation of Ancient Rome
A. D. Lee

Imperial Rome AD 193 to 284
The Critical Century

Clifford Ando

EDINBURGH
University Press

Edinburgh University Press Ltd
22 George Square, Edinburgh EH8 9LF

www.euppublishing.com

Reprinted 2013

Typeset in Sabon
by Norman Tilley Graphics Ltd, Northampton,
and printed and bound in Great Britain
by CPI Group (UK) Ltd, Croydon, CR0 4YY

A CIP record for this book is available from the
British Library

ISBN 978 0 7486 2050 0 (hardback)
ISBN 978 0 7486 2051 7 (paperback)
ISBN 978 0 7486 2920 6 (webready PDF)
ISBN 978 0 7486 5534 2 (epub)
ISBN 978 0 7486 5535 9 (Amazon ebook)

Published with the support of the Edinburgh University
Scholarly Publishing Initiatives Fund.

Contents

Figures

Series editor's preface

Rome, the city and its empire, stands at the center of the history of Europe, of the Mediterranean, and of lands which we now call the Middle East. Its influence through the ages which followed its transformation into the Byzantine Empire down to modern times can be seen across the world. This series is designed to present for students and all who are interested in the history of western civilization the changing shape of the entity that was Rome, through its earliest years, the development and extension of the republic, the shift into the Augustan Empire, the development of the imperial state which grew from that, and the differing patterns of that state which emerged in east and west in the fourth to sixth centuries. It covers not only the political and military history of that shifting and complex society but also the contributions of the economic and social history of the Roman world to that change and growth and the intellectual contexts of these developments. The team of contributors, all scholars at the forefront of research in archaeology and history in the English-speaking world, present in the eight volumes of the series an accessible and challenging account of Rome across a millennium and a half of its expansion and transformation. Each book stands on its own as a picture of the period it covers and together the series aims to answer the fundamental question: what was Rome, and how did a small city in central Italy become one of the most powerful and significant entities in the history of the world?

John Richardson, General Editor

Acknowledgements

Once upon a time, it was my great privilege to read many of the literary texts cited in this work in the company of David Potter, whose work has done so much to illuminate the history of the third century. In preparing to write this book, I returned for the first time in many years to *Prophecy and History in the Crisis of the Roman Empire* and found it, if anything, an even more impressive achievement than on first encounter. To David, my thanks.

The invitation to write this volume came from John Richardson, and it was supervised at the Press by Carol MacDonald. Without John, it would not have been written; and without Carol, it would not have been finished. I owe debts of a different kind to Thomas Keith, who read the text and compiled the list of works cited; to Kate Milco, who helped with the chronology; and to Bernhard Palme, who solved various papyrological problems when I despaired of an answer.

Formal acknowledgement for maps and photographs appears below, but as many will appreciate, assembling even a limited program of maps and illustrations requires aid and kindness that no such list can properly convey. For permissions, assistance, photographs and friendship, I wish to express deep gratitude to Matthew Canepa, Olivier Hekster, Andy Meadows, John Nicols, David Potter, Richard Talbert and Brian Turner.

This book was written in July and August 2011 in Berkeley, California, in the company of my son Theodore. We are grateful to Irma Reyna for her hospitality and likewise to Ari Bryen for conversation and good cheer. Nor could we have left Chicago behind without unshakeable confidence in Ruth's infinite care for cats.

My primary debt is to Theodore. It cannot be easy to watch someone else write a book. He was nonetheless an ideal companion in writing, eating, shopping and playing. I would not wish another such summer on him, but it was precious to me.

Maps 1 and 2 are © 2011, Ancient World Mapping Center (www. unc.edu/awmc). My thanks to Richard Talbert and Brian Turner for their assistance with customization. Terrain depiction calculated from Environmental Systems Research Institute. SRTM Shaded Relief, on ESRI Data & Maps 2006 [DVD-ROM]. Redlands, CA.

Maps 3 and 4 were provided by John Nicols and Olivier Hekster.

The figures not in the public domain include 1, which is reproduced with the kind permission of Kelley Ross; 7, which was supplied by the Bildportal der Kunstmuseen and is reproduced with its permission; 8 and 15, which were supplied by the British Museum and are reproduced with its permission; 10 and 14, which were supplied by Matthew Canepa; 11, which is reproduced with the permission of the Papyrology Collection, Graduate Library, University of Michigan; and 12 and 13, which are reproduced with the permission of the American Numismatic Society.

Abbreviations

Abbreviations follow those in the *Oxford Classical Dictionary*, 3rd edn; exceptions are listed below.

APIS	Advanced Papyrological Information System
CFA	John Scheid, ed., *Commentarii Fratrum Arvalium Qui Supersunt*
CPR	*Corpus Papyrorum Raineri*
Dodgeon-Lieu	See Dodgeon and Lieu 1991
Gardner-Lieu	See Gardner and Lieu 2004
Girard-Sens	P. F. Girard and F. Senn, *Les lois des Romains*
HD	*Epigraphische Datenbank Heidelberg*
HGM	L. Dindorf, ed., *Historici Graeci Minores*
IAM	*Inscriptions antiques du Maroc*
IGBR	*Inscriptiones Graecae in Bulgaria repertae*
IGLS	*Inscriptions grecques et latines de la Syrie*
ILTun.	*Inscriptions latines de la Tunisie*
OLD	P. G. W. Glare, ed., *Oxford Latin Dictionary*
P.Abinnaeus	H. I. Bell et al., eds, *The Abinnaeus Archive*
P. Apokrimata	W. L. Westermann and A. A. Schiller, eds, *Apokrimata: Decisions of Septimius Severus on Legal Matters*
P.Euphrates	See Feissel and Gascou 1995
P.Hever	*Aramaic, Hebrew and Greek Documentary Texts from Nahal Hever and Other Sites, with an Appendix containing Alleged Qumran Texts*
P.Yadin	*The Documents from the Bar Kochba Period in the Cave of Letters, I. Greek Papyri*
RS	Michael Crawford, ed., *Roman Statutes*
SB	F. Preisigke et al., *Sammelbuch griechischen Urkunden aus Ägypten*
Sel.Pap.	A. S. Hunt and C. C. Edgar, eds, *Select Papyri*
SPP	*Studien zur Palaeographie und Papyruskunde*

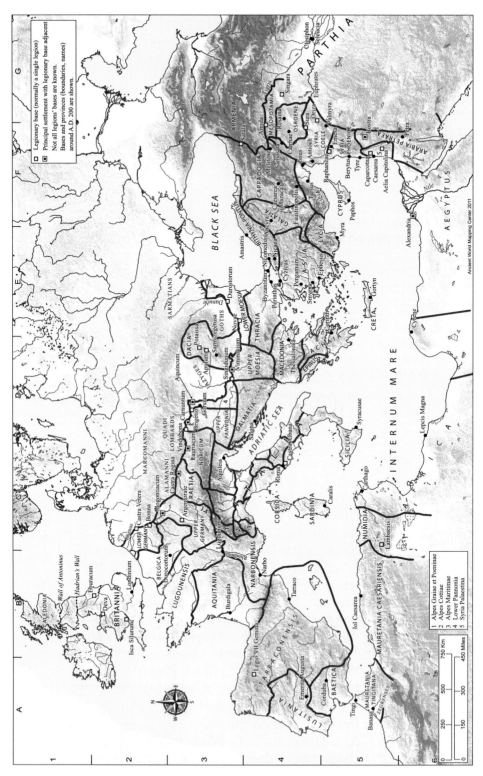

Map 1 The Roman Empire in the age of Septimius Severus

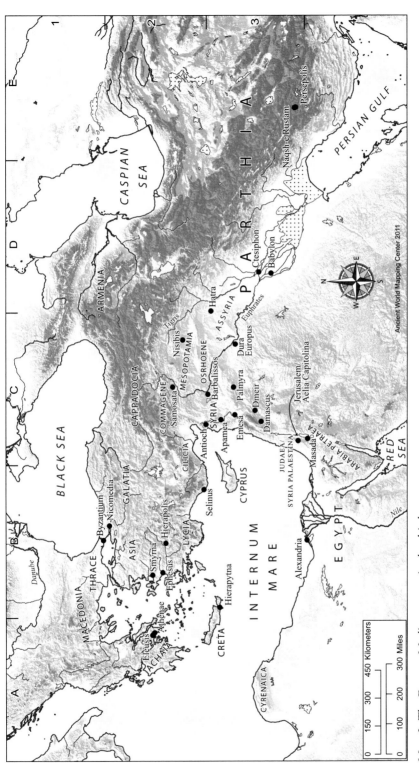

Map 2 The Eastern Mediterranean in the third century AD

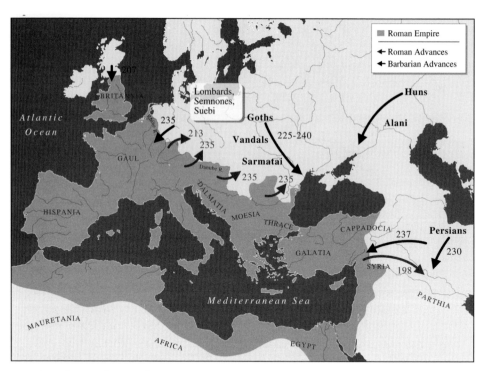

Map 3 Military advances from Septimius Severus to Gordian III. Courtesy of John Nicols and Olivier Hekster

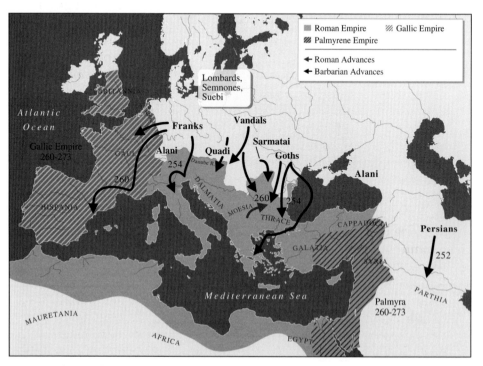

Map 4 Military advances from Papienus to Diocletian. Courtesy of John Nicols and Olivier Hekster

CHAPTER 1

A critical century

The period of roughly a century between the death of Commodus on December 31, 192 and the accession of Diocletian on November 20, 284 transformed the Roman empire. This was so on a number of levels. Here I name four; still others will be explored in the pages that follow. First, the empire was frequently attacked, sometimes simultaneously on multiple borders. Its resources were thereby seriously depleted and select populations placed under enormous pressure. The territorial integrity of the empire was threatened and might well have collapsed. Processes of experimentation in government at virtually all levels, from office-holding to monetary policy, accelerated. The state that emerged at the end of the century was in fundamental respects a new polity. It would be transformed again in the half century that followed.

Second, the long-standing unwillingness of the governing class to articulate and sustain rules of succession had long produced, with regular irregularity, irruptions of political instability. These occurred in the third century as well, but their severity and impact were greatly exacerbated by the pressures of war. This was so for the simple reason that many emperors and would-be emperors died in battle. It was also so for the complex reason that success in war and defense of empire were among the principal foundations of imperial legitimacy. An emperor who could not defend the empire was open to challenge; generals victorious in some regional effort of defense might well imagine themselves – might rightly imagine themselves – acceding to imperial rule.

Third, in AD 212, under circumstances that remain obscure (even the date is open to question), the emperor Caracalla extended Roman citizenship to nearly all free-born residents of the empire. This was clearly an event of enormous symbolic importance: if an empire to be an empire must rule over someone, the Antonine Constitution – as Caracalla's decree is now commonly denominated – might be regarded as no less than an unprecedented act of imperial self-abrogation. Its consequences for social, legal and political life are difficult to trace, but momentous nonetheless.

Fourth, in complex relation to developments in social history (of which the universal grant of citizenship was one), the religious landscape of the Roman world changed dramatically across the third century. Here I single out two trends, but others will be discussed later. On the one hand, in keeping with long-standing developments in civic cult, individuals and institutions at all levels of society experimented with ritual forms in order to articulate the nature of political and social belonging in a state that sought at last to embrace all its members, even as it confronted what seemed existential threats. And on the other, numerous cults dissociated from narrowly civic or governmental structures expanded their reach, likewise capitalizing on very precisely the possibilities provided by empire. (One of those cults, that of Christ, described its own genesis in the age of Augustus as an act of Providence: on this view, God gave his only son to the world at the very moment when it was unified by Rome, precisely to provide a context for the spread of Christianity.)

This volume attempts to trace the events and chart the trends that might substantiate these claims. In keeping with the aims of the series, its ambition is not to rehearse a narrative of war and action, but to explore and explain broad-scale changes in state and society. That said, in this volume (as in select others), events in war and politics will often move to the fore. This must be so in part because the purely political and military history of the third century is enormously complex, and even in simplified form must strain the patience (and indeed the credulity) of the intelligent reader. But it must also happen because the vast upheaval suffered by the structures of the state played an essential causal role in shaping just those broad-scale changes that are this volume's main focus. This is true, I think, even though it lies in the nature of causation of this kind that it cannot be strictly documented – all the more so given the state of evidence prevailing for the third-century Roman empire (on this see further below, pp. 12–13).

This tension between an interest in social historical change and the irreducibility of politics tracks another, in form. The history of war and politics – of usurpers killing emperors and, having themselves become rulers, themselves being killed in turn – lends itself to narrative. But changes in political culture; the rise and fall in prominence of particular trade routes; shifts in the popularity of particular cults – histories of phenomena such as these must take a different form. Nor can a close relation always be maintained between the chronological frameworks of the two schemes: the facts of ancient economic or legal history, as it were, are not keyed to the events of imperial history. The chapters of this volume seek to balance among themselves, and within themselves, the desire to unfold a sequential narrative of politics and the challenge of describing developments in social and cultural conduct.

In what remains of this introduction, I offer a series of remarks, observations and sketches of the Roman empire on the eve of the third-century crisis. The resulting picture is not intended to be comprehensive, nor do I restrict all reflection on earlier history to this chapter (for example, on legal relations before Caracalla see pp. 76–93). I concentrate rather on those issues regarding which some knowledge is essential in order to understand the import and consequences of the actions and events narrated in the immediately following chapters.

Imperial politics in the Antonine Age

The system of imperial rule instituted by Augustus and both solidified and modified over the first two centuries of this era might be described in a number of ways. Here I focus on the dynamics of imperial succession. The reasons for this are two. First, the civil wars that erupted when the succession was contested wreaked untold devastation – through irregular exactions, in loss of life and destruction of property, and disruption to agricultural and other productivity – and this effect was greatly multiplied in the third century, when rapid turnover and military weakness undermined, through negative feedback, the ability of any given emperor to consolidate his claim to legitimacy and grip on power.[1] Figure 1 offers a schematic representation of *one* aspect of imperial politics in the third century, namely, an ordering of the men who claimed the throne, the approximate length of their reigns, the degree to which their periods of rule overlapped with those of others advancing more or less the same claim, and the manners of their deaths. This chaos

---

1. Fergus Millar, *Rome, the Greek World, and the East*, vol. 1: *The Roman Republic and the Augustan Revolution*, eds Hannah M. Cotton and Guy M. Rogers (Chapel Hill: University of North Carolina Press, 2002), 215–37; Clifford Ando, "From Republic to empire," in Michael Peachin, ed., *Oxford Handbook of Social Relations in the Roman World* (Oxford: Oxford University Press, 2010), 37–66 at 37–41.

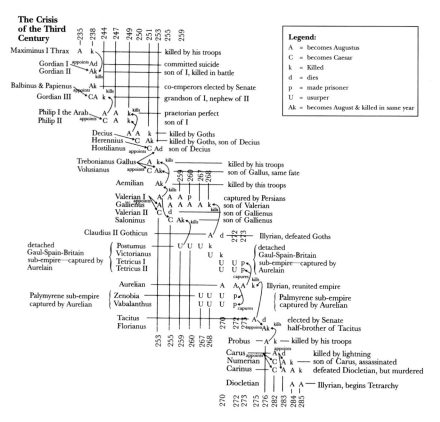

Figure 1 Emperors and usurpers, AD 235–85 (copyright Kelley L. Ross; reproduced with permission)

resulted in part from the failure of earlier generations to secure a consensus on rules of succession.

The second reason to concentrate for a moment on politics at the center of power is the following. Whatever one's understanding of the nature of ancient government, the military and infrastructural power of the Roman state so empowered the single person of the ruler that, in Gibbon's judgment, "on his personal qualities the happiness or misery of the Roman world must ultimately depend."[2] Reflecting on the death of Commodus in particular, Gibbon wrote:

> Such was the fate of the son of Marcus, and so easy was it to destroy a hated tyrant, who, by the artificial powers of government, had

2. Edward Gibbon, *The History of the Decline and Fall of the Roman Empire*, ed. David Womersley, 3 volumes (London: Allen Lane, 1994), 1:172.

> oppressed, during thirteen years, so many millions of subjects, each
> of whom was equal to their master in personal strength and personal
> abilities. (Gibbon, *Decline and Fall*, 1:120)

I shall not here engage the questions of how great was the power, or what were the means, whereby the emperor might in fact affect the lives of his subjects (but cf. below, pp. 13–17, regarding the interpretive paradigm of "crisis" as applied to this period). Up to a point, those questions are moot in this period, as the problematic of war, foreign and civil, comes violently to the fore. But it also bears remembering that the personality of the emperor looms large in ancient evidence. This is naturally true of literature because of the conventions of ancient historical narrative, which fixated on personality as a factor in history, and also because the producers of literature generally sprang from the social classes more proximate to the throne and more likely to be affected by the idiosyncrasies of its occupant. But the person of the emperor was also an important focus of religious practice, which reveals individuals and groups throughout the empire to have conceived their own existential concerns as somehow bound up with the fate of the emperor or, at times, with that of the polity that he embodied and led. The question of the degree of their delusion in so subscribing to an ideology of monarchic rule is largely beside the point: their internalization of that ideology is a factor in history in its own right.

The Antonine empire – which is to say, the age that ended with Commodus but included the reigns of Nerva, Trajan, Hadrian, Antoninus Pius and Marcus Aurelius – occupied a special place in historical memory already in antiquity, and again in the historiography of the Enlightenment and the modern world. This was so in part because it was perceived to have been an age of uncommon internal peace and stability. In consequence, demographic expansion and productivity gains brought the Mediterranean world to a level of urbanism and material and demographic prosperity that it would not see again for centuries, indeed, in some areas for well over a millennium. What is more, the prosperity of the empire in that age became an enduring theme of the *laus imperii*, the praise of empire, in varied branches of imperial rhetoric. The Christian Tertullian, for example, writing in North Africa at the start of our period, offered the following reflection in an aside in a treatise entitled "On the Soul":

> Certainly the world itself is patently daily more cultivated and more
> built up than earlier. All places are now accessible, all are known; all

> open to commerce; very pleasing farms have wiped from memory
> what were once stricken wastelands; fields have conquered woods;
> herds have put wild beasts to flight; sands are sown; rocks broken;
> marshes drained; and there are as many cities as there once were
> cottages. Islands no longer arouse dread, nor do crags terrify. Every-
> where is domestic life; everywhere the populace; everywhere *res
> publica* (the state), everywhere life. (Tertullian, *De anima* 30.3)

The spread of human habitation, human flourishing itself, is here
connected with the spread of commerce and urbanism, and both are
bound to a specifically Roman ideal of republican life.

The other dominant theme in ancient and modern reflections
on the Antonine period concerns the nature of imperial rule. For a
remarkable run – Trajan as successor to Nerva, Hadrian to Trajan,
and on down to Marcus Aurelius – the succession had been determined not by dynastic means (or so runs the standard claim), but by
selection of the "best man." Again, one might quote Gibbon: "The
true interest of an absolute monarch generally coincides with that
of his people. Their numbers, their wealth, their order, and their
security, are the best and only foundations of his real greatness;
and were he totally devoid of virtue, prudence might supply its place,
and would dictate the same rule of conduct" (1:144); even so, the
"united reigns" of Nerva, Trajan, Hadrian, Antoninus and Marcus
were "possibly the only period in history in which the happiness of
a great people was the sole object of government" (1:101–2).

As it happens, Commodus the tyrant was the son of Marcus
Aurelius, and reflection on his case reveals two facts: first, for all his
fame then and later, Marcus seems never to have considered any
possibility other than to surrender the world into the despotic power
of his errant child. Second, Marcus was in fact the first ruler in all
that long run to have had a child to whom he could give the succession. In other words, selection of the "best man" had only been
the default when true dynastic succession, succession by blood, was
not an option.

That said, emperors in the third century were able to secure stable
successions neither for their children nor for hand-picked successors.
How had the system worked in the second century such that it failed
in the third?

As regards the stability and legitimacy of the imperial office, the
dynamics of imperial politics can be usefully reduced at the level of
analysis to two stages: how were emperors made in the first place,
and how did they legitimize and stabilize their position so as to

discourage and delegitimize potential usurpers? (The following remarks are not intended to be exhaustive. These are obviously issues to which we shall often return.)

In the bluntest possible terms, emperors were made through victory in war, which often enough meant war against rival Romans. When rulership was contested, the contest was resolved by force. Reflecting in the early second century AD upon the civil war that erupted after the death of Nero, Tacitus urged that it had revealed a "secret of empire," namely, that emperors could be made elsewhere than Rome (Tacitus, *Historiae* 1.4: *evulgato imperii arcano posse principem alibi quam Romae fieri*). He might more accurately have said that the secret was revealed that emperors were made by armies, wherever those happened to be. In reflecting on the process by which Augustus came to power, for example, authors of the high Roman empire described him as victorious in a sequence of civil wars in which other potential emperors had been eliminated until Augustus alone was left standing. Servius, the late antique commentator on Vergil, for example, in one place describes Augustus as victor in five civil wars: against Antony at Mutina; against Lucius Antonius at Perusia; against Sextus Pompey; against Brutus and Cassius; and against Antony and Cleopatra (*ad Georg.* 4. 13). Elsewhere, when commenting on the phrase "grow accustomed to war," Servius describes the struggles of 49–31 BC as comprising seven separate civil wars, three fought by Caesar and four by Augustus, omitting Mutina (*ad Aen.* 6. 832).

That said, it was in virtually no one's interest – except perhaps the army's, though it was crucially not a unitary body – to acknowledge this fact. Hence, in the system negotiated by Augustus and consolidated through practice over subsequent generations, two further repositories of social authority and political legitimacy were brought into play: the citizen body and the Senate. The history of these issues has been explored already in other volumes in this series. I will therefore confine my remarks to select problems only.

First, Augustus and his successors described their office in numerous ways, but in official contexts they were long careful not to describe it as an office at all. Rather, they represented themselves as occupying a number of traditional offices – or perhaps as holding the agglomerated powers of a number of traditional offices – at the same time. Nor was this mere talk: the records of celebratory sacrifices by the Arval Brethren, a priestly college of high-ranking Romans whose cult site lay in the suburbs of Rome, reveal even emperors in the civil

wars of 69 to have arranged for their formal election to separate
offices on separate days. The ritual should of course be understood
as part and parcel of the Augustan effort to establish continuities
between Republic and Principate. But it should also be understood
as symbolically locating sovereign power in electoral processes to be
conducted at Rome: armies might (illegally) depose an emperor, but
they could not choose one. In the judgment of Gibbon, "[Augustus]
wished to deceive the people by an image of civil liberty, and the
armies by an image of civil government."[3]

Second, the emperors of the first two centuries AD worked hard to
enhance the authority and nominal powers of the Roman Senate.[4]
Most importantly, emperors commencing with Augustus negotiated
with the Senate certain prerogatives in respect not only of their role
in senatorial debate, but also of the legality of their actions in
matters of state. The history of this process is known to us from
perhaps the most famous of all Latin inscriptions, a bronze tablet
that preserves part of the law granting specific powers and privileges
to Vespasian now denominated (misleadingly) the *lex de imperio
Vespasiani* (RS 39).[5] Its language and operation to one side, what it
and kindred texts pointedly reveal is the compromise struck between
emperor and Senate, whereby the emperor conceded publicly that
the Senate was the final repository of authority in the State (and
hence able to grant and also to withhold powers from any given
candidate), which concession the Senate met by its own grant of
virtually unlimited power to just that candidate. Again, the effect
was to rob mere violence or military force – even victory – of
decisionist power in contests for the throne.

The collusion between emperor and Senate went farther still.
The *lex de imperio Vespasiani* itself gestures at this, insofar as true
statutes conferring power of command had not traditionally been
crafted in the Senate. Across the first two centuries, varied forms of
political, judicial and legislative activity that had once belonged to

3. Gibbon, *Decline and Fall*, 1:96. I set aside here the myriad ways, including the monumental elaboration of the Forum, by which Augustus in particular altered the processes
and mechanics of voting at Rome. Needless to say, the opportunity to vote was not open,
nor was the process transparent.
4. On the history of the Senate in the first two centuries of the monarchy see R. J. A.
Talbert, *The Senate of Imperial Rome* (Princeton: Princeton University Press, 1984).
5. On the *lex de imperio Vespasiani* see Peter Brunt, "*Lex de imperio Vespasiani*," *JRS*
67 (1977), 95–116, and on the legal mechanism by which it operated, see Clifford Ando,
Law, Language and Empire in the Roman Tradition (Philadelphia: University of Pennsylvania Press, 2011), 7.

the people as a sovereign body, deliberating and voting in the Forum, were transferred to the Senate. Again, this was a process in which emperors colluded. Perhaps the most significant evidence of this process is an inscription from the reign of Marcus Aurelius, publishing a response by Marcus to a petition from the city of Miletus.

> Having read your letter concerning the contest, we considered it our duty to address the sacred Senate in order that it might grant you what you were asking. It was necessary to address it also concerning several other matters. Since it did not ratify each of the proposals individually, but a *senatus consultum* (a decree of the Senate) was passed concerning everything we said that day in common and collectively, the section of the speech relevant to your request has been attached to this reply for your information.[6]

In formal terms, what had occurred was this: Marcus as emperor had been granted the right to address the Senate first at any given meeting, and the unrestricted right to make a motion. Under the Republic, addresses to the Senate were followed by debate, after which a motion was crafted, and in consequence of the motion, a decree. What is stunning about the inscription is that it records a section of the speech made by Marcus, in which many issues were raised at one go. What is more, the inscription reports that Marcus then made a single omnibus motion regarding all the matters he had raised. In other words, the entire process of consultation and deliberation on individual matters was dropped, even as a formality. Marcus merely had to speak and the Senate voted. The process had been shortened to its essentials: Marcus elevated the Senate by asking its opinion, which gesture it acknowledged by concurring instantly and absolutely. The foreshortening of the process was even concretized in the language of the text, for the text does not possess the grammatical form of a classical senatorial decree: it presents, rather, the *oratio* of Marcus. The emperor's speech before the Senate was thus assimilated to an authoritative utterance of the Senate itself.

Nor was this pure charade, or charade without effect. The Roman Senate achieved an empire-wide prominence in the first two centuries AD that it had not had before in the days of its true power: it was under the Principate, and not the Republic, that the Senate became the object of cult.

---

6. Oliver, no. 192 ll. 12–20 (*AE* 1977, 801; translation Oliver, with modifications). This letter was followed by a Latin extract, now damaged, of Marcus' oration to the Senate.

To speak in these terms risks giving a misleading impression of imperial politics in a number of ways. Hence it must be emphasized that one should not see even battles for the throne as a two-stage process, in which individuals first nakedly employed violence and later deployed the justificatory tropes of imperial apologetic. Contests for power were always contests for public opinion, and in that arena a narrow range of principles of legitimacy were consistently advanced, and chief among those at all times was blood relation to an earlier emperor.

At this point we return to the paradox of the Antonine age. For all that people praised the selection of the so-called best man over against dynastic succession as more rational, more fair and more conducive to the common weal, over the course of the first three centuries of monarchy, dynastic succession was simply never questioned. Indeed, commencing already with Augustus and continuing robustly into the Antonine age, the conventions of Roman practice with regard to adoption were manipulated in such a way that the selection of a successor outside one's agnatic line was in fact realized through the adoption by the ruling emperor of some adult as his son, simultaneously with legislative acts that conferred upon that individual select or full imperial powers.

The army

Once upon a time, service in arms had been an essential duty of the citizen. Indeed, Romans of the classical period imagined (more or less correctly) that the institutions of the early Republic had in various respects echoed the structures of the citizen body under arms. As a corollary, the army had in various periods been understood as standing for, or existing in synedochic relation to, the citizen body as sovereign within the state. How had it come to pass that the legions could not claim – or could not regularly carry the claim – that the choice of monarch was theirs to make in consequence of their status as an organized collective of citizens under arms?

Rome had confronted this problem at length before, most notably during the chaotic civil wars of the late Republic, and it had been one of the signal achievements of Augustus to break, as far as one might, the ties of personal loyalty and financial dependence that had bound legionaries to individual dynasts in the late Republic. In so doing, Augustus forged a new social consensus about the nature of public power and about the state's monopoly on legitimate violence, two issues on which earlier understandings had more or less ruptured in the fall of the Republic. Crucially as regards the capacity of the legions to become actors in politics, what Augustus produced was most pointedly not a return to some republican *status quo ante*, in which soldiering was a component of citizenship and all citizens were always potential soldiers. Rather, the mechanisms that he developed – the institution of regular terms of service, and the use of taxes to pay both salaries and discharge bonuses – effectively sundered military service from the performance of citizenship. As a result, the citizen became a civilian and soldiering became a career, while both violence and the purveyors of violence became instruments of the state.

Taken together with the (apparent) formal requirement that imperial office be endowed through election by purely civilian bodies, the system established by Augustus effected a radical transposition, removing from the legions the influence they had acquired under the triumvirate (however it be understood), and locating the legitimacy of his office precisely in the operations of civil society. By positing civilian corporate bodies as the final repositories of authority in the state, Augustus and his successors sought to persuade potential usurpers – and those who would support them – that neither assassination nor revolt would earn the throne. Guilty of murder or treason, the usurper would have to watch the Senate nominate and the people elect a man whose first official act would be gratefully to execute his benefactor. In Edward Gibbon's view, it was this constitutional "distance" between military and civilian authority that saved, as their proximity would later damn, the feeble or truculent men whom fate placed on the throne (Gibbon, *Decline and Fall* 1:128).

This had further implications within a wider, imperial political culture, both early in the Principate, when most provincials were legally alien and subject in respect to Rome, and later, as more and more and eventually all became citizens. In that broader perspective, the creation of a complex bureaucracy at the level of the central state, mediated at the local level by the multiple instruments of tax collection, nurtured a widespread understanding of the state as a depersonalized institution whose primary role was the cultivation of social order within the empire and peace with the powers without. The complex system of transfer payments between center and periphery that enabled this system to work in turn relied on the relatively high levels of commerce and monetization that were themselves a product of Roman peace and imperial institutions.

Sources

I will introduce the more important individual sources as they are cited in the text, and further information is supplied in the Guide to Further Reading. Here I offer a characterization of the landscape only.

The chaos that prevailed in imperial politics in the period covered by this volume is, alas, largely matched by the confusion and deficiencies of surviving sources. One might find some marginal comfort in this condition by reflecting that the writing of history, like all forms of cultural production, was affected by the disruption that characterized this period. To that extent, the condition of our sources would seem to confirm an interpretive position that views this century as one of crisis (on which issue see the final section of this chapter, below). But it is frankly little comfort to the student or historian who seeks order and information.

The first decades covered by this work are, in fact, remarkably well documented on multiple levels, and are notably well served by contemporary historians, namely Cassius Dio and Herodian. But after the end of Herodian's narrative in 238, the situation is far more difficult. A number of continuous Latin narratives of the period survive from the second half of the fourth century – those by Aurelius Victor and Eutropius as well as the so-called *Epitome de Caesaribus* and the *Historia Augusta*, to name the four most important – but these all rely to a very great extent upon a single earlier narrative, now lost, which was written in the mid-fourth century. Not only are we not well positioned to assess its scope and reliability or investigate its sources, but its existence means that the later Latin sources cannot be treated as autonomous from each other, their "facts" weighed one against the other as though resting upon independent sources of differing reliability.

This situation is made all the more complex by the fact that the *Historia Augusta* is a work of satire, whose multiple targets include imperial politics as well as the pretensions of literary culture, source criticism and imperial biography. Like all great satire, the *Historia Augusta* works in part through the careful cultivation of plausibility: where it does no harm or serves his purpose, the author conveys much that is true. But the book is least reliable as a source of information – if most interesting as an essay on politics – precisely when our other sources fail, which is to say, exactly when we should like it to be true.

It should also be emphasized that at a very general level, the Greek and Latin historical traditions for this period operate independently of each other. (Dio made extensive use of Latin literary sources for events before his lifetime, but less so for events to which he was witness.) That said, the *Historia Augusta* made extensive use of Herodian, and the late antique historian of the Goths Jordanes relates considerable information that is likely to have come from Dexippus of Athens.

Most interestingly, we also possess for this century three oppositional voices, for lack of a better word, of a kind lacking for much of Roman history. I refer to the *Ecclesiastical History* of Eusebius (to which one might add the Christian martyr acts), the eschatological thirteenth Sibylline Oracle, and the record of his own achievements authored by Sapor, the second king of the Sasanian dynasty, and preserved in a monumental trilingual inscription at Naqsh-e Rustam. In quite different ways, each of these texts can and should be understood as occupying a position of self-conscious ideological opposition to, and therefore also as mirroring, authorized voices and genres in Roman imperial culture. Each also supplies plausible information available from no other source.

To these one might add an extraordinary abundance of legal and documentary sources, whether on stone or papyrus, as well as an abundance of coins – but the volume of all these types of evidence too varies with the political stability of the empire as a whole or, to be more precise, with the social and economic fortunes of the regions in which they were produced.

The crisis in critical

Historiography on the third-century Roman empire has been dominated in recent years by a single interpretive question, namely whether the period as a whole is rightly characterized as a time of crisis.[7] Like much revisionism, this debate has been characterized by

7. Wolf Liebeschuetz, "Was there a crisis of the third century?" in Olivier Hekster, Gerda de Kleijn and Daniëlle Slootjes, eds, *Crises and the Roman Empire* (Leiden: Brill, 2007), 11–20, reviews the literature. See also Thomas Gerhardt, "Zur Geschichte des Krisenbegriffs," in Klaus-Peter Johne, Thomas Gerhardt and Udo Hartmann, eds, *Deleto paene imperio Romano: Transformationsprozesse des Römischen Reiches im 3. Jahrhun-*

rhetorical excess. Again, like much revisionism, it has also produced trenchant critiques of earlier certainties (and earlier rhetorical excesses) as well as substantial and valuable empirical work.[8] To a point, as many have observed, the question of whether the difficulties of the empire amounted to a "crisis" should be asked region by region, and when that is done, the answer will vary. There can be little doubt that the provinces along the Rhine and Danube frontiers, or peninsular Greece, which faced foreign invasion for the first time in centuries, or the provinces invaded by Sasanian armies, suffered tremendously in the years in particular from 235 to 284, while Spain, say, or North Africa experienced little direct pressure from foreign powers in those same years.

That said, Wim Jongman has usefully responded that such regional particularism is not in itself sufficient to understand the period. As he demonstrates through various efforts at aggregation (some his own, others performed by others and summarized by him), the empire experienced huge declines in population and economic output in this period, and its population appears to have suffered substantial declines in nutrition and overall health, commencing already in the late second century.[9] The causes must have been manifold, and many were non-political, including the plague that ravaged the empire starting in AD 165 and, it seems, a shift in climate.[10] But the effects of such environmental factors were deeply exacerbated by the social and economic disruption caused by war.

Again, there being little or no evidence for the destruction of buildings in war in a number of provinces, for example, we must pose the question of whether substantial and widespread disruption

dert und ihre Rezeption in der Neuzeit (Stuttgart: Steiner, 2006), 381–410; and Andrea Giardina, "Préface," in Marie-Henriette Quet, ed., *La crise de l'empire romain de Marc Aurèle à Constantin* (Paris: PUPS, 2006), 11–18.

8. Here I might single out for special praise the immensely valuable work of Christian Witschel, who has provided regional surveys of archaeological and epigraphic evidence. See especially *Krise, Rezession, Stagnation? Der Westen des römischen Reiches im 3. Jahrhundert n. Chr.* (Frankfurt: Marthe Clauss, 1999) and "Zur Situation im römischen Afrika während des 3. Jahrhunderts," in Johne et al., *Deleto paene imperio Romano*, 145–221. Witschel offers a superb overview of his monograph in English in "Re-evaluating the Roman west in the 3rd c. A.D.," *Journal of Roman Archaeology* 17 (2004), 251–81.

9. Wim Jongman, "Gibbon was right: The decline and fall of the Roman economy," in Hekster et al., *Crises*, 183–99.

10. On the contribution of the so-called Antonine plague to the history of the third century see Christer Bruun, "The Antonine plague and the 'third-century crisis,'" in Hekster et al., *Crises*, 201–17, citing earlier bibliography.

to social and economic life in one region heavily affected others in ways not readily visible in the material record. The answer depends at least in part on how we understand the empire to have functioned as a social, political and economic unit in the period of its prosperity. There are substantial reasons to believe that the empire promoted the growth and continuance of macro-regional trade networks, and that in consequence it effectively encouraged particular regions toward forms of manufacturing and single-crop agriculture that would have been unsustainable absent the ability of the empire *qua* superordinate state to reduce the risks and transaction costs of long-distance trade. The data from shipwrecks, and even patterns in long-distance trade across the Red Sea, suggest substantial declines in long-distance trade in the third century even in regions bracketed from the immediate material effects of war.[11] Those facts lend credence at once to robust claims regarding the effects of empire on connectivity and production, as also to models that suggest that economic crisis in one region is likely to have had substantial ripple effects in the empire as a whole.

Finally, political instability and warfare had disastrous effects on the Roman money supply. To continue a theme from above, however much the degree of adoption of Roman coin varied from region to region across the first and second centuries, by the end of the second century the Roman economy was heavily monetized and Roman coin served as the currency of exchange in all high-value and long-distance exchange throughout the empire. During the third century, the combination of huge outlays to soldiery, periodic and region-specific collapses in precious-metal mining (coupled with overall long-term decline), and the difficulty of moving bullion and coin as the territorial integrity of the empire fell apart placed enormous strain on money supply and currency transfer and forced a number of *ad hoc* currency reforms. These constitute evidence at once of the size, duration and meaning of the crisis, as also of the integration and connectivity of the empire theretofore.

---

11. In addition to Jongman's essay, see Dario Nappo, "The impact of the third century crisis on the international trade with the east," in Hekster et al., *Crises*, 233–44; Andrea Giardina, "The crisis of the third century," in Walter Scheidel, Ian Morris and Richard Saller, eds, *The Cambridge Economic History of the Greco-Roman World* (Cambridge: Cambridge University Press, 2007), 757–64.

Surviving the third century

We should not take the survival of the Roman state for granted. Its emergence as a unitary political formation after a period of serious disintegration and truly profound political upheaval demands explanation. Certainly the next time its borders proved so porous – the next time enemies reached the gates of Rome, in the early fifth century – the integrity of the empire collapsed, and breakaway states of varying stability formed across the west. Likewise, when Britain fell away – admittedly the least Romanized of all regions of the empire (if such a thing can be quantified) – neither did it seek to return nor did its culture persist on some Roman trajectory, nor, it must be said, did anyone seek to get it back. The will toward unity in the political culture writ large had evaporated.

We will return to this issue in the Conclusion, data in hand. Let me now gesture toward some important themes when reading with this end in mind. One might suppose that it was a matter of indifference to the population at large whether any given locality sent its taxes to Rome or some other macro-regional center. After all, there is little evidence of local resistance to the rise of splinter states or shadow governments in Gaul and Palmyra in the 260s. One might even go farther and suggest that this indifference stemmed neither from apathy nor from despair (all governments being equally rapacious) but from true lack of import: in this view, imperial politics and even imperial administration were simply epiphenomenal to the social-material realities of life for the great mass of population in the greater Mediterranean.

But one can maintain this view only by ignoring very considerable evidence for the penetration of the state into the pragmatics of local life, such that even micro-regional relations, village to village, and interpersonal relations within communities were affected – to say nothing of the cognitive and pragmatic dynamics of self-fashioning at the level of the individual. Curiously, and importantly, evidence for the operation of the state on this level continues – albeit in lesser quantity than previously – throughout the third century.

This brings me to a second observation. The pragmatics that generated this evidence for the ongoing functioning of the imperial state would appear to continue altogether independently of the identity of the occupant of the imperial office. When villagers from Thrace implored Gordian III to act in accordance with his avowed desire to support the flourishing of village and municipal life – in texts they do not cite – did it matter whether Gordian had ever made such a declaration (see p. 227)? It was, rather, the sort of thing emperors said – indeed, many are on record doing just that. In their suppositions about imperial policy, and about the constraints that imperial ideology placed upon the idiosyncratic desires of any given emperor, the villagers were likely correct. Certainly in their correspondence with Gordian they were successful.

Which brings me to a final suggestion. There is another, more complex aspect to this faith in the ongoing functioning of government at an institutional level. By the mid-third century, the operations of Roman government had long since become cultural archetypes for the functioning of institutions: the protocols of meetings of non-statal collectivities look like the protocols of the Roman Senate because that was the dominant picture everyone had of how a meeting should be conducted and its minutes recorded. But if this is true, it will have had recursive effects, in some feed-back loop, upon the vitality of Roman institutions: they could not fail – they could not be allowed to fail – because of the essential homology they both inspired and sustained with the broad structures of social and economic conduct writ large. Their failure would have provoked an existential crisis in the reproduction of culture. Hence, one might say, if Roman institutions had to fail, some other state claiming both to be Rome and to act as Rome would have had to replace it, even on a region-by-region basis. To these issues we shall return in closing.

CHAPTER 2

The principal author of the decline and fall

The accession and death of Pertinax (December 31, 192– March 28, 193)

January 1 was a day heavy with meaning in the high Roman empire. It had traditionally been – and it remained – the day when new consuls entered office, in a pageant of religious ritual and political ceremony. As the eponymous magistrates of the Roman year, the entry of the consuls into office continued to structure Roman historical memory. Of course, the historian Tacitus had used the conventions of consular dating to denounce as a charade the continuance of republican offices within the reality of monarchy, but the system continued regardless. The varied populations of Rome, Italy and the empire at large also marked the new year with a series of political and religious vows – of loyalty to the acts of the emperor and prayers for his health – distributed on the first and third day of the month.

The emperor Commodus died – was poisoned and then strangled – after dinner on December 31, 192. The historian and senator Cassius Dio was present in Rome at the time, and represents the act as undertaken without a clear plan for its aftermath. It was, rather, a desperate response to Commodus' apparent descent into total madness. Dio ends his narrative of the reign with a conventional reckoning of the length of his life: "He had lived thirty-one years and four months, and with him the dynasty of the genuine Aurelii came to an end" (Dio–Xiphilinus, 73(72).22.6). As we shall see, the adjective "genuine" gestures to a phenomenon Dio witnessed in the months and years to come, namely, the effort by new emperors to legitimate themselves by retrospectively – posthumously? – adopting themselves into the family of a predecessor.

Dio deserves a further word before we commence in earnest. A Greek from Nicaea in the province of Bithynia, Dio entered the Roman Senate under Commodus and held positions of authority and

influence under nearly every emperor until his death: he was designated praetor by Pertinax in spring 193 (which office Dio held in
194 or 195); he was suffect consul under Septimius Severus in 205
or 206; and he held a series of offices under Alexander Severus – as
governor in Africa, 223/4; as legate in Dalmatia and then Pannonia
at points between 224 and 228 – before holding the ordinary
consulate as partner to the emperor himself in 229. Dio also spent
time with Caracalla in Asia during the latter's tour of the east in
214/15. He was thus a remarkably well-placed observer. He was also
a diligent researcher: he claims to have spent ten years on research
and twelve years in the writing of his greatest work, a history of
Rome from the beginning to his own day (the exact end point is not
known, but he does refer to events during his consulate in 229). The
work survives only in part: several complete books survive (notably
nearly all of books 36–60, covering the years 68 BC to AD 47); and
excerpts from the whole were quoted in compendia or summarized
in compressed histories and the like produced in Byzantium, and
many of those survive.[1] In what follows, I shall indicate the source
of the extract (whether the epitome by Xiphilinus or some collection
of quotations like the Excerpta Valesiana) where it might possibly
impinge on the relationship between the wording used and the
ipsissima verba of Dio himself. The material that does survive
reveals him to be an exceptionally clear-headed and percipient
observer of imperial government. As a Greek and a senator, he
combined an insider's information with an outsider's skepticism of
specifically Roman pretensions.

If we are to believe Dio, those responsible for the death of
Commodus had acted so spontaneously that they had made no plan
for his replacement. In the event, they turned to Publius Helvius
Pertinax, an elderly senator (born August 1, 126) who had led a
remarkably varied career – principally on the military side of things
– under Antoninus Pius, Marcus Aurelius and Commodus. Indeed,
there is every reason to believe that all three factors played a role in
his selection: he was old, and so would not occupy the throne for
long; his earlier career would give him credibility with the army; and
his association with Antoninus Pius and Marcus would recall earlier,
better days. Pertinax represented the establishment.

1. Peter Michael Swan, *The Augustan Succession: An Historical Commentary on
Cassius Dio's Roman History, Books 55–56 (9 B.C.–A.D. 14)* (New York: Oxford University Press, 2004), 36–8, 383–5 provides a guide to the state of Dio's text and its modern
editions.

That said, the first act of the conspirators is telling: Pertinax went to the camp of the Praetorian Guard and sought their approval, which came willingly enough when he offered a donative of 12,000 sesterces a man. Only then did he return to the city and address the Senate. "I have been named emperor by the soldiers," he began, after which he offered to resign and in so doing invited the Senate to insist that he remain (Dio–Xiphilinus, 74[73].1.4).

The few actions attributed to Pertinax before his murder by the very soldiery whose approval he had purchased suggest an ostentatious (and in large measure) salutary effort to reverse and correct the excesses of the previous reign. The act of the greatest immediate symbolic importance was the official condemnation of Commodus' memory, an act realized through the desecration of his images and the defacing of his name on public monuments (SHA *Pertinax* 6.3; see also *Commodus* 20.4–5). We are told that Pertinax found only a million sesterces in the treasury, whereupon he held an auction of properties, luxury goods and gladiatorial gear accumulated by Commodus (Dio–Xiphilinus, 73.5.4–5; SHA *Pertinax* 7.8–9) – an action that both raised money and very publicly repudiated the persona of his predecessor. He enacted a series of reforms of administrative law and practice in two directions above all: securing private property rights against the imperial purse on the one hand, and restoring and maintaining an appropriate correlation between legal rank and social status on the other.[2] (It was a perpetual complaint against bad emperors that they created an atmosphere favorable to, and betimes directly encouraged, the upending of social distinctions between slaves and free, freedmen and patrons, lower and upper class, and so forth.)

In the brief time available to him, Pertinax clearly devised policies for and directed messages toward multiple constituencies: the Senate, the populace of Rome (meaning especially the wealthy) and the army. With the last-named, he failed. The brief narratives of his reign suggest ongoing tension with the Praetorian Guard, which seems to have feared the imposition of an austerity program. The Guard may have resented the death of Commodus and in consequence distrusted whoever replaced him, or perhaps it simply remained open to possibility: perhaps the soldiers felt they had settled for too little. Whatever the cause, we are told that the Guard remained open to whispers of rebellion, until some hundreds

2. These are listed above all in SHA *Pertinax* 7–9.

suddenly marched on the palace and slew Pertinax on March 28, 193.

The historian Herodian, who lived and worked well outside the corridors of power but who may have been an imperial functionary of equestrian rank, observed of the reign of Pertinax: "As the report of his gentle rule traveled round the peoples of the empire, including both subjects and allies, and round the garrisons, they were all convinced that he ruled with divine authority" (Herodian, 2.4.2). The remark raises complex issues regarding the nature of communication under Rome, to which we shall return in greater depth when we consider the rise of Septimius Severus. Here let it suffice to point out that "the report" that "traveled round" was probably authored by, or at least for, Pertinax himself. Cassius Dio, writing from the center, describes the reception by governors in the provinces of what must have been a coordinated announcement of the new reign: governors, fearing a trick designed by Commodus to test their loyalty, imprisoned the messengers (Dio–Xiphilinus, 74(73).2.5).

In any event, Dio's assessment of Pertinax's reign is more measured and vastly more astute:

> Thus died Pertinax, having attempted to restore all things at one go. He did not recognize, although he was most experienced in affairs, that it is impossible safely to correct a mass of things all at once, and that restoration of political affairs in particular requires both time and wisdom. He lived sixty-seven years less four months and three days, and he reigned eighty-seven days. (Dio–Xiphilinus, 74(73).10.3)

As had happened at the death of Nero, the death of Commodus and the collapse of the Antonine "dynasty" revealed at an abstract level the peril and the cost of never having instituted a mechanism of widespread acceptance for choosing a new emperor. The ease with which Pertinax was killed – or Galba, or Otho, or Vitellius, or many others yet to come – instead laid bare the hollowness of popular sovereignty as an ongoing concern, and likewise of the Senate's self-interested constitutionalism. Absent a significant social consensus, there was no reason for any and all constituencies not to hazard a claim upon a new and unsettled emperor or, that failing, upon the throne.

That said, it will not do simply to indict the system. The peril needs to be named: the soldiery was willing to use violence, and likewise to withhold it, for a price; and there were men, nearly always commanders, willing to exploit that venality. Nor does Pertinax deserve our sympathy: he knew the rules and had played the game. (The judgment of Dio, that Pertinax did everything "a good emperor should do," speaks precisely to the conventional nature of the expectations that governed an emperor's entry into office [Dio–Xiphilinus, (74)73.5.2].) Would Pertinax have survived longer, had he paid more? Or paid again? The resources and skills that Pertinax was able to bring to bear were simply insufficient. As always in Roman civil wars, others would go on paying the price.

Auctioning the empire (March–June 193)

Before he died, Pertinax had sent his father-in-law, Titus Flavius Sulpicianus, whom he appointed prefect of the city, to speak to the Guard in its camp. Apprised during his visit of the death of his son-in-law, Sulpicianus began to negotiate the succession for himself. Meanwhile, according to the *Historia Augusta*, one Didius Julianus, the hand-picked colleague of Pertinax in the consulate and himself a man of wide-ranging experience in civil government and in both unarmed and militarized provinces, had heard of a disturbance and came to the Senate to investigate. Encountering there two tribunes who urged him to throw his hat in the ring, he rushed to the camp. Finding the gate barred, Julianus announced his candidacy by placard: he signaled to the soldiers on the walls that they should beware a candidate who would seek to avenge Pertinax, and he vaunted that he would restore dignity to the memory and name of Commodus (SHA *Didius Julianus* 2.4–6).

> There followed a most disgraceful affair and one unworthy of Rome. For as if in a market or some auction house, both the city and its entire empire were auctioned off. They were sold by the men who had killed their emperor; those wishing to buy were Sulpicianus and Julianus, who strove against each other, one from inside and the other outside the camp. (Dio–Xiphilinus, 74(73).11.3; see also SHA *Didius Julianus* 2.6)

The soldiers selected Julianus but extracted from him a promise that he would not kill Sulpicianus, and indeed, Sulpicianus survived Julianus by some years, only (as it seems) to be killed by the victor in the next round of civil wars, Septimius Severus, perhaps for having supported a rival candidate, Clodius Albinus (Dio–Xiphilinus, 76[75].8.4).

Other than the rehabilitation of Commodus and execution of his assassins, very nearly the only acts credited to Julianus between his accession on March 28, deposition on June 1 and death a day later are defensive ones, taken against rivals. For nearly as soon as word can have reached the provinces, three generals apparently declared their intent to seek the throne: Septimius Severus, governor of Illyricum, on April 9; Clodius Albinus, governor of Britain, at about the same time; and Pescennius Niger in Syria, on or around April 19. We are told that Severus rapidly struck an alliance of convenience with Albinus, according to which Albinus took the rank of Caesar, in subordination to Severus as Augustus (Dio–Xiphilinus, 74[73].15.1–3). This left the latter free to march on Rome, without fear of action in his rear. We are also told that Severus paid an immediate and large donative to his soldiers – a remarkably naked act of bribery and claim to power, since only the emperor could grant a donative (SHA *Severus* 5.2).

The publicity campaigns undertaken by Severus and Niger are notable for their ideological foundations: Severus credited the legitimacy of Pertinax and the mechanisms of his selection and accused the Praetorian Guard of illegality twice over, first in murdering Pertinax and then in presuming to select Julianus. (Before we accuse Severus of too great cynicism, one should know that Severus had served under Pertinax when the latter was governor in Syria between 180 and 182.) Niger for his part put it forth that he had been summoned to rescue the city and people of Rome:

> Niger tried to win over his legionary commanders by telling them the news he was receiving from Rome [namely, that the people were chanting his name in the Circus]. In so doing he intended the news to come to the ears of the soldiers and the rest of the inhabitants of the eastern provinces … In this way Niger hoped that no one would have any difficulty in supporting him, if they heard that he for his part was not making some insidious bid for power, but going to assist the Romans in response to their call. (Herodian, 2.7.7–8)

As Niger later put it, in an address to his soldiers and the city of Antioch where he was based: "It is not some trivial, vain hope that beckons me on, but the Roman people, into whose hands the gods have given the sovereignty over all things, including the office of emperor" (Herodian, 2.8.4).

As Severus marched into Italy and Niger prepared for the much longer and more complex campaign he would have to undertake –

a campaign pre-empted by the swiftness of his rival – the situation in Rome collapsed. The farce of March 28 had left the Guard and Julianus utterly co-dependent but without legitimacy in the minds of others, at Rome or in the empire at large; and in the face of mounting pressure, neither proved capable of commanding or trusting the other, or anyone else, for that matter. Before Severus had crossed the Alps, Julianus induced the Senate to declare Severus a public enemy, but by the time Severus had reached Ravenna, the Senate openly disobeyed. According to Dio, who was present in the Senate, Julianus tried to bargain and have Severus named co-emperor. Meanwhile, Severus had written letters to the Guard: if they surrendered the assassins of Pertinax and kept the peace (and did not resist Severus as he approached), they would suffer no harm. Looking to their own skins, they sent word of their acquiescence to the consul rather than the emperor they had made. The Senate, delivered from fear, symbolically stripped Julianus of power on June 1 and ordered his death, while voting the consecration of Pertinax (Dio–Xiphilinus, 74[73].17).

Severus entered Rome on June 9 and remained there exactly one month. Even before he formally entered the city, he confronted the Praetorian Guard, which, conscious of its guilt and confronted by Severus' veteran legions, met him at his command unarmed and outside the city. He executed the murderers of Pertinax and discharged the rest, without weapon or uniform; he then replaced the Guard, which had long been composed of recruits primarily from Italy, wholesale with men drawn from his own legions. To his legions as a whole, he also gave a massive donative – perhaps under duress (Herodian, 2.14.5; SHA *Severus* 7.6–7). Severus would surely have rewarded his troops; it was, as we have seen, traditional, and we are told that the soldiery pressed their claim in just those terms. But the narratives available to us imply that the money was hard to raise, as surely it would have been, a massive donative having been paid from the treasury already twice in six months. But Severus was himself under pressure: he may have co-opted Clodius Albinus, but Niger remained – and we are told that even as Niger received news from Rome and spread abroad his own versions of that news, so too he was writing to Rome, offering to do what Severus had just done, namely, arrive as emperor acclaimed by his troops, to rescue the state from oppression (SHA *Severus* 6.8).

Needing to deal with Niger, Severus knew he had to leave not simply Albinus in his rear, but Rome itself – and Rome remained important even in Severus' own propaganda as the essential site where legitimate imperial power was claimed, that claim was redeemed, and power was exercised. Severus needed to ensure that the institutions of government at Rome – or, perhaps, key constituencies at Rome – remained loyal.

His principal solution at the level of politics was to burnish his relations with the Senate, and his means were twofold. First, Severus "promised such things as the good emperors before had done," most particularly that he would not execute any senator without a trial before the Senate. (Dio observes in the same breath that Severus soon broke this promise, and did so often [Dio–Xiphilinus, 75(74).2.1–2].)

The second act whereby Severus sought to cement his good relations with the Senate, and to solidify his legitimacy more generally, was to rehabilitate Pertinax and tie his own standing to his. The former he accomplished through a formal consecration, carrying out in ritual the act the Senate had voted the week before he arrived in Rome. This rite, which in formal terms declared the honorand to have become – or been made – a god (or perhaps it might even be said that the ritual declared no more than that the honorand was the object of the ritual: Roman law operated with a deeply self-conscious understanding of the efficacy of performative legal language) had become already under Augustus the means whereby a dead emperor's successor and survivors passed judgment on his reign. As we have already seen, the negative option was condemnation of his memory. Hence, the first act of a new reign was always the decision how to honor, slight or condemn one's predecessor – and hence, too, the sharp irony of Tacitus' claim regarding Tiberius that the first *crime* of the new reign was murder (Tacitus, *Ann.* 1.6.1). Dio's description of the consecration of Pertinax is the fullest to survive and deserves quotation in full:

> Having established himself in rulership, Severus built a shrine to Pertinax and ordered that his name should be invoked in all prayers and oaths, that a golden portrait of him should be led into the Circus on a chariot pulled by elephants, and that three gilded thrones for him should be paraded into all other arenas. Although he had been dead a long time, a funeral was held as follows:
>
> A wooden platform was erected in the Roman forum by the marble rostra, and on it was set a shrine without walls decorated with ivory and gold, and in it was placed a similarly fashioned couch. It was surrounded by the heads of beasts from both land and sea and

covered by cloths of purple and gold, and on it was set an image of
Pertinax, made of wax and dressed in triumphal robes, and a hand-
some boy chased away the flies from it with peacock feathers, as if it
were in fact sleeping.

The image lying there, Severus and we senators and our wives
approached in mourning clothes; the women then seated themselves
under porticoes and we under the open sky. After this there was a
procession first of statues of all outstanding Romans of old, then a
chorus of boys and men singing some hymn to Pertinax. After that
followed all the subject nations in the form of bronze images, dressed
in native fashion, and then the guilds of the city itself, those of the
lictors and scribes and heralds and others of this sort. Then came
images of other men whom some deed or invention or conduct of life
had made famous, and after them the cavalry and foot-soldiers in
armor, and race-horses, and the funeral offerings that the emperor
and we and our wives and the honorable equestrians and peoples
and corporate bodies of the city had sent. A gilded altar followed,
decorated in ivory and Indian gems.

When these had passed, Severus mounted the rostrum and read a
eulogy of Pertinax. We cried aloud often during his address, now
praising Pertinax and now lamenting him, but most of all when he
finished. Finally, as the couch was about to be moved, we all grieved
and wept. The *pontifices* (a college of priests) and magistrates, both
those in office and those designated for the following year, accompanied it from the platform, and they gave it to select equestrians
to carry. The rest of us preceded it, some beating their breasts and
others playing the flute; the emperor came last; and thus we came to
the Campus Martius.

There a three-story tower-like pyre had been erected, decorated
with ivory and gold and statues, and at its peak was a gilded chariot
which Pertinax used to drive. The funeral offerings were placed
within, together with the couch, after which Severus and the relatives
of Pertinax kissed the image.

The emperor ascended a tribunal and we the Senate – excepting
the magistrates – mounted wooden stands, in order to watch both
safely and conveniently. Finally, the magistrates and the equestrians,
decked out in a fashion befitting them, together with the cavalry and
foot-soldiers passed around the pyre, performing maneuvers of both
war and peace. Then the consuls hurled fire upon it. When this was
done, an eagle flew from it on high, and thus was Pertinax made
immortal. (Dio–Xiphilinus, 75(74).5; see also Herodian, 4.2, an
equally full – but not first-person – description of the consecration of
Severus)

During this visit to Rome, Severus also arranged that the Senate should vote him the name Pertinax, which he appears in fact to have started using even before he left Pannonia. That said, he did not go so far as to arrange a posthumous adoption: he called himself "Severus Pertinax," rather than "Severus *divi filius,* Severus son of the god."[3] According to Herodian, it was also at this moment that Severus authorized Clodius Albinus to strike coins in his own name – an important token of legitimacy and, it might seem, a major concession (Herodian, 2.15.5). Indeed, coins displaying Albinus' portrait and bearing the legend "Decimus Clodius Septimius Albinus Caesar" were minted even at Rome, which can only have happened with the permission of Severus,[4] and the rank of Caesar was attributed to Clodius on inscriptions in areas under Severus' control (see, e.g., *ILS* 414 from Rome and 415 from Africa Proconsularis).

The scripts enacted and deployed by Severus and his enablers in Senate and army brought together in simultaneous articulation various truths – and various kinds of truth – about the construction and nature of social and political power in the high Roman empire. The assassinations of Commodus and Pertinax and execution of Julianus (if so it be called) had cast into doubt the efficacy of the traditional mechanisms for the legitimation of imperial power. Severus and Niger might still deploy the tropes, and various interest groups might welcome their doing so, but their effectiveness in restraining the license of the army and thereby effacing the work of force and role of bribery in the making of emperors was rapidly eroding.

Seemingly motivated by just these concerns, and unable because of circumstance to arrange or invent an adoption (as Nerva and Trajan had done, and Trajan and Hadrian, and so on), the emperors of 193 also experimented with the legitimating power of the past. Of this, Severus proved the master. In celebrating Pertinax, the legitimacy thus conferred upon a ruler so short-lived as to be pure cipher rebounded upon Severus, and in this the Senate conspired, for its own reasons. Nor was the policy meaningless in practice: clearly the Senate preferred that Severus should honor Pertinax, when like Julianus he might have followed Commodus. The one set a gentler precedent than the other. What is more, the son of Pertinax survived and was brought forth as a token of continuity, holding the

3. Herodian, 2.10.1; SHA *Pertinax* 15.2. Coins: *BM Coins, Rom. Emp.* V, Wars of Succession nos 1–180 and 215–65.
4. On the coinage of Albinus, see Mattingly, *BM Coins, Rom. Emp.* V, lxxvii–lxxviii, lxxxv, and lxxxviii–xci.

consulate as suffect together with Caracalla in 212, only to be killed by the self-same emperor in that very year.

By these means – the official removal of Julianus from office; the execution of the murderers of Pertinax; the rehabilitation of Pertinax – the record of the auction and the efficacy of sale were officially effaced as precedents. Their erasure from memory was an altogether different story.

The wars of choice of Septimius Severus (June 193–January 202)

Severus spent nearly the entirety of his reign in constant motion, and much of it on campaign. Two of those wars were civil, undertaken to eliminate rivals: Pescennius Niger in the east in 193/4, the final battle taking place in April at Issus, the site of Alexander the Great's victory over Darius, king of Persia; and Clodius Albinus in the west, who fell to Severus at least by February 197. (When Severus promoted his son Bassianus – whom posterity knows as Caracalla – to the rank of Caesar in 195, Albinus read the writing on the wall and declared himself emperor in Britain and Gaul.) Other wars were mere shows of force, undertaken as much or more for domestic reasons as for those of geopolitics: the campaigns against Parthia in 194/5 and 197/9 were, in the grand Roman tradition, vanity projects, though naturally not without important consequences for the populations destroyed and the regions annexed, and ultimately for Rome itself, when a new empire rose in Persia and sought (like Severus) to revise the balance of power that had theretofore obtained between Rome and Parthia. Of terribly great importance, too, were the repeated concessions and gifts Severus made to the army after each war.[5] To this problem we will return in Chapter 3. After a break of over half a decade, which included significant time in his native North Africa, Severus departed in 208 for Britain, where he died three years later.

We shall have occasion in later chapters to study developments in law and religion under Severus and Caracalla; and there and elsewhere, in describing Roman relations with the new Sasanian empire, we shall consider the long-term effects of their wars in the east. Here I wish to concentrate on another aspect of Severus' early campaigns, namely, the use he made of them to bolster his claims

5. In addition to those already mentioned, another round of gifts followed the war with Albinus: Herodian, 3.8.4–5.

upon the throne and the content and consequences of the efforts he made to communicate those claims. In so doing, I seek not simply to draw attention to the deeds of a single Roman emperor, but to reveal the dynamics of communicative practice between the emperor and his subjects in the high empire.

A primary source – very likely *the* source of information of first recourse – for provincial populations regarding the deeds of the emperor specifically and the imperial government generally was communications directly distributed by that government. Of course, emperors broadcast news of their victories in order to burnish their credentials as protectors of the Roman world: the integrity of the borders, the maintaining of security on a geopolitical scale, remained the pre-eminent justification of the empire's existence, so success in war was a qualification *sine qua non* for any emperor. But such announcements also made them money: cities and corporate entities receiving such news were expected on these and other significant occasions to send the emperor thanks, congratulations and a gift of gold.

Such exchanges were not without opportunity for the recipients of imperial communiqués. Communities throughout the empire (pre-eminently cities, but also corporate bodies, religious communities and significant minority populations) filled the ostensibly congratu-latory letters with requests – for tax relief, subventions for building projects, change of administrative status, and on and on. We know about the imperial communiqués not because they themselves survive, but because communities whose requests were granted inscribed a record of those grants on some permanent medium, and often enough considerable information about the history of the correspondence is embedded in any given document within such an exchange. Taken together, such documents reveal essential infor-mation about the history of particular cities, about the policies of emperors, and about the structures of imperial government in the broadest possible sense. They also reveal much about imperial practice in communication, not least the penchant of emperors to communicate different messages to different constituencies.

In order to situate official documents of the imperial era within patterns of geographic and chronological dispersal – and in order to study just this question of whom the emperor addressed, with what message and when – modern historians rely in very large measure on a set of markers embedded in imperial titulature – information, one might say, transmitted in the protocols or headers of official documents – rather than on their substantive content. The protocols of the Severan period carried five pieces of information of relevance in what follows. First, emperors were acclaimed as "Imperator" by their soldiers after victories. These events had a stylized, formal quality, so much so that emperors added imperatorial acclamations to their titulature: Imperator IV meaning four times acclaimed Imperator. (The word originally meant "commander" and came to be used exclusively of the emperor and hence to mean "Emperor." It is of course the word from which the English word derives.) Second, emperors took additional names or titles to signify their status as victorious over select foreign enemies: "Germanicus" or "Parthicus," for example, meant "Victor over the Germans" or "Victor over the Parthians." Such names naturally speak to the history of warfare, as also the history of publicizing war. What is more, insofar as the right to give such names was contested, as with all other imperial powers, their history reveals something of the competition among interest groups across time.

Third, these elements of an emperor's titulature sat alongside notations regarding the emperor's status as consul for the first, second or third time – the consulate being an office they could occupy at will, though most held it only infrequently. Fourth, ever since Augustus, emperors had indicated the length of their reign by recording the number of years they had held the tribunician power. Fifth and last, any given emperor might take a partner in rule, who would generally be a son or, if not, would be adopted as such. The presence or absence of such partners is of course a marker of the context of a document's generation, and any given partner in rule would have titulature of his own, with its chronological markers.

Once aggregated, and taken together with the substantive content of specific documents, this information – however fragmentarily preserved on any given stone, whether wholly or partially reproduced in any given context – can permit a fairly robust reconstruction of the communicative practice of a regime. What follows is an attempt to wed a narrative of Severus' wars against Pescennius Niger and Clodius Albinus and his efforts to establish a dynasty for and through his sons with an exploration of the communicative acts whereby the wars were known to the provinces and the claims the dynasty put forward.

Departing Rome on July 9, 193, Severus rushed east to deal with Pescennius Niger and spent the winter of 193/4 in Perinthus; in early 194 he marched to Syria where, having defeated the forces of

Niger, he made preparations for a campaign against Parthia.

In the course of his war with Niger Severus had been hailed as *Imperator* by his army three times; the last such occasion, the battle of Issus, was in the fall of 194. The so-called first Parthian war, which began in the spring of 195, accomplished nothing; it was presumably planned primarily to allow Roman legions that had so recently fought each other to fight against a common enemy.[6] Indeed, there seems to have been little fighting – Herodian, for one, omits this campaign altogether – but Severus had to make a show of power against two vassals of Parthia who had supported Niger, the Arabians and Adiabenes. Some glorified the campaign by calling it a Parthian war, and Severus allowed his army to acclaim him *Imperator* for the fifth, sixth and seventh times in the summer of 195 and an eighth time before the end of that year. (We know this also from claims to distinction made by his lieutenants, who boasted of having served in multiple wars in just these years.[7]) Severus presented himself more humbly before the Senate, apparently worried lest he seem to glorify a victory in a civil war. When he returned to Rome in 196 the Senate voted him several titles and a triumph, but he refused the triumph.[8] Severus, however, did not wait for the Senate's approval before notifying the provinces about his victories: his name starts to appear with the titles *Arabicus Adiabenicus*, or *Parthicus Arabicus Parthicus Adiabenicus*, in the summer of 195, a year before his return to Rome, on inscriptions from Africa, southern Italy, Rome, Cisalpine Gaul and Gallia Narbonensis, the Danubian provinces and throughout the east.[9]

---

6. The suggestion of A. R. Birley, *The African Emperor: Septimius Severus* (2nd edition, London: Batsford, 1988), 115.

7. Tiberius Claudius Candidus was army commander in the Asian campaign (against Niger), in the Parthian campaign (i.e., the first Parthian war) and in the Gallic campaign (against Albinus): *ILS 1140*. For Severus' titulature in 195 see Zvi Rubin, *Civil-War Propaganda and Historiography* (Brussels: Revue d'Études Latines, 1980), 205–9.

8. SHA *Severus* 9.9–11. He issued coins celebrating his acts in Rome: his arrival, a distribution to the public and the celebration of games: *BM Coins, Rom. Emp.* V, Severus nos 595–8, 602–3 and *RIC* V.1 Severus nos 73, 80, 81a–b and 91.

9. Data compiled by P. Kneissl, *Die Siegestitulatur der römischen Kaiser* (Göttingen: Vandenhoeck & Ruprecht, 1969), 135–6, with supplements: *(Parthicus) Arabicus (Parthicus) Adiabenicus* with *Imperator* V: *ILS* 417 (Africa); *CIL* VIII 4364 (Africa); *CIL* X 7272 (Sicily); *ILTun.* 613 (Africa); *AE* 1982, 817 (Pannonia Inferior); *AE* 1984, 373 (Italy–Umbria). *Arabicus Adiabenicus* with *Imperator* VI: *IGRom.* IV 672 (Phrygia); *CIL* VIII 9317 (Africa). *Arabicus Adiabenicus* with *Imperator* VII: *CIL* III 905 (Dacia); *CIL* V 4868 (Cisalpine Gaul); *CIL* VIII 1333, 24004 (Africa); *CIL* XII 56 (Gallia Narbonensis); *AE* 1946, 202 (Spain); *AE* 1984, 919 (Syria). *Arabicus Adiabenicus* with *Imperator* VIII: *CIL* VIII 8835 (Africa); *IGRom.* IV 566 (Phrygia). Definitely from 195

Severus' anxiety about waging further civil wars was not mis-
placed. Even as he returned to Rome, he began a propaganda
campaign against Albinus, charging him, among other things, with
having murdered Pertinax.[10] But Dio, who says emphatically that he
was present in Rome and "heard clearly everything that was said,"
reports that the populace was unpersuaded: the people in the Circus
chanted against further warfare (Dio–Xiphilinus, 76[75].4.1–6).

The spread of this titulature aptly illustrates the dynamics governing relations between an emperor and his various constituencies.
Monopoly over the limited means of rapid communication in that
day allowed Severus to behave deferentially, as partner, before the
Senate, which had once assumed control over the awarding of
victory-*cognomina* and which seems to have continued to claim that
privilege for itself.[11] (The term "victory-*cognomina*" refers to names
added to an emperor's official titulature in commemoration of a
victory: "Germanicus" meaning "Victor over the Germans".) At
precisely the same time Severus could boast to the provinces about
the same deeds with very different rhetoric: he needed their gold, and
they would give it only to someone with clear and undisputed
achievements in war. Finally, the immediate presence of his army
constrained Severus to accept their displays of loyalty, that is, their
acclamations, even as both he and his army knew full well that
such actions demanded from him a corresponding reward for his
enthusiastic soldiery. This pattern in Severus' behavior, of distribut-
ing information selectively and modulating his self-presentation,
continued to obtain for the next four years.

His quick success against Niger gave Severus the confidence to
break with Albinus and to name his son, Bassianus, his official

but without numeration of imperatorial acclamation is *CIL* III 14507 (cf. B. Lörincz,
"C. Gabinius Barbarus Pompeianus, Statthalter von Moesia Superior," *ZPE* 33 [1979],
157–60), and very likely also *AE* 1983, 830 (from Dacia). On the evidence from Egypt,
see P. Bureth, *Les titulatures impériales dans les papyrus, les ostraca, et les inscriptions
d'Égypte: 30 a.C.–284 p.C.* (Brussels: Fondation Égyptologique Reine Élisabeth, 1964),
94. Kneissl also lists *CIL* VI 1026 (from Rome), which contains the titles *Arabicus
Adiabenicus* along with *Imperator* IIII; the stone is, I believe, no longer extant, and it is
very unlikely that Severus claimed these titles prior to the start of the Parthian campaign.
10. Birley, *African Emperor*, 118 n. 23.
11. Senatorial control: R. J. A. Talbert, *The Senate of Imperial Rome* (Princeton: Princeton University Press, 1984), 364 n. 27. The continued role of the Senate, attributed
directly to the reign of Severus: SHA *Severus* 9.9–11. The historical pattern, however,
had long been that the army would acclaim the emperor as victor and the emperor would
in turn reward the army with a donative: J. B. Campbell, *The Emperor and the Roman
Army, 31 B.C.–A.D. 235* (Oxford: Clarendon Press, 1984), 122–42.

successor. To strengthen his claim as the only legitimate holder of imperial power, Severus also announced the adoption of himself and his family into the line of Marcus Aurelius and the deification of Commodus, and encouraged his army to declare Albinus an enemy of the state.[12] At roughly the same time – in this case we know the precise date, April 14, 195 – Severus honored his wife Julia Domna with the title *mater castrorum* (mother of the camps), a title held previously only by one woman, Faustina, the wife of Marcus Aurelius.[13] Severus probably also arranged that his official portrait and the portraits of his family should closely resemble the portraiture of Marcus Aurelius, Faustina and Commodus.[14]

The efficacy of the legal actions relating to the adoption, taken without the authorization of the Senate, was highly debatable, and it is just possible that Severus chose to keep the Senate in the dark about his self-adoption for the time being. Certainly Cassius Dio, who was in Rome at this time, seems to have thought that Severus informed the Senate about his wishes for the first time only after the defeat of Albinus in 197.[15] Severus clearly informed his partisans and those under his control elsewhere: four inscriptions survive from different parts of the empire, all reflecting developments in Severus' self-presentation within 195. The earliest originates with the First Cohort of Syrians, which was stationed at this time at Ulcisia Castra, located halfway along the road between Aquincum and Cirpi in Lower Pannonia, next to Severus' old province. The precise impulse that occasioned the inscription is unknown – perhaps the happy coincidence of a Severan victory on the twentieth anniversary of the creation of the cohort – but its text is clear:

> To Imperator Caesar Lucius Septimius Severus Pertinax Augustus, *pater patriae* (father of the fatherland), Arabicus Adiabenicus,

12. Severus first hinted at his connection to Marcus in his autobiography (Dio–Xiphilinus, 75[74].3.1). For Albinus as *hostis publicus*, see Herodian, 3.6.8, before Severus departed for the west.
13. Birley, *African Emperor*, 115–16.
14. D. Baharal, *Victory of Propaganda. The Dynastic Aspect of the Imperial Propaganda of the Severi: The Literary and Archaeological Evidence*, A.D. *193–225* (Oxford: Tempus Reparatum, 1996), 20–33.
15. Dio, 76(75).7.4. See Mattingly, *BM Coins, Rom. Emp.* V, xciii: "There is not a hint of any attempt by Septimius to win over the Senate. Even more than the people, it was secretly friendly to Albinus: had the fortune of Septimius shown serious signs of wavering, it would have been quick to declare against him." The *Historia Augusta* insists that Severus announced the adoption during his return to the west in the spring of 196, during a stop at Viminacium on the border between Dacia and Upper Moesia (SHA *Severus* 10.3).

> *Imperator* V, consul for the second time, holding the tribunician power for the second year, *pontifex maximus* (chief priest of the college of *pontifices*), and Marcus Aurelius Antoninus Caesar, the First Cohort of the Syrians, the Aurelian Antonine, makes this dedication, when Piso and Julianus are consuls. (*AE* 1982, 817 = HD001756)

The reference to Severus' fifth acclamation as *Imperator* proves that Severus dispatched news to the army in Pannonia of his latest victory while still in the middle of the summer's campaign. The application of Antonine nomenclature to Caracalla alone merely suggests that the carver put as much on the stone as possible and that the document was of local origin, even if written in reaction to news sent from the imperial court. Certainly epigraphic texts dedicated by army units later in the same year credit Severus, too, with Antonine ancestry (*CIL* III 14507, from Upper Moesia). Finally, the use of similar victory titles, again in conjunction with Severus' fifth acclamation but without any reference to his self-adoption or to Caracalla, in a publicly funded inscription from Umbria, strengthens the possibility that Severus deliberately tailored his news bulletins for particular audiences around the empire (*AE* 1984, 373). Severus might well have been trying to make less explicit claims to Antonine ancestry or to the establishment of a dynasty in texts sent to Italy, prior to arranging an appropriate reception for the news on the part of the Senate.

Severus no doubt published another announcement after his next acclamation. The reception of that announcement is reflected on an inscription dedicated by the town magistrates of Kastellum, between Tipasa and Caesarea in Mauretania Caesariensis. It is the earliest extant text to record what would become the common refrain of all those allying themselves with the Antonine monarchy:

> To Imperator Caesar, son of the Divine Marcus Antoninus Pius Sarmaticus Germanicus, brother of the divine Commodus, grandson of the divine Antoninus Pius, great-grandson of the divine Hadrian, descendant of the divine Trajan Parthicus, descendant of the divine Nerva, Lucius Septimius Severus Pius Pertinax Augustus, Arabicus Adiabenicus, *pontifex maximus*, holding the tribunician power for the third time, *Imperator* VI, consul for the second time, proconsul, the bravest ... unconquered general. Dedicated by C. Iulius Ianuarius and L. Cassius Augustinus, *magistri quinquennales* (five-yearly magistrates). (*CIL* VIII 9317)

The nomenclature advertises Severus' fictive connection to the Antonine house, and the sixth acclamation as *Imperator* points to a time later than the text from Ulcisia Castra. The text is quite lavish – abbreviations are kept to a minimum. Why then is Caracalla not mentioned? First, the inscription from Ulcisia Castra probably misrepresented the situation: Caracalla, only seven years old in 195, undoubtedly did not yet have a true share in his father's power. Rather, Severus had simply marked him out as his designated successor: the name Caesar, which Caracalla acquired at this time, therefore had no more and no less significance than the title *imperator destinatus*, "emperor designate," which was attached to his name in some inscriptions until at least 197.[16] Second, even if Caracalla had been mentioned in the announcement that Ianuarius and Augustinus commemorated, they may not have known what his titulature signified. After all, Commodus had been the last child of an emperor to rule jointly with his father, and even he had not appeared at the head of an epistle until proclaimed Augustus in 177, when he was sixteen years old.[17]

It is, however, by no means clear that Severus attempted to claim that Caracalla was ruling jointly with him at this time before *every* audience. A fragmentary inscription from Prymnessus, in Phrygia in the province of Asia, preserves the beginning of a letter from Severus to the town. Though only the beginnings of the lines are preserved, it is clear that the text dates from the second half of 195: Severus' connections to the Antonine house are specified, but he is still listed as consul for the second time. Most importantly, there is no space at all for any mention of Caracalla at the head of the letter (Oliver, no. 214). Similarly, when Julius Pacatianus, the man installed by Severus as the first governor of Osrhoene following the annexation of that territory in the late summer of 195, surveyed the border between Osrhoene and the kingdom of Abgar of Emesa, he cited the authority of Severus alone (*AE* 1984, 919).

The fragmentary state of Severus' letter to Prymnessus does not allow any clarity regarding its purpose. However, the likelihood that Severus was responding to an embassy sent by Prymnessus, which had itself been dispatched in response to some announcement about his victories and about the new status of Caracalla, is greatly increased by the existence of a complete letter from Severus later

16. J. Šašel, "Dolichenus-Heiligtum in Praetorium Latobicorum: Caracalla, Caesar, *imperator destinatus*," ZPE 50 (1983), 203–8, publishing a text from Praetorium Latobicorum. See also HD033021, from Africa Proconsularis.
17. *ILS* 375, on which see P. Herrmann, "Eine Kaiserurkunde der Zeit Marc Aurels aus Milet," *MDAI(I)* 25 (1975), 149–66 at 152–3.

in the same year, addressed to the city of Aezani, approximately 100 km from Prymnessus. In it Severus advertised his eighth acclamation as *Imperator*, placing his response sometime after the fall of Byzantium in late 195 but before December 10 of that year. He thanked Aezani for its embassy:

> The pleasure that you take in my success and in the rise of my son Marcus Aurelius Antoninus with good fortune to the hopes of the empire and to a position alongside his father, I have seen most clearly in your decree. I am in addition pleased that you have conducted a public celebration and sacrificed thanks-offerings to the gods, since your city is famous and has long been useful to the Roman Empire. Because I saw that a Victory had come to be a witness to my success, along with your decree, I have sent this letter to you to be placed among your local gods. (Oliver, no. 213)

The Victory to which Severus refers is almost undoubtedly a golden statue of the sort that Tripolis, in the account provided by Ammianus, sent to Valentinian as its contribution of so-called "crown gold" on the occasion of his accession (Ammianus, 28.6.7). Though the Aezanitae had clearly been informed about the change in Caracalla's status and mentioned that change in their decree, Severus alone responded, indicating unsurprisingly once again that Caracalla did not yet actively participate in the exercise of power (*ILS* 8805).

Severus waited to leave the east until he had certain news of the fall of Byzantium, which had sided with Niger (perhaps from expediency) and held out long against the forces of Severus (Dio–Xiphilinus, 75[74].14.1–2). The news of his self-adoption into the Antonine house spread farther around the empire: awareness of the consecration of Commodus is abundantly attested in inscriptions during this year.[18] Though coins from the mint at Rome prove that Severus stopped in Rome in the winter of 196/7 prior to proceeding against Albinus in Gaul, that visit has left no trace in our literary sources. The history of Cassius Dio, whose narrative would no doubt have revealed much, is preserved only in fragments for this period, and both Herodian and the *Historia Augusta* depict Severus proceeding directly from the east to Gaul.[19] It is significant, in light of what was said before about Severus' tailoring his self-presentation

---

18. J. Hasebroek, *Untersuchungen zur Geschichte des Kaisers Septimius Severus* (Heidelberg: C. Winter, 1921), 89 n. 4.
19. Mattingly, *BM Coins, Rom. Emp.* V, xcii–xciii; Birley, *African Emperor*, 123.

to conform to constitutional niceties that would flatter the Roman Senate, that on a dedication to Nerva that Severus made at Rome in the fall of 196 he did not use the nomenclature that claimed Antonine ancestry and that is so abundantly attested in other parts of the empire at just this time: he called Nerva his "forefather," *atavus*, a term that staked a much less direct claim to ancestry than the official *abnepos*, "descendant," and he designated himself merely L. Septimius Severus Pius Pertinax Augustus (*ILS* 418).

The situation had clearly changed once again in Severus' favor following the defeat of Albinus. Severus sent the head of Albinus to Rome to be displayed on a pole, along with a letter intimating the punishment of the friends of Albinus that was to come. It may be that he informed the Senate officially of his wishes with regard to his own adoption into the Antonine house and his desires for Caracalla for the first time in this letter.[20] The Senate, no doubt hoping to appease him prior to his return to the imperial city, sent an embassy both to him and to Antoninus Caesar, *imperator destinatus*.[21] The creation of a title for Caracalla, that of official successor to the throne, would be insulting if it had been officially known to the Senate that Caracalla already shared in the imperial power. Having declared Albinus an enemy of the state on his own initiative, Severus allowed his soldiers to rejoice in their victorious Gallic campaign (*ILS* 1140 and 3029; *AE* 1914, 248). The authority of Severus and the new position of Caracalla are firmly attested in a dedication from Lugdunum, the site of Albinus' final defeat on February 19: on May 4, 197, a group of local priests and priestesses in the imperial cult vowed a *taurobolium* (a specific form of sacrifice of a bull) for the health and safety of Imperator L. Septimius Severus Pius Pertinax Augustus, M. Aurelius Antoninus *Imperator destinatus*, Julia Augusta *mater castrorum*, and the whole of the *domus divina* (the 'divine' or imperial house), and for the condition of their colony (*ILS* 4134).

It is during his narrative of the year 197, immediately following his description of Severus' mutilation of the body of Albinus and

20. Herodian, 3.8.1. Dio–Xiphilinus, 76(75).5.3–8.4, alas, does not make it clear whether Severus' announcement of his self-adoption and desires for Caracalla were contained in the same speech that he read out to the Senate in the summer of 197, in which he ridiculed the clemency of Pompey and Caesar and defended the memory of Commodus: see F. Millar, *A Study of Cassius Dio* (Oxford: Clarendon Press, 1964), 142.
21. The embassy is recorded on a dedication which narrates the career of one of the ambassadors, P. Porcius Optatus (*ILS* 1143).

the sending of his head to Rome, that Dio comments on Severus' affiliation with the house of Marcus and in particular on the praise the latter now bestowed on Commodus, in strong contrast to the rhetoric adopted by Severus in the immediate aftermath of the death of Pertinax. Dio casts his remarks in the first person plural, referring to himself and his fellow senators:

> It especially upset us that he described himself as the son of Marcus and brother of Commodus and that he gave divine honors to Commodus, whom he had recently abused. Reading a speech to the Senate, and praising the severity and cruelty of Sulla and Marius and Augustus as being safer, and denigrating the gentleness of Pompey and Caesar as having been the bane of those men, he gave a speech of defense on Commodus' behalf in which he attacked the senate for having unjustly dishonored that man. (Dio–Xiphilinus, 76[75].7.4– 8.1)

Then, in a display of tyrannical power – tyrannical insofar as its only rationale lay in the whim of the ruler – Severus released from custody thirty-five senators affiliated with Albinus but killed twenty-nine others, among whom was Sulpicianus, the father-in-law of Pertinax.

Finally, chance has preserved three further documents written in the context of Severus' second Parthian war, in the latter half of 197 and lasting through early 198. Sometime in the late fall of 197 Severus was acclaimed *Imperator* for the tenth time, probably following the fall of Ctesiphon.[22] News of this event then circulated. Severus subsequently chose to celebrate his victories in the east in grander style on the anniversary of the official date of the accession of Trajan, the last man to win a major victory over Parthia. On January 28, therefore, Severus was acclaimed again and, in what was no doubt a splendid ceremony, he elevated Caracalla to Augustus and his younger son, Geta, to the rank of Caesar. He thus further associated himself and his sons with the identity, achievements and institutional memory of the Antonine dynasty.[23]

22. Zvi Rubin, "Dio, Herodian, and Severus' second Parthian war," *Chiron* 5 (1975), 419–41 at 436.
23. R. O. Fink, A. S. Hoey and W. F. Snyder, "The *Feriale Duranum*," *YClS* 7 (1940), 1–222 at 77–81. Trajan, too, had manipulated calendrical data for propagandistic reasons. He celebrated his birthday on September 18, the day Domitian had died and Nerva had been promoted to the throne: "it would be a very remarkable coincidence, if Trajan's own birthday had actually fallen on that critical date" (Harold Mattingly, "The imperial '*vota*'," *Proceedings of the British Academy* 36 [1950], 155–95 at 183 n. 12).

In response to a message announcing Severus' tenth acclamation, the city of Aphrodisias in Caria issued a decree and dispatched an embassy to deliver it. The ability of such embassies – like that from Alexandria which reached Augustus in Gaul – to find the emperor in itself suggests something of the frequency and content of his dispatches to them. The Aphrodisian embassy reached Severus after the elevation of Caracalla, for the answer to it was issued jointly by Severus and Caracalla, but it makes reference only to the joy of Aphrodisias at Severus' success against the barbarians.[24] The ceremony on January 28, 198, must have been widely publicized: Aphrodisias, either in response to news of that event, or because the earlier response from the Augusti revealed Caracalla's new status, wrote another decree and sent another embassy. This time they specifically acknowledged the promotion of Caracalla, and it was he who ostensibly authored the reply: it was most fitting, he wrote, for a city that had already celebrated the victory over the barbarians and the establishment of universal peace now to congratulate him on his promotion.[25]

An embassy in response to the ceremony of January 28 also reached Severus from Nicopolis ad Istrum, in Lower Moesia. That embassy thanked him for all his recent benefactions, to which Severus responded:

> We see your goodwill towards us most clearly from your decree, for thus have you shown yourselves to be loyal and pious and anxious to better yourselves in our judgment, by rejoicing in the present conditions and by celebrating a public festival at the good news of our benefactions: an all-embracing peace existing for all mankind, created through the defeat of those barbarians who always harass the empire, and the joining of ourselves in this just partnership, because we have a Caesar who is from our house and legitimate. Therefore we have read your decree with appropriate respect and have accepted your contribution of 700,000 [N.B. no unit of value is stated] as from loyal men. (Oliver, no. 217, ll. 21–35)

Apart from its other information, the ideological importance of dynastic succession is here stressed (at least implicitly in opposition to mere adoption of the best man – including, posthumously, Albinus) in the reference to the elevation of Caracalla's younger

24. J. Reynolds, *Aphrodisias and Rome* (London: Society for the Promotion of Roman Studies, 1982), no. 17.
25. Reynolds, *Aphrodisias and Rome*, no. 18.

brother Geta to the position of Caesar in subordination to his brother and father: Geta is a Caesar "from our house and legitimate."

Beyond the data they provide regarding the movements, wars and titulature of Severus and his sons, the more general importance of these texts lies in their illustration of the continuous nature of the dialogue between emperor and provincials over his good deeds and the nature of the claims and actions advanced and undertaken in the course of those exchanges. Quite apart from the need of emperors at the start of their reigns to advertise their strengths and achievements, they could only raise such *ad hoc* monies in a regular way if they continued to communicate; for their part, local governments had to respond to announcements with a decree that acknowledged a specific event, be it an anniversary or a victory. Participants in those municipal councils cannot have failed to notice that the titulature at the head of any news bulletin evolved to reflect and record significant moments in the reign. Significant resources of shared historical memory and political self-consciousness were thus constructed.

Ending in peace and war (February 202–February 211)

Severus returned from his second Parthian war to Rome overland, reaching the city in 202. There he celebrated the tenth anniversary of his accession, which event included the dedication of a victory arch in his honor, granted him by the Senate and people of Rome (Dedicatory inscription: *ILS* 425; Figures 2 and 3). Then he departed for North Africa. There he inspected construction work in his home town, Lepcis Magna: he had set in motion, and provided financing for, a massive monumentalization project, which included an extraordinary colonnaded street, a magnificent theater and a new forum with related buildings around (a basilica; a market). The city for its part voted him a triumphal arch, which he graciously financed. The abandonment of the city in late antiquity has left its ruins among the best preserved in North Africa, and the ensemble presents a startling testament to Roman urbanism (Figures 4–6).

Severus returned to Rome by June 203. That year if not earlier he began preparations to celebrate the end of one era and the start of a new one, in the form of the so-called Secular Games (*ludi Saeculares*). The games themselves were celebrated June 1–3, 204, in a splendid and expensive ensemble with *ludi honorarii* (ad hoc games provided through the generosity of a magistrate) on June

Figure 2 The dedicatory inscription from the arch of Septimius Severus in the forum at Rome (Photograph: Clifford Ando)

Figure 3 The north-west frieze of the arch of Septimius Severus in the forum at Rome (Photograph: Clifford Ando)

Figure 4 The arch of Septimius Severus at Lepcis Magna (Photograph: David Gunn; public domain)

4–10 and the *lusus Troiae* (Trojan games) on June 11. Despite attempts by scholars and religious experts in antiquity to endow the *ludi Saeculares* with a systematizing rationale, they remain something of a paradox: formally, they marked the end of one *saeculum* and the start of another, but the seemingly crucial question of how many years (or what other criterion) made a *saeculum* was debated without ever being decisively answered. Nonetheless, because emperors used these occasions to mark their reigns as having historic, even cosmic significance, they remain among the very best-attested

Figure 5 The theater at Lepcis Magna (Photograph: David Gunn; public domain)

Figure 6 The market at Lepcis Magna (Photograph: Sascha Coachman; public domain)

religious rituals in all of antiquity.[26] Hugely detailed records were made of the rituals performed: full enough for the games under Augustus, the records for the games under Severus are without parallel. Remarkably, these still lack even a competent survey. For some incidental reflections on their meaning in comparison with other ritual acts undertaken by Caracalla and Decius, see Chapters 3 and 6 (pp. 55–7, 123–5 and 139–41).

The years in Rome were notable as well for a drama at once domestic and political. At nearly every step of his career, Severus had been assisted by a boyhood friend from Lepcis Magna, Gaius Fulvius Plautianus, to whom Severus may have been related through his mother. Severus made Plautianus prefect of the guard in Rome in 195, and in 197 elevated him to praetorian prefect; and Plautianus repaid this trust with loyal service in every war – against Niger and Albinus and on both Parthian campaigns. In the years of peace Plautianus' power greatly increased, as he extended networks of patronage throughout the upper classes at Rome and massively extended his reach into the imperial economy: his position seemed to be cemented in 201 when his daughter Fulvia was engaged to Caracalla, and the marriage was carried out in 202. The meaning of the marriage tie was perceptible to all: an honorific inscription from Aquileia describes Plautianus as "the intimate of our emperors, in-law and father-in-law of the Augusti" (AE 1979, 294; see also HD018959, 021344 and elsewhere). But rival interests within the imperial house began to turn against him, most importantly Severus' own brother and the savage Caracalla. In January 205, Plautianus was denounced for having plotted against Severus and was murdered at Caracalla's command.

> Thus this man, who was the most powerful of all people in my life-time, such that all feared and trembled more before him than before the emperors themselves, and who had been raised to still greater hopes, was murdered by his son-in-law and tossed from the palace into the street, for only later was he carried away and buried at the command of Severus. (Dio–Xiphilinus, 77[76].4)

Immense numbers of his adherents were caught up in his ruin, as occurred also in the demise of Sejanus under Tiberius. Plautianus' properties were so extensive that a special procurator had to be

---

26. The epigraphic records for all the Secular Games were collected and edited by G. B. Pighi, *De ludis saecularibus populi Romani Quiritium* (Milan: Società Editrice Vita e Pensiero, 1941; reprint Amsterdam: P. Schippers, 1965).

appointed to locate and collect them (*ILS* 1370 = *HD*005839).

Dio asserts that Severus undertook the war in Britain merely to make war: to give the legions and his sons something to do. Arriving in Britain in 208, he lingered there for three years, venturing north into Scotland but achieving nothing more than provoking sufficient resistance to justify venturing north again. Dio's narrative concentrates wholly on the growing enmity between Caracalla and his brother Geta and the tension this produced between Caracalla and Severus. (Dio also asserts, not wholly implausibly, that Caracalla openly indicated his desire to murder them both.) Severus' final instructions to his sons – his very words, according to Dio – concentrated on just those problems: "Get along with each other; enrich the soldiery; despise all others" (Dio–Xiphilinus, 77[76].15.2). Caracalla was unpersuaded and murdered his brother in their mother's arms. To that event, and to the lingering fate of the house of Severus, we turn in the next chapter.

Dio's obituary for Severus contains two facts at seeming odds with the general tone of his narrative. First, Severus left the finances of the empire strong: massively depleted by civil war upon his accession, the treasury contained a substantial surplus at his death (Dio–Xiphilinus, 77[76].16.4). Second, as emperor he spent every morning until midday judging legal disputes. And indeed, though not strictly for his personal involvement alone, the age of Severus and his dynasty looms large in the history of law, which topic will form the subject of Chapter 4. But it should be noted already here that exercising jurisdiction – holding court, hearing appeals, responding to petitions – was throughout the history of Rome an absolutely essential function of the imperial office, and the reign of Severus gives particularly rich evidence of the emperor's personal involvement, in the form of dozens of responses on papyrus, delivered on the occasion of his visit to Egypt in 199–201.[27]

Commencing his narrative proper on January 1, 193, Gibbon regarded the reign of Severus as a turning point in Roman power.

> Till the reign of Severus, the virtue and even the good sense of the emperors had been distinguished by their zeal or affected reverence for the senate, and by a tender regard to the nice frame of civil policy instituted by Augustus. But the youth of Severus had been trained

27. See esp. *P.Apokrimata* = *SB* 6.9526 = Oliver, nos 226–38. In general see Jean-Pierre Coriat, *Le prince législateur: La technique législative des Sévères et les méthodes de création du droit impérial à la fin du principat* (Rome: École française de Rome, 1997).

> in the implicit obedience of camps, and his riper years spent in the despotism of military command. His haughty and inflexible spirit could not discover, or would not acknowledge, the advantage of preserving an intermediate power, however imaginary, between the emperor and the army. He disdained to profess himself the servant of an assembly that detested his person and trembled at his frown; he issued his commands, where his requests would have proved as effectual; assumed the conduct and style of a sovereign and a conqueror, and exercised, without disguise, the whole legislative, as well as the executive power. (Gibbon, *Decline and Fall*, 1:147)

> The contemporaries of Severus, in the enjoyment of the peace and glory of his reign, forgave the cruelties by which it had been introduced. Posterity, who experienced the fatal effects of his maxims and example, justly considered him as the principal author of the decline of the Roman empire. (Gibbon, *Decline and Fall*, 1:148)

Typically, Gibbon here insists that the importance of events was not necessarily apparent to contemporaries, who regularly lacked percipience and in any event did not see the effects of events even of their own lifetime. What is more, it is important to recognize that Gibbon's judgment is complex and qualitative: Severus revealed the working of power relations among interest groups within the state more nakedly than ever before; he more openly mocked or discounted the discursive and institutional structure by which those relations had been channeled, controlled and disguised.

Pursuing for a moment Gibbon's line of analysis, we might note that like Marcus Aurelius, Severus, too, cited the authority of the Senate in making law. In a famous text preserved in several copies (not least bilingual ones), Severus dressed down an inquirer for not knowing a decree of the Senate that forbade the billeting of persons in the houses of senators without their permission:

> *Sacrae Litterae*
> You seem to us not to know the decree of the Senate in accordance with which, if you had consulted a legal expert, you would know that it is not compulsory for a senator of the Roman people unwillingly to take in a guest. Given on the day before the Kalends of June in Rome when Fabius Cilo (for the second time) and Annius Libo were consuls (AD 204).[28]

---

28. Thomas Drew-Bear, W. Eck and P. Herrmann, "*Sacrae Litterae*," *Chiron* 7 (1977), 355–83; C. P. Jones, "The *Sacrae Litterae* of 204: Two colonial copies," *Chiron* 14 (1984), 93–9.

What is striking about these texts is the heading, *Sacrae Litterae*, "Sacred Letters," which phrase marks out the text as an utterance of the emperor himself (or, in this case, the emperors themselves). As we saw in Chapter 1, Marcus Aurelius had, by contrast, taken great pains that even the form of his text should respect the power of the Senate to make his proposal into law; and, what is more, his wishes in that regard were to a point respected in its inscription in the provinces. Without placing too great an emphasis on a single document (albeit one extant in multiple copies), even provincials understood that power in the Severan empire derived from the emperor alone.

CHAPTER 3

The legacies of Septimius Severus

Severus left the empire a paradoxical legacy. He had certainly not lost any wars – the territorial integrity of the empire remained intact. What is more, at the moment of his death, the empire's finances were not obviously precarious.

And yet, it might also be said that he had planted the seeds of its (short- and medium-term) ruin. The dynasty that he established was incompetent. His subversion of an earlier balance between interest groups grossly increased the power in politics of army units and their commanders and accelerated the increase in cost of maintaining the army overall. Finally, his exploitation of a declining Parthian empire for domestic political gain sowed the seeds of a disastrous antagonism with its successor in the east. The instability of the Roman empire in the third century is due in no small measure to the repeated disasters it suffered on the eastern front, which claimed vast numbers of lives and stores of money and sapped legitimacy and prestige from the imperial system as a whole.

The murder of Geta (February–December 211)

The marriage that produced the emperors Caracalla and Geta was in fact Severus' second. The first, to Paccia Marciana, a woman of his home town, ended with her death and was without issue. In 187 (probably, but perhaps 185) he married again: his bride was Julia Domna, born of the royal house of Emesa in Syria. The rumor later circulated that Severus sought her out after he learned that her horoscope predicted she would marry a king (SHA *Severus* 3.9). He may have met her when he served in Syria earlier in the decade. She bore him two sons, Bassianus, who was probably born in 188 but perhaps in 186 – he was later called Caracalla after the name of a Celtic-style robe that he invented (Dio 79[78].3.3) – and Geta, born in 189. Julia Domna was prized and honored by Severus and acquired immense public prestige, being granted unprecedented public titles that culminated in the weighty "mother of the camps and Senate and fatherland."[1] She also had a sister, one Julia Maesa, whose influence would eclipse anything recorded for Julia Domna; to her story we shall return.

Although Severus advanced Caracalla to each new honor first (Caracalla being the older), he had clearly wished the brothers to rule together after his death: quite apart from Dio's report regarding Severus' last words to the brothers (see p. 45), Severus had named them ordinary consuls together in both 205 and 208 and at some point during the campaign in Britain (208–11) named Geta to honors fully equivalent to those of his brother: Imperator Caesar Publius Septimius Geta Augustus, proconsul, father of his fatherland (*IlAlg* 4664).

Nor is there any doubt, or any dispute, what happened next. Severus died at Eburacum in Britain on February 4, 211. Caracalla and Geta immediately began joint rule, but narratives of the next nine months attribute virtually all agency to Caracalla. They also focus nearly relentlessly on his hostility to his brother. The former imbalance may to a point reflect political reality: Caracalla was the elder and had ruled longer. And even the latter imbalance may not distort: the most important actions of the joint reign were no doubt to end the war in Britain and return to Rome, there to consecrate their father, even as their father had consecrated Pertinax (Herodian, 4.2). That said, despite the focus of our narrative sources on their personal relations, each is known rapidly to have established an independent administrative apparatus, and the fundamental business of empire – including judicial business – must have gone on. What is more, however decisions were produced, they will have been promulgated in the name of both rulers.

Things came to a head in December. In order to isolate Geta from his bodyguard, Caracalla tricked their mother into inviting the two of them, unaccompanied, to her apartments for a reconciliation. Caracalla had stationed soldiers at the ready: these rushed upon Geta and slew him in their mother's arms.

> After the murder Caracalla was the first to jump up and run from the chamber. Rushing through the whole palace, he shouted out that he had escaped a great danger and only just been saved … The soldiers

1. Dio clearly thought Julia Domna a woman of good character and he spares kind words for her, largely by way of reflecting on her inability to restrain her monstrous son (see, e.g., Dio–Xiphilinus, 78[77].18.2–3).

> believed him, since they had no idea what had been done inside, and
> so they all rushed outside with him ... Bursting into the camp and the
> temple [at the center of the camp] where the standards and divine
> images belonging to the legion are stored, Caracalla threw himself on
> the ground. Then he offered thanks and made a sacrifice for his
> safety. (Herodian, 4.4.3–6)

As news trickled in through fugitives from the palace and the guard
became restive, Caracalla offered a massive donative and, according
to Herodian, authorized the soldiers to seize it themselves from the
treasuries. "The soldiers saluted him as sole emperor and declared
Geta a public enemy" (4.4.7).

Although Dio was better positioned to know the details, his
intense (and fully justified) hatred of Caracalla concentrates overly
much on Caracalla's pathological co-dependency on the legions,
and theirs on him. This may in fact have been appropriate as an
interpretive position with regard to Caracalla's reign as a whole, but
one wants to know the very words by which Caracalla made this
dependency explicit:

> Although it was evening, Caracalla seized control of the legions [near
> Rome], crying the whole way as if he had been the object of a plot
> and in danger. Reaching the wall of the camp, he said, "Rejoice,
> fellow-soldiers: for now I am able to do well by you." Then, before
> they heard all that had happened, he stopped their mouths with so
> many and so great promises that they could neither plan nor speak
> proper pieties for the deceased. "I am one of you," he said, "and
> for you alone I am willing to go on living, so that I might grant
> you many things. For all the treasuries are yours." (Dio–Xiphilinus,
> 78(77).3.1–2)

Caracalla immediately embarked on a massive purge of Geta's
supporters and all those others who had been somehow protected
from his dislike by his father's lingering influence, as well as nearly
anyone who could claim relation by blood, however distant, with a
former emperor. Dio, Herodian and the *Historia Augusta* report in
horrific terms on the extent of the purge, Dio numbering the dead at
20,000 (Dio–Xiphilinus, 78(77).3.4; Herodian, 4.6; SHA *Caracalla*
3.3–4.9). Whatever the exact number, the savagery on this occasion
is of a piece with the slaughter of civilians in Alexandria ordered by
Caracalla on the occasion of his visit there in 215 (on which see
below, p. 60).

Much is made by Dio of the impossible position in which

Caracalla placed his mother, and indeed, Julia Domna must have been forced to play her part: "To her alone, the Augusta, the wife of an emperor and the mother of emperors, was it not permitted to cry even in private over such a loss" (Dio–Xiphilinus, 78(77).2.6). Though we have no source of information regarding her feelings, we do know that her relatives – Caracalla's aunt, Julia Maesa, and her many descendents – were banished from Rome, though not killed. But Julia Domna and Severus remained the ideological foundations on which Caracalla rested his claim to rule, even if *de facto* he relied more and more on force and violence. As a result, although Caracalla officially condemned the memory of his brother (in Roman terms, enacted a *damnatio memoriae*), and so required the defacing of Geta's images and name from any public record, monuments carrying the image of the house persisted, but with Geta erased: it was now, and was in official memory of the past, a house of three. Perhaps the most famous record of this act is a painted tondo reproduced on the cover of this volume, very likely of Egyptian origin, that originally depicted Geta and Caracalla standing in front of Julia Domna and Severus, from which Geta's face was subsequently erased (Figure 7). Epigraphic testimonials to the condemnation of Geta's memory abound (Figure 8).

The spin that Caracalla placed on the murder of Geta at that initial moment in the camp, namely, that Geta had plotted against him and Caracalla had been saved through divine good favor, set in motion two further processes deserving consideration here. First, the salvation of the emperor from any danger had always been met with public rites of thanksgiving. The obligation is made explicit in words attributed by Herodian to Caracalla when addressing the Senate after Geta's death. After citing actions taken by earlier emperors to forestall plots against them, Caracalla continued:

> I, too, have warded off an enemy, when poisons had been prepared and his sword drawn. Enemy is the name his deeds have won for him. You must now thank the gods, because they have saved at least one of your emperors: cease all sectarian feelings and thoughts and, looking toward one emperor, live undisturbed. For Zeus created rulership among men even as he is among the gods, one over all. (Herodian, 4.5.7)

Second, Caracalla decided to amplify the scope of the religious act by enlarging the community embraced by his command, and so granted citizenship to nearly all free residents of the empire. To that remarkable act we now turn.

Figure 7 A tondo of the Severan period, probably Egyptian. It once depicted Geta and Caracalla standing before Julia Domna and Septimius Severus, but Geta's face has been rubbed out. Antikensammlung Berlin inv. 31329 (Photograph: Bildportal der Kunstmuseen, reproduced with permission)

The Antonine Constitution (212)

For a seemingly momentous occasion – the absolute erasure of distinction between conqueror and conquered within a world empire – Caracalla's grant of universal citizenship is shrouded in mystery. Few contemporary texts even mention it. Two contemporary witnesses of impeccable credentials and reliability do – the historian Dio and the lawyer Ulpian, an advisor to emperors and ultimately praetorian prefect of Rome – but they refer to the act only in passing, the one with disdain and the other as mere matter of fact.[2] Even

2. Dio's remarks on the Antonine Constitution are quoted below, p. 58. Ulpian: "All those who are in the Roman world have been made Roman citizens as a result of a constitution of the Emperor Antoninus (Caracalla)" (Ulpian, *Ad Edictum* book 22 fr. 657 Lenel = *Dig.* 1.5.17).

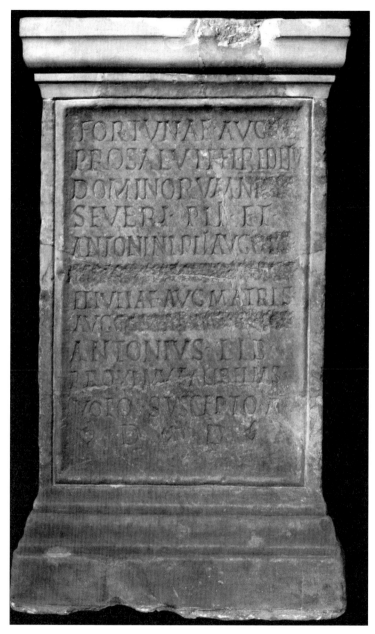

Figure 8 An altar, now in the British Museum, whose inscription was mutilated to efface Geta's name (Photograph: British Museum, reproduced with permission)

the publication in 1910 of a papyrus copy of what seems to be the very edict has raised more questions than it has answered.[3] A translation of the badly damaged text might read as follows:

> Imperator Caesar Marcus Aurelius Augustus Antoninus Pius says: [- - - - -] rather [- - - - - -] the causes and the considerations [- - - - -] I might give thanks to the immortal gods because they preserved me [from so] great [a conspiracy]. Therefore, believing that I would be able to respond [with piety and grandeur?] appropriate to their greatness if I were to lead [to the temples of the gods] [all those] now among my people, and as many as shall come into that number, I give Roman c[itizen]ship to all those dwelling under my rule, with [the rights of their communit]ies <upon them> remaining unimpaired, excepting only the [...]. (PGiss. 40 = Oliver, no. 260)

The major difficulty raised by the papyrus derives not from this text, but from the position of this edict within the papyrus itself. In its present form, it collects three edicts by Caracalla, which appear to be in chronological order – but the sequence is only three items long, and several known edicts of Caracalla from just this period are not found on it.[4] If the items are not in chronological order, a strong argument for a very specific date in 212 fails, and if that is so, the conspiracy might not have been Geta's, or the appropriate restoration might not be "conspiracy" at all. Outside some well-worn anecdotes, the next three years of Caracalla's life are poorly known, beyond the fact that he campaigned in Germany and traveled to the east. What are the perils, real or imagined, that he might have suffered in that period? (A second difficulty concerns the exception in the last line, which would appear to have bracketed two groups of persons from the grant of citizenship: foreigners who had surrendered themselves in war, as well as freed slaves found guilty of certain crimes. In a fashion typical of Roman law, the latter had once needed to be classified and assigned rights before the law and had been lumped in with a group and under a title – *dediticii*, "foreigners who had surrendered in war" – with whom they had nothing in common.)

That said, the social-historical consequences of an act can be analyzed independently from any reconstruction of its motivation or

---

3. A literature review covering the first half century of publications treated some ninety items, and many of the questions identified in that review remain pertinent: C. Sasse, "Literaturübersicht zur C.A.," *Journal of Juristic Papyrology* 14 (1962), 109–49.
4. On the date, see Fergus Millar, "The date of the Constitutio Antoniniana," *Journal of Egyptian Archaeology* 48 (1962), 124–31, and below, p. 57.

the specific context of its performance.⁵ Indeed, Caracalla need not
have considered or even imagined what the consequences of his act
might be. These were complex. Because understanding the legal
ramifications of the universal grant of citizenship requires considerable supplementary exposition, Chapter 4 considers the Antonine
Constitution as a moment in legal history on its own. Here I concentrate on two aspects: the intelligibility of his act as he describes it,
namely, as an act in the religious sphere; and the tracing of its effects
in space, time and across sectors of the population.

Commencing perhaps in the mid-Republic, Roman religion drew
an important distinction between public and private, for which their
terms were *publicus* and *privatus*. (Some such distinction had no
doubt existed before, but one does get a sense of its emergence as an
officially sanctioned distinction, in what becomes a stable form, in
perhaps the third or more likely the second century BC.) But we must
not be misled by the fact of etymological ancestry into assuming that
our terms map onto their terms and hence that our distinction maps
onto theirs. For them, "public" meant of and for the citizen body, no
more, no less. Hence "public rites," "the rites of the Roman people,"
those rites conducted by magistrates, were performed on behalf of
the citizen body as a whole, and, as a corollary, all citizens as individuals were understood to assent to those rites and, by synecdochic
representation, to participate in them.⁶ This was as fundamental a
feature of Roman religion as individual assent to law was to citizenship. One could not choose on a case-by-case basis whether to obey
a law, even if one had voted against it. No more with religion.
Indeed, the example of assent to law, and honoring of legal language
and form, was explicitly cited by the Romans as capturing the nature
of communal religious life: in this respect, and with this precise
meaning, they even described the gods of Rome as their fellow
citizens.⁷

5. A point already formulated with cogency and insight by A. N. Sherwin-White, *The
Roman Citizenship*, 2nd edition (Oxford: Clarendon Press, 1973): "The document
[*PGiss.* 40] has added little to the understanding of this act of Caracalla, which can be
evaluated independently of the papyrus" (279). "This remarkable controversy, which has
added singularly little to historical knowledge, has been concerned more with the formulation of Caracalla's pronouncement, his motives and intentions, than with the practical
effects of it in the Roman world" (380).
6. Festus s.v. *publica sacra* (284L): "Public rites are those performed at public expense
on behalf of the people," where the seeming unhelpfulness of employing *publicus/popu-
lus* to define what is *publicus* suggests rather an inability to imagine a world without this
conceptual foundation.
7. On the status of gods as citizens and their incorporation within Roman conceptions

There were, of course, numerous special occasions on which it was felt insufficient to allow magistrates to perform rites on behalf of the people. In some cases – the early *lectisternia* (rites at which gods were feasted), for example (Livy, 5.13.5–8) – it was officially enjoined that all households should perform rites in fractal relation to the public ones. Far the most common such was the *supplicatio*, a rite of supplication or propitiation in response to an ominous sign.[8] On other occasions, individuals and groups appear spontaneously to have performed their own rites, of whatever form, in harmony of sentiment with public rites. Here, thanksgivings celebrated on the occasion of Augustus' safe return to Rome, or the saving of the city from some danger, or prayers for the emperor's health, might be cited.[9] But the issue of actual material participation at the level of the individual, however important within some frameworks of historical inquiry, is wholly separable from the ideological and (one might say) doctrinal issue, of fundamental importance, that public religious acts embraced all citizens, and only citizens.

Here it would be worth emphasizing that classical Latin developed no term for "pagan" as a marker for self-identification among participants in Roman public cult. This was because the term "Roman" when applied to persons in its proper usage meant absolutely and necessarily "Roman citizen," and all citizens were religiously Roman. (Hence, in the passage of Dio quoted below [p. 58], the phrase "[Caracalla] made everyone ... Roman" means exactly the same thing as "Caracalla gave everyone Roman citizenship." It does not mean he made them culturally Roman, or made them more Roman by changing their dress or system of education or some such. Again, in legalitarian usage, there were no degrees of Romanness. There were no degrees of citizenship – only differential protections and entailments.)

Within this framework, Caracalla's assertion that his salvation from danger merited thanksgiving, and further an act of thanksgiving amplified by actual participation by all citizens, and that such

of the political community, see John Scheid, "Numa et Jupiter ou les dieux citoyens de Rome," *Archives de Sciences Sociales des Religions* 59 (1985), 41–53, and Scheid, *Religion et piété à Rome*, 2nd edition (Paris: Albin Michel, 2001). On the public–private distinction see Clifford Ando and Jörg Rüpke, *Religion and Law in Classical and Christian Rome* (Stuttgart: Steiner, 2006), 4–13.
8. The same term/rite was employed in thanksgiving, with differences that require no elaboration here.
9. See, e.g., Augustus, *Res Gestae* 4.2, 9, 11, 12.

an act would be further amplified by an increase in the number of citizens, is fully intelligible and wholly unsurprising.

Tracing the effects of the Antonine Constitution in social relations is rather more difficult. Here, scholars depend almost entirely on two bodies of evidence: personal legal documents, almost exclusively on papyrus, which testify to changes in the private law framework of social and economic relations among formerly non-Roman peoples; and nomenclature. Roman names were distinctive within the Mediterranean world. This was true, up to a point, insofar as they were Latin, but Latinity was neither necessary nor sufficient to make a name Roman. As a legal matter, Roman names had (at least) three parts – *praenomen, nomen, cognomen* – while most other systems of personal names in the ancient Mediterranean had two, very often a personal name and a patronymic (of the form "X son of Y"). It was traditional for aliens who received Roman citizenship through the patronage of a particular Roman to take the *nomen* of that individual. There survive from the first two decades of the third century two sets of documents from which one can make a systematic study of changes in nomenclature: both are rosters of military units, one (from Rome) containing tens of names, the other (from Syria) hundreds. Both suggest massive change: in each case, units that contained a majority of non-Roman names before 212 display, by late 213 or 214, a huge preponderance of "Aurelii," which is to say, new citizens who took the *nomen* of Caracalla.[10] A handful of further epigraphic and papyrological texts bear witness to such changes, not in a systematic way like the military rosters, but often (and spectacularly) with very precise dates.[11] Taken together, these suggest a remarkable reception – and remarkable publicity – for the Constitution; recursively, they help to pinpoint the date of the Constitution as absolutely no later than January 213.

Caracalla on campaign (January 213–April 217)

The five years of Caracalla's sole reign are notable almost exclusively for financial mismanagement, rapine, theft and massacre, and for

10. J. F. Gilliam, "Dura rosters and the 'Constitutio Antoniniana'," *Historia* 14 (1965), 74–92; Olivier Hekster, *Rome and its Empire, AD 193–284* (Edinburgh: Edinburgh University Press, 2008), 50–5.

11. Some early epigraphic material is cited in Gilliam, "Rosters," p. 87; see also Peter Herrmann, "Überlegungen zur Datierung der Constitutio Antoniniana," *Chiron* 2 (1972), 519–30. The earliest Egyptian evidence known in 1962 is cited in Millar, "Date," 128–9. See also below p. 95.

continuing a militaristic foreign policy instigated by his father that sowed the seeds for defeat and disaster for decades to come. In all these respects, the reign of Caracalla differs largely in degree, rather than in kind, from those of his successors in his mother's family (and many that followed). Nonetheless, the portrayals of his reign and of that of Elagabalus are remarkably negative, a fact largely to be explained by the stunning hostility they aroused – often enough knowingly – in the governing classes of the empire at large. (The same might be said of Maximinus the Thracian.)

As an illustration pertinent to many strands of this volume, one might cite one of Dio's many denunciations of Caracalla, this one concentrating on the emperor's greed and financial maladministration (as opposed to his sexual crimes, which Dio often mentions and just as often disdains to catalog):

> In the first place, there were the gold crowns that he was repeatedly demanding, on the constant pretext that he had conquered some enemy or other; and I am not referring to the actual manufacture of crowns – why would that matter? – but to the vast sums of money given under that name, with which cities were accustomed to "crown" emperors. Next there were the provisions that we were to provide often and everywhere, which he would regularly distribute to the soldiers or simply give away. And of course the gifts that he demanded from both wealthy individuals and from communities. And then the taxes! Both the others that he promulgated, as well as the tenth that he exacted – rather than the former twentieth – on the emancipation of slaves, legacies left to anyone whatsoever and all gifts. For he abolished rights of succession and the tax-free status of legacies granted to those closely related to the deceased. It was for this reason that he made everyone in his empire Roman: he claimed it was an honor, but in fact he did so in order to increase his income from these sources, because aliens did not pay most of these taxes. But beyond all these things, we were compelled to build luxurious houses for him whenever he set out from Rome, and to furnish expensive accommodation during even the shortest of journeys, and yet the absurdity extended so far that he not only never lived in them, but in some cases would never even see them. In addition, we built amphitheaters and racecourses everywhere that he wintered or even expected to winter, receiving nothing from him by way of aid, and all these were immediately demolished. This occurred for one reason only, so that we might be impoverished. (Dio–Excerpta Valesiana, 78[77].9.2–7)

Although Dio elsewhere displays real knowledge of the mechanics of rule, and a deep understanding of imperial politics, here his interest lies solely in substantiating an indictment of Caracalla for irrational greed. Indeed, a startling number of the *bons mots* attributed by Dio to Caracalla concern his desire to ruin everyone else and give to the army: "No one in the world but I should have money, so that I might give it to the soldiers" (Dio–Xiphilinus, 78[77].10.4). (In fairness, in so acting Caracalla did honor two of the three final commands of his father: see p. 45.) In reflecting on the role of an emperor's relations with the governing class in particular in shaping a literary legacy, one would do well to mark in this passage the sheer number of first-person verbs. "We" refers to men of the senatorial class, not all Romans. Dio does not approve of financial mismanagement, but he feels special indignation for the abuse of himself and his peers.

More broadly, one should take note of three further aspects of this text, two of general significance, one of more narrow relevance. First, Dio's complaint with respect to crown gold confirms two related claims advanced with regard to crown gold in Chapter 2: it was potentially a source of great revenue, and it was so only so long as emperors communicated with their subjects.[12] Second, like his father, Caracalla spent much of his reign on the move. Chapter 2 emphasized the ability of provincials to communicate with the emperor despite this fact. Dio's complaint draws attention to two further aspects of the emperor's travel (to both of which we shall return): it was very expensive (even when the emperor was not insane), and, because of the number of troops, administrators and hangers-on involved, it presented enormous logistical challenges. Even if the emperor did not require gladiators or exotic animals for combat, in an era without refrigeration, assembling the requisite volume of food for a sudden increase in local population was difficult and burdensome under the best of circumstances.

Finally, Dio's inclination to view all of Caracalla's actions through the lens of fiscal malfeasance serves him ill when he turns to the citizenship decree. The emperor had all manner of means for raising revenue, and of course could impose any tax he wanted on Romans and non-Romans alike. The idea that Caracalla had to give citizenship to the subject populations – to make them Roman – in order to

12. The tendency of emperors to lie about their military achievements – and the difficulty of learning the truth under a monarchy – are the object of frequent commentary in Dio's narrative: see Clifford Ando, *Imperial Ideology and Provincial Loyalty in the Roman Empire* (Berkeley: University of California Press, 2000), 125–6, 154 and 181–2.

render them liable to a tax he might have extended without so doing strains credulity.

Caracalla left Rome to campaign in Germany in 213: on October 6 of that year, a priestly college at Rome celebrated the arrival of news of an imperial victory (*CFA* no. 99a, ll. 22–9). The following year he departed for the east, traveling overland in order to visit the Danubian provinces. Dio was in the east at this time and reports on Caracalla's goings-on in detail: his quoting of poetry during a visit to Pergamum; sacrifices at the tomb of Achilles at Troy; gladiatorial games in Nicomedia where he wintered.[13] And all the while, preparations went on for an expedition against Armenia and Parthia: these encompassed actions both serious and costly (the building of siege engines and gathering of supplies; the military rosters preserved at Dura show greatly heightened recruitment) and idiotic and vainglorious (Caracalla indulged his fascination with Alexander the Great by training some soldiers to mimic the Macedonian phalanx; the gesture may have seemed particularly appropriate in a campaign against an empire in the east).

Caracalla passed south and north along the Syrian coast between 215 and 216, visiting Egypt along the way. There, under circumstances that remain obscure, he ordered a massacre of the local population of Alexandria. The cause seems to have been some display of disrespect – inappropriate jeering, perhaps. (Similar episodes are known from Rome in the early empire and from Antioch and Constantinople in late antiquity: the emperor Julian's bitter satire "The Beard-Hater" was directed at the population of Antioch in response to one such occasion.) But Caracalla did not write a pamphlet in response, or impose punishing taxes, or reduce the city's legal status. He loosed the army. Exactly what happened is not clear. Dio disdains to describe the slaughter itself or its mechanics but revels in attendant details, including the valuable aside that Caracalla allowed resident foreigners to leave the city before the massacre began (Dio–Xiphilinus, 78[77].22–3). According to Herodian, Caracalla announced the formation of a special army unit in honor of Alexander the Great, to be recruited from the city he had founded: having arranged all the young men in the city in rows for inspection, he directed the army to kill them all (Herodian, 4.9.4–8).

13. Dio–Excerpta Valesiana, 78(77).16.7; Dio–Excerpta Valesiana, 78(77).16.8; Dio–Xiphilinus, 78(77).17–19.

Caracalla's return journey from Egypt to Antioch is notable for an event that was in some sense wholly typical: the emperor supervised a judicial proceeding. The case concerned a temple in the village of Dmeir in the region of Rif Dimaschq in south-western Syria, where a remarkable inscription was erected in commemoration of the event. The case was heard at Antioch on May 27, 216: it arose from a dispute between a local tribe, the Goharieni, who were represented by a "defender of their interests," an Aurelius with a Semitic name, and, on the other side, a tax collector, apparently over the status of some temple lands. (A very great deal of the law on religion from the ancient world – and the modern – arises from disputes over the tax-free status of lands owned by religious properties: it is in that context that Roman legal institutions were forced to confront the question whether some religion was a real religion, or whether its god was a real god.) Much of the surviving text concentrates not on the substantive issue under dispute, however, but the question of what the appropriate venue for the case should be.

The inscription itself is notable for two related reasons.[14] First, it presents the case in the form *not* of a summary or even full quotation of the judgment alone – which would have been normal in epigraphic records – but in the costlier, lengthier form of a verbatim transcript of the proceedings. Second, the text is bilingual: but again, it does not conform to standard patterns. For example, it does not present parallel Greek and Latin texts (common enough in antiquity). Rather, the protocols of the text – the heading and dating formula, the announcement of the occasion and record of participants – are all in Latin, while the words of the participants are recorded in Greek. Indeed, even the notations of a change in speaker: "Lollianus said," "Antoninus said," are in Latin, but what follows is in Greek. (It is only fair to observe that Caracalla's interventions are wholly apposite and clearly formulated.)

The form of the text may have been unusual for an inscription. The transcript of a proceeding was, however, a fundamental genre of administrative record within Roman government. We will see in Chapter 4 that the emperor Antoninus Pius when governor of Asia required local officials to keep transcripts of interrogations whenever cases were likely subsequently to come before a Roman governor. Chapter 6 will take up the broader cultural significance of the use of

---

14. P. Roussel and F. de Visscher, "Les inscriptions du temple de Dmeir," *Syria* 23 (1942/3), 173–200 = *SEG* 17.759.

Roman forms by non-Roman or non-governmental organizations, not least Christian communities. Here let it suffice to observe that while the language of conversation in Antioch was Greek, Latin was the language of Roman government, and the use of Latin on the inscription was part and parcel of those formal aspects of the text that endowed it – and the decision it recorded – with enduring legitimacy.

The rest of Caracalla's life was consumed with military posturing on the eastern frontier. Considered in isolation, some of this activity was wholly traditional. The frontier zone between Rome and Parthia had long been filled by assorted buffer states of varying stability, size and longevity – Armenia, Osrhoene, Hatra and so forth – and the great game of foreign relations between Rome and Parthia had long consisted in minor contests over the right to place one's candidate on the throne of those kingdoms. Vologaeses the king of Parthia had died in 208, and the succession had been contested between 208 and 213 between two of his sons, Vologaeses and Artabanus. (The contest served to weaken the already diminished Arsacid house, which in turn allowed Ardashir, ruler of the breakaway province of Fars, to consolidate his control there. To his story we shall return.) Such contests for succession were also traditional moments for outside interference and the renegotiation of status markers, and these were largely the terms in which Caracalla justified his campaign to the Senate (Dio–Xiphilinus, 78[77].12.3–5, 78[77].19; Dio–Excerpta Valesiana, 78[77].21).

But in the longer trajectory, Caracalla's actions in the east and interference in Parthian affairs contributed to a broader destabilization of the Arsacid house and reorientation of Roman relations with its eastern neighbor. The annexation of new territories in the middle Euphrates by Severus had, in essence, removed the traditional buffers between Rome and Parthia. This was bad enough, but it was perceived on the Parthian and Persian side as an unjustified encroachment on tradition. (The eastern campaigns of Trajan had done much the same, but Hadrian had had the wisdom to abandon the territories annexed by Trajan immediately after Trajan's death.) Led on by the hubris and idiocy of Severus and Caracalla, the Romans opened the question of what the boundary between Rome and the empire to the east should be. They would soon wish they had not done so.

Caracalla never returned from his eastern campaign. On April 8, 218, while on the march from Edessa to Carrhae, Caracalla took to the bushes "to satisfy the needs of nature." There he was killed, in suitable ignominy but not soon enough, by one Julius Martialis, a soldier attached to the Praetorian Guard. The weakness of the Senate – its paralysis in the face of the contest for power that followed – left Caracalla for a time in limbo, neither officially consecrated nor officially condemned.[15]

Interlude: Marcus Opellius Macrinus (April 217–June 218)

We are told that Julius Martialis was one among a number of disaffected soldiers whose hatred of Caracalla was encouraged by one Marcus Opellius Macrinus (Dio, 79[78].5.1–5; Herodian, 4.12.3–13.2). This claim is now impossible to assess, not least because we are also told that no evidence existed connecting Macrinus to Martialis, else Macrinus would have been killed. Nonetheless, in the short term Macrinus profited greatly from Caracalla's death, ruling (as it were) the empire for a few days shy of fourteen months between Caracalla's demise and his own. An imperial functionary of no particular distinction, Macrinus ranks among those third-century emperors whose only talents were murder and bribery and whose only useful official act – and very nearly only act – was his own death.

Early in his career, Macrinus had worked for the praetorian prefect Fulvius Plautianus, who, after having been raised to unprecedented heights by Septimius Severus, fell spectacularly from favor. Many followers and dependents were associated in his ruin. Macrinus' career recovered, but there can be little doubt that he felt as acutely as anyone the danger of proximity to Caracalla. His service on the Parthian campaign earned him consular honors, but the closer one came to a tyrant, the faster and harder one might fall. It is not for us now to second-guess his motivation for the plot.

For three days after the assassination, Macrinus bided his time, lest any claimant appear to have killed Caracalla for his own advancement. "During that time, the affairs of the Romans were utterly *anarchta* – literally 'unruled' or perhaps 'ungoverned' – though they did not know it." But by April 11, 217, Macrinus had cemented support and was acclaimed *Imperator* – the first non-senator to reach the throne (Dio, 79[78].11; Herodian, 4.14.1–3).

Macrinus was in a difficult position, having assumed the throne in

15. Death: Dio, 79(78).5; SHA *Caracalla* 6.6. Posthumous limbo: Dio, 79(78).9.

the midst of a pointless campaign, one in clear contravention of an earlier treaty. His own interests clearly lay in extricating himself as soon as possible from Parthian soil and returning to Roman territory, lest some other candidate should appear before his claim was secure. He thus moved along three fronts: first, he continued the war in Parthia even as he commenced negotiations to end it, which he eventually did in early spring 218 on unfavorable terms, paying perhaps as much as 50,000,000 *denarii* in reparations for the Roman war of aggression (Dio, 79[78].26.2–27.4; Herodian, 4.15).[16] Second, he began seeking the Senate's support, informing it of his actions and seeking its imprimatur; and third, he anticipated the Senate (to put the matter politely) by assuming the prerogatives of office and, most importantly, by appointing his 10-year-old son Diadumenianus as Caesar.[17] Dio does not say so, but it may be that the Senate moved slowly in voting Macrinus the regular honors of office, perhaps from offense at his presumption, or perhaps because the Senate was far from the action and fully aware of the dangers of committing itself in the face of uncertainty. Whatever the cause, Macrinus appears to have received the title "father of the fatherland" in midsummer and to have been co-opted into the priestly colleges only in December.

Like Pertinax – and Julianus and Severus, for that matter – Macrinus thought he had ended a dynasty, and like them he faced the difficulty that dynastic continuity was an immensely important source of legitimacy. What is more, like Pertinax, Macrinus did not want to claim even a fictive tie to his immediate predecessor (namely, Caracalla): Macrinus therefore took the official name Imperator Caesar Marcus Opellius *Severus* Augustus; later, sensing the restiveness of the soldiery, he bestowed the name Antoninus on his son (Dio, 79[78].17.2 and 19.1–2).

Events rapidly slipped beyond Macrinus' control. At some point after the murder of Geta, Julia Domna's sister, Julia Maesa, had returned from Rome to Emesa with her two daughters, Julia Soaemias and Julia Mamaea, Soaemias being the elder of the two (Dio, 79[78].30.2–4; Herodian, 5.3.2). Each of them had a son, whose given names are not knowable with certainty: Dio reports

16. Thomas Pekáry, "Le tribut aux Perses et les finances de Philippe l'Arab," *Syria* 38 (1961), 275–83 at 278.
17. Dio, 79(78).15–16 is sadly lacunose, but it is clear that Dio describes the reception by the Senate of letters from Macrinus, which Macrinus signed using the titles of office: "without awaiting any vote on our part, as would have been appropriate."

them as Varius Avitus (known to posterity as Elagabalus) and Bassianus, but Herodian names the elder Bassianus and the other Alexianus. The uncertainty is at once a sign of confusion in the centers of power regarding the structure of that most peculiar household, as well as evidence of the power of new imperial truths to efface mere social realities: in this case, the power of imperial titulature and the empire's communicative apparatus worked together to erase a former identity in favor of a constructed, dynastic one.

In any event, at some point early in 218, Maesa began to circulate the rumor that Elagabalus and his cousin were both natural sons of Caracalla. The rumor found a ready audience in the rank-and-file soldiers stationed in the region, who had not shared Macrinus' dislike of Caracalla and were apparently distressed at his harping on about the state of the imperial finances. This is not the first time, nor will it be the last, that the army reacted badly to the prospect of an austerity program. As the rumor spread of the boys' relation to Caracalla, along with reports of Julia Maesa's great wealth, the troops indicated favor – and by May the deal was struck. The boy was brought to the legionary camp at Emesa and acclaimed Antoninus, and a donative was granted (Herodian, 5.3.9–12).

When Macrinus heard the news from Emesa, he sent a force to put down the incipient insurrection, but his troops instead joined Elagabalus. Their commander escaped but was seized by another unit at Apamea, which had likewise exchanged its loyalty: they cut off his head and it was given to Macrinus. He was not so daft as not to understand the message (Dio, 79[78].34.1–6). Macrinus also wrote to the Senate, letters that Dio seems to have felt betrayed a mind rapidly losing its grip: and yet, Macrinus was emperor, and solemn imprecations were made against Elagabalus and his cousin and both their mothers, "as is customary when such things happen" (Dio, 79[78].38.1). Within days, the Senate changed its mind and declared Macrinus and his son public enemies: we might add, "as was customary when such things happened."

Macrinus tried to endow his position with the solidity of a dynasty by promoting his son Diadumenianus to the rank of Augustus even as he prepared for battle. The armies of the two emperors met near Antioch on June 8, 218 (Dio, 79[78].37.3–39.1). While the battle's outcome was still unknown, Macrinus disappeared, whether to rally more troops or in flight. He was seized only after he had crossed the Hellespont and was executed.

And so, fleeing rather than conquered, Macrinus made off like a runaway slave through the provinces that he had ruled, and was arrested like some bandit at first encounter ... He was condemned to die, who had possessed the power to punish or pardon any Roman whatsoever; and he was arrested and beheaded by centurions, whom he had the power to kill, along with others of greater and lesser rank. And his son died with him. (Dio, 79[78].40.5)

The dynasty of Julia Maesa, 1: Elagabalus (March 218–March 222)

Even as third-century Roman emperors go, Elagabalus cuts an unusual figure. Inappropriate for the office to a highly unusual degree, his arrival on the throne testifies to the staggering sclerosis of imperial politics. His survival there for nearly four years must testify at least in part to a desire on the part of many for a respite (a desire Elagabalus in the end could not satisfy). It must also testify to the ongoing competence of Rome's administrative apparatus, however minimal and geographically attenuated. Four rescripts in the Code bear witness to the functioning of the imperial judicial apparatus under Elagabalus.[18] By contrast, none is preserved from the reign of Macrinus.

Before Elagabalus was acclaimed on May 16, 218, his primary occupation had been the performance of his duties as high priest of an Emesene cult of the god Elagabal, who was worshipped in the form of a baityl or unfigured rock. (In origin, the cult was probably directed at a sacred mountain, though some Greek dedications identify the god with the sun.) Elagabalus continued in this role as emperor. Indeed, he appears to have insisted that the title "Most High Priest of the God Unconquered Sun Elagabalus" be added to his official titulature. A very great deal of ancient testimony about his reign concerns the exoticness of the cult and the strangeness of his own deportment (Dio–Xiphilinus, 80[79].11; Herodian, 5.5–6). Indeed, just about the only rational act attributed to him is an awareness of how his dress and deportment were likely to be received at Rome: in consequence, he attempted to forestall all amazement by having a huge picture painted of himself in his finery and sent to Rome in advance of his arrival. Once there, he conducted

---

18. Two from Elagabalus as sole ruler, and two more issued jointly by Elagabalus and Severus Alexander. To these one might add two responses cited by jurists quoted in the *Digest*. For these data I rely on the Palingenesia published in Tony Honoré, *Emperors and Lawyers*, 2nd edition (Oxford: Clarendon Press, 1994).

rites to the god each day, sacrificing a hekatomb to the clashing of cymbals and drums. He and his female attendants wore Phoenician dress, and he required high-ranking political and military officials to dress likewise and to carry the entrails of the victims in golden bowls.

His behavior rapidly deteriorated. What had been an expensive and potentially containable affectation rapidly spun out of control. His mother had arranged a marriage to a high-ranking Roman woman, one Julia Cornelia Paula. She was set aside in order that Elagabalus might force a marriage with the Vestal Virgin Aquilia Severa (Dio–Xiphilinus, 80[79].9). The performance of cult became an obsessive preoccupation, while Elagabalus delivered authority into the hands of low-ranking hangers-on, most famously a freedman and former mime, Valerius Comazon, whom Elagabalus made ordinary consul along with himself in 220. If Dio is to be trusted, the exoticness of the emperor's dress – it was, we are told, a source of concern to his mother, because the army might perceive it as effeminate – might be due in part to Elagabalus' desire not to be a man at all: with a startling degree of coolness, he reports that Elagabalus sought to go beyond the circumcision required by his cult and to castrate himself, if only he could find a doctor who could create for him a vagina, and among the catalog of his marriages is the claim that he also married in the role of wife (Dio–Xiphilinus, 80[79].11.1; Dio–Xiphilinus, 80[79].14.4–15.4; Dio–Zonaras, 80[79].16.7).

By 221, we are told, his grandmother and mother had lost all ability to restrain him. The best they could do was to persuade him to take his younger cousin as partner in power. The son of Julia Mamaea was therefore adopted under the name Marcus Aurelius Alexander in late June 221. Although Elagabalus designated himself and his cousin joint ordinary consuls for 222, relations between them were strained. We are told, for example that former adherents like Comazon were accused of attending too closely to the new Caesar. Likewise, various units of soldiery are described as anxious that the cousins should get along, recalling, no doubt, the murder of Geta by Caracalla a decade earlier.

The elevation may have eased anxiety about the degree of chaos that would erupt were Elagabalus to be set aside. In the event, one day – March 11, 222 – when Alexander was not seen in public, the guard rioted, fearing that Elagabalus had done some harm to his cousin. Elagabalus went to the camp, where he was violently detained until his mother, Julia Soaemias, appeared with Alexander. Their arrival triggered a release of pent-up passion, and in the ensuing fury Elagabalus, his mother, the prefect of the guard and several other officials were slaughtered, the emperor's body being mutilated before being thrown in the Tiber.

The last preserved sentence of Dio's narrative for his reign draws a fitting curtain on the story: "Elagabalus himself [namely, the god] was banished from Rome completely" (Dio–Xiphilinus, 80[79].21.2).

The dynasty of Julia Maesa, 2: Severus Alexander (March 222–spring 235)

Elagabalus was dead by the start of the day, March 12, 222. Alexander was then 13 years old. He was officially elevated to sole rule the next day, on which occasion he officially took the name Imperator Caesar Marcus Aurelius Severus Alexander, linking himself across the generations to his only competent predecessors of the prior sixty years.

The child ruler appears to have functioned for much of his reign as a cipher for other interests. This is true as a characterization of his practice, such as it was, and also as a characterization of the historiographic tradition. To address the latter first, the preface to his *Life* in the *Historia Augusta* offers (as often) a cogent and insightful reading of both the politics of the events themselves and of earlier historiography. Having reported that Severus Alexander received all the traditional honors of his office at one go, the author pauses:

> Now, lest this rush of honors seem precipitate, I will set out the reasons that compelled the Senate so to act and him to concede. For it befitted neither the *gravitas* of the Senate to confer all things at once, nor a good emperor to snatch so many honors at once. But the soldiers had by then become accustomed to make emperors for themselves by their own rash judgment, and likewise to change them – not infrequently alleging in their own defense that they had not known that the Senate had named a *princeps*. For they had made emperors of Pescennius Niger and Clodius Albinus and Avidius Cassius and earlier Lucius Vindex and Lucius Antonius, and even Severus himself, although the Senate had named Julianus *princeps* ... To this must be added the excessive eagerness of Senate and People after that disaster (Elagabalus), who had not only brought shame on

the name of the Antonines but also disgraced the Roman empire. (SHA *Severus Alexander* 1.4–2.2)

This tendency to freight Severus Alexander with hopes that he could not possibly fulfill was then exacerbated in the aftermath by the chaos and unpleasantness that followed.

The enormously positive judgment accorded Severus Alexander arises largely from an effect of his youth, namely, that he proved exceedingly easy to manipulate. This might of course have been a disaster, but as it happens his mother and grandmother collaborated with a number of experienced, high-ranking officials to usher in a period of approximately sane administration. (Many of those officials had held high office under Severus: thus, though they had ties to the family, it was to a more responsible age, but also, in the eyes of the army, a less generous one.) The problem for modern historians is that ancient accounts of his reign were crafted in light of just those long-standing expectations that produced statements of the sort we have already quoted: the new emperor did all those things "a good emperor should do"; all things unfolded "as is customary when such things happen." Favorable judgments were issued in accordance with the fulfillment of such expectations, and those expectations were fulfilled because Alexander's mother and grandmother delivered power into the hands of such men as subsequently wrote the major sources of the period. As a result, outside foreign affairs, where by definition exogenous agency can dictate the course of events, the reign of Alexander is nearly unnarratable.[19]

Allow me therefore to deliver a pair of contrasting remarks on the nature of government under Alexander before turning to foreign affairs.

Alexander needed to establish a firm break with his predecessors along a number of axes, not least the rationality and fairness of financial administration and the abuse of foreign policy toward that end. We can see him making such a break immediately after his accession on precisely a policy and practice abused by Caracalla, namely, crown gold. (Not coincidentally, the topic obsessed Cassius Dio.) The break with prior practice was announced by an edict, a copy of which is preserved on a papyrus from the Fayum:

---

19. We also face the difficulty that, though Cassius Dio continued his narrative to 229, due to a number of factors (office outside Rome, illness, and friction with the soldiery when in Rome) he spent much of this period away from the city and was not an eye-witness to events (Dio–Xiphilinus, 80[80].1.1–2.1).

Imperator Caesar Marcus Aurelius Severus Alexander proclaims:

[Nearly the whole of the first column is missing.]

> ... in order that communities not be compelled to make contributions greater than they can afford through their desire to express joy at my entering into rule. Hence arises this plan of mine, in designing which I did not lack for precedents, among whom I will be imitating especially Trajan and Marcus, my ancestors, emperors most worthy of admiration, whose practice in other respects, too, I plan to emulate.
>
> If the state of the public finances did not interfere, I would make a clearer display of magnanimity and would not hesitate to cancel whatever contributions of this type [i.e., crown gold] were still coming in, being owed from the past, and to cancel as well any monies for crowns that were voted in connection with my elevation as Caesar, or were yet to be voted upon ... But because of what I mentioned just now, I do not think this will be possible.

Alexander therefore announces that he will accept – indeed, require – payment of all crown gold already voted upon in connection with his elevation to Caesar in 221, but releases cities from the obligation to pay further crown gold in connection with his elevation to Augustus in 222. He continues:

> For neither my own welfare nor anything else will be a concern for me except to increase the empire through love of humankind and doing good, in order that my own conduct might stand as an example of the greatest moderation for the governors of the provinces and the procurators sent out by me, whom I dispatch after a most rigorous examination. Let the governors of the provinces learn more and more with how great zeal they should look after the provinces over which they are appointed, when it is possible for them all to see the emperor conducting the duties of kingship with so much orderliness and wisdom and self-control. (Oliver, no. 275)

Alexander hits all the standard talking points, not least in his invocation of the canonically good emperors Trajan and Marcus Aurelius. To the larger issue toward which he gestures, namely, the reform of provincial government through his own example, we will turn in Chapter 10.

That said, ancient narratives of Alexander's reign also betray the yawning chasm that had opened up between the notional location of sovereign authority in a duly appointed ruler and the license of the soldiery – a chasm that an emperor still on the threshold of puberty was hardly fit to bridge. Most famously, Elagabalus and Alexander had nominated as praetorian prefect for 222 the remarkable jurist Domitius Ulpianus. His relations with the Praetorian Guard rapidly deteriorated: he apparently put to death commanders popular with the guard, and, in circumstances that remain wholly obscure, fights broke out between the Guard and the population of the city. The Guard came off worse and had its revenge first by setting fire to portions of Rome and then by attacking Ulpian, and though the prefect fled to the emperor's palace, the Guard attacked him in front of the emperor and Julia Maesa and cut him down. The emperor's authority was so weak that he was unable to punish the chief instigator, one Epagathus, except by nominally promoting him to the prefecture of Egypt and only executing him away from Rome (Dio–Xiphilinus, 80[80].2.2–4).

Finally, Alexander's reign also witnessed the rise of a new power in the east – the establishment of a new empire, on the shoulders of a new religion – upon the ruins of the Arsacid house. The story of Rome's confrontation with the new Sasanian empire, and in particular its wars with the founder of that empire and his son, Ardashir and Sapor, will run in counterpoint through nearly the whole remaining narrative of this volume. We will devote some time to general considerations regarding Rome and its neighbors in Chapter 5. Here let us examine the rise of Ardashir only so far as necessary to bring Alexander to the east, where his military failures fatally undermined his capacity to rule and led rapidly to his overthrow in 235.

The regions traditionally embraced by empires of the Fertile Crescent present several fundamental contrasts with those of the Mediterranean. In particular, the dependence of the former on land-based technologies of transport and communication – to say nothing of the alternation of vastly fertile plains with inhospitable highlands, mountains and deserts – presented formidable challenges to governance. In consequence, the empires of Iran had long surrendered vastly greater autonomy to regional governors (whatever their title) than was traditional at Rome; the dynamics of relations between those governors and regional aristocracies played a greater role in imperial history; and Iranian ideologies of imperial rule had, at least in the past, sustained correspondingly articulated visions of imperial culture and imperial power.

As we have already seen, the Parthian empire was distracted in 208 by a war of succession for the Arsacid throne. The fight between

Artabanus and Vologaeses did more, however, than provide an opening for Caracalla. More importantly, their distraction seems to have
provided an opening for an ambitious local dynast, Ardashir of the
province of Fars (or Persia), to bring to heel the other powers of his
province and then to declare a break with Arsacid overlordship. The
chronology of these events is deeply unclear: the evidence consists
of very much later narratives, in a bewildering variety of languages,
which themselves rely on sources of dubious accuracy, together
with a simply remarkable series of monumental relief sculptures and
inscriptions erected by Ardashir and his son Sapor.[20]

Nonetheless, what is clear is that by 224, Ardashir had advanced
beyond the province of Fars and engineered a confrontation with
Artabanus, which was resolved in an unknown number of battles
with the complete overthrow of the centralized power of the Arsacid
house. Ardashir celebrated this victory by granting himself the traditional Persian title "King of Kings" and commemorated the
moment with reliefs that endowed the event with a cosmic significance. In the image from Naqsh-e Rustam, for example, Ardashir
receives his crown and right to rule directly from the god Ahura
Mazda (Figure 9). They face each other on horseback; they are larger
than all other figures but equal in size to each other. Each tramples
a defeated enemy under foot: Ardashir crushes Artabanus; Ahura
Mazda, Ahriman (Zoroastrianism's "demon of demons"). As Ahura
Mazda destroys evil and restores order on a cosmic plane, so
Ardashir his servant restores order on earth. The text inscribed with
the image – which just might have been added by Ardashir's son,
Sapor – reads: "This is the visage of the Mazda-worshipping lord
Ardashir, the King of Kings of Iran, who is of the radiant image of
gods, son of the lord Papag, the king."[21]

In point of fact, the victory over Artabanus in 224 may have given
Ardashir control over the Iranian heartland, but virtually all the
perimeter of the empire was openly rebellious, including a string of
principalities along its western border with Rome, not least Hatra,
Media and Armenia. Ardashir ruled for another sixteen years, and a
significant portion of his campaigns over that period was directed

---

20. On the reliefs see esp. Matthew Canepa, *The Two Eyes of the Earth: Art and Ritual
of Kingship Between Rome and Sasanian Iran* (Berkeley: University of California Press,
2009) and Canepa, "Technologies of memory in early Sasanian Iran: Achaemenid sites
and Sasanian identity," *American Journal of Archaeology* 114 (2010), 563–96.
21. Translation from Canepa, "Technologies of memory," 576.

Figure 9 The commemoration in relief of the investiture of Ardashir by Ahura Mazda at Naqsh-e Rustam (Photograph: Photo Ginolerhino 2002; public domain)

toward consolidating control over his own empire and subduing by whatever means remnants of the Arsacid house and its allies. What is more, the Sasanian empire had long and complex borders to both north and east, along which there was nearly continuous pressure. In short, we should not make the mistake of assuming that Ardashir (or his son Sapor) had foreign policy considerations foremost in his mind at all times or, for that matter, that Rome was central even when they were. These caveats should be kept in mind whenever we turn to the eastern frontier.

Ardashir's campaigns in the west of his empire in 226/7 and beyond registered with ever increasing urgency among Rome's eastern provinces. Virtually the last information Dio relates before he left Rome in 229 concerns information arriving in Rome from the east: first, the new king of Persia, Artaxerxes (as the Roman tradition termed the region and its king), was determined to reconquer all the regions once held by Persia, as far as the shores of the Mediterranean; and second, the region was in disarray from fear of invasion, while the local legions grew restive and those in Mesopotamia had slain their commander (Dio–Xiphilinus, 80[80].4; Herodian similarly dates the arrival of news about the change in rulership in the east and reports the same rumor about his intentions, 6.2.1–2).[22]

The sources for the next events are defective, but when Ardashir struck (probably in 230), he moved first against Nisibis, then Cappadocia and Syria.[23] Severus Alexander departed for the east the next year. A three-pronged campaign of retaliation was launched the following summer, in 232: one army advanced through Armenia, another down the Euphrates, and a third, commanded by Alexander himself, was to advance via Hatra. The first two armies did remarkably well under difficult conditions but were left horribly exposed when Alexander inexplicably failed to advance (Herodian, 6.5). Alexander lasted another two years, but Herodian suggests the die had been cast. It was put about that Alexander was forced to break off the eastern campaign because he had been summoned west to deal with an invasion in Germany, but the official story failed to take. No army wishes to be taken to war by a commander in whom it has no confidence.

Alexander passed through Rome, where he improbably and impolitically celebrated a triumph. (The pause in Rome is marginally more intelligible if the German campaign was in fact merely a pretext to abandon the eastern campaign and engage a more disorganized foe. That is to say, if Germany were in fact being invaded, Alexander could not have justified the detour to Rome. Nevertheless, even bracketing the question of the German invasion's reality, it is difficult to see how the pause could have been justified to civilians or soldiers without a real loss of face, given the rumors circulating at the time.) Alexander arrived in Germany in late fall 234 and bridged the Rhine, but the arrival of deep winter put a stop to any progress. That pause allowed a growing unrest within the army and officer corps to fester. The unrest appears to have been motivated in large measure by a pervasive sense that Alexander was weak and neither would defend the empire's honor – it was rumored that he commenced negotiations with the Germans before he had even begun campaigning – nor was capable of honorable action, should he be

---

22. The rumor regarding Ardashir's intent to rule some version of an historical greater Persian empire, like those that circulated later regarding Sapor, has been shown to be false (David S. Potter, *Prophecy and History in the Crisis of the Roman Empire: A Historical Commentary on the Thirteenth Sibylline Oracle* [Oxford: Clarendon Press, 1990], 370–6). The currency of those rumors will be taken up in Chapter 5.
23. Zonaras 12.15; George Syncellus 1.674; Potter, *Prophecy*, 20–1.

spurred to undertake action at all. This loss of confidence among the men whose lives Alexander was risking was fatal.

Unrest among the Pannonian legions found a focus in one Julius Verus Maximinus. An apparently terrifying physical specimen, Maximinus had risen through the ranks until he was placed by Alexander himself in charge of the training of new recruits in Pannonia. Those recruits now acclaimed their commander, who at first resisted before relenting – and promising an enormous donative (Herodian, 6.8.5–8). In late February or early March, Maximinus seized control. When he marched on the camp of Alexander, no one resisted. Alexander and his mother were strangled in their tent (Herodian, 6.9.5–6).[24]

---

24. According to the pseudo-prophetic twelth Sibylline oracle, Alexander was murdered *because* of his mother (*Oracula Sibyllina* 12.285–8).

CHAPTER 4

Law, citizenship and the Antonine revolution

Law and legal institutions occupy a paradoxical place in the study of ancient empires. On the one hand, outsiders tend to regard law as an instrument of the imperial power, imposing metropolitan systems of norms on subjugated cultures and helping to sustain inequitable distributions of wealth and power both within colonized societies and between those societies and the colonizing power. Ancient historians, on the other hand, have over the last generation acquired a deep skepticism regarding the efficacy and reach of ancient government. This last arose at once from minimalist assessments of ancient government's infrastructural power, and also from attendant considerations regarding the material conditions under which government operated: prevailing levels of literacy were low; rural communities, where the bulk of the population lived, were remote; and so forth. Where one group has urged that law must be a principal instrument of imperial oppression, the other has urged that it cannot have been such.

These difficulties have been exacerbated by problems of evidence. In short, until the systematic reading of papyri began, the evidence for legal history under Rome was generated nearly wholly by Roman authorities. Not only do those sources signally fail to address practice in the provinces outside a tiny handful of references, their privileged position within European culture seemed to confirm contemporary suspicions regarding the myopia of metropolitan cultures. What is more, even as scholars discovered and began to decipher the documentary record of Roman Egypt, debates erupted about the nature of its legal culture: how Roman was it? If it was Roman, how debased? And was its legal culture unique, even as its evidentiary regime was?

The problems of evidence began to dissolve perhaps a quarter century ago. In particular, the discovery of legal documents on papyrus in the Judaean desert and middle Euphrates utterly collapsed any argument bracketing the Egyptian evidence as somehow unique to a single province.[1] What is more, the new papyri often reveal remarkable awareness of Roman law and astonishingly robust legal institutions. In part as a result of the excitement generated by legal-historical study of those texts, people have begun to revisit – and perchance to collate for the first time – epigraphic evidence for the nature and history of legal institutions in other provinces.[2]

These same handicaps to a robust legal history of the Roman empire have likewise hampered the study of the Antonine Constitution. It had once seemed, and still might seem, a likely turning point in the history of the empire. After all, if an empire – to be an empire – must rule over someone, then the Roman empire must have become some other sort of state at that moment when Caracalla erased the most important legal distinction between conquerors and those once conquered. The moment seemed all the more salient when regarded in light of the subsequent history of European empires: many of those had dissolved at just that moment when the imperial powers were confronted by demands to fulfill in some meaningful way their avowed imperial projects.

That said, at an earlier moment in the publication history of ancient papyri, and likewise before serious aggregation of epigraphic evidence with regard to non-elite nomenclature, even a superb historian could write of the Antonine Constitution that it should have been a tremendous revolution, an immense about-face … but where was the evidence?[3] Echoes and reactions among contemporary writers were stunningly few. How had it not been an ideological watershed?

Here again, the gradual accumulation of epigraphic and papyrological evidence, as well as the development of social-historical frameworks for its analysis, have allowed for cautious new assessments.

---

1. I refer above all to the texts published in *P.Euphrates*, *P.Hever* and *P.Yadin*. A useful but now dated survey may be found in Hannah Cotton, Walter Cockle and Fergus Millar, "The papyrology of the Roman Near East: A survey," *JRS* 95 (1995), 214–35.

2. See in particular Julien Fournier, *Entre tutelle romaine et autonomie civique: L'administration judiciaire dans les provinces hellénophones de l'empire romain (129 av. J.-C.–235 apr. J.-C.)* (Athens: École Française d'Athènes, 2010) and Georgy Kantor, *Roman and Local Law in Asia Minor, 133 BC–AD 212* (Oxford: Oxford University Press, forthcoming).

3. Ludwig Mitteis, *Reichsrecht und Volksrecht in den östlichen Provinzen des römischen Kaiserreichs* (Leipzig: Teubner, 1891), part II, chapter 6, "Die Constitutio Antonina und ihre Wirkungen."

It will not be possible in a single chapter to offer a comprehensive survey of all those arenas of social and economic activity affected by the grant of universal citizenship. The rest of this chapter seeks instead to offer a framework for understanding the forces at work in legal history that might stand in loosely paradigmatic relation to changes in other domains. We commence with a review of the basic frameworks within which it was decided what system of law would apply in any given case in the early Principate. At issue was a fundamental expectation that each political community should have its own system of law and that citizens in any given community should regulate their conduct according to its body of law. The next section considers the pressures for change that arose in actual legal practice prior to the Antonine Constitution, whereby Roman legal forms came to influence provincial life even outside the framework of citizenship. We then turn to the Antonine Constitution and its aftermath.

Legal pluralism and the dynamics of empire

One might begin by sketching a basic normative framework for the separation of the empire into separate jurisdictions as the Romans themselves theorized the issue. The most famous and most concise formulation in a classical text is that provided by the jurist Gaius, the author of the only surviving textbook on law from classical antiquity,[4] at the opening of his *Institutes* (Gaius' *floruit* appears to have been the two decades immediately prior to the reign of Septimius Severus – his remarks here should therefore be taken as late, second-order observations on long-developed practice):

> All peoples who are governed by statutes and customs observe partly their own peculiar law and partly the common law of all human beings. The law that a people establishes for itself is peculiar to it, and is called "civil law" (*ius civile*), being, as it were, the special law of that *civitas*, that community of citizens, while the law that natural reason establishes among all human beings is followed by all peoples alike, and is called *ius gentium*, being, as it were, the law observed by all peoples. Thus the Roman people observes partly

4. The term "classical antiquity" is adopted in order to exclude Justinian's *Institutes*, which text has, of course, much to tell about law in the classical period, but whose relationship to procedure in that period is extraordinarily attenuated. That fact alone raises significant problems of interpretation for the historian of law in the Antonine and Severan ages, quite apart from the complex imbrication of historical layers in the text at the level of doctrine.

its own peculiar law and partly the common law of humankind. (*Institutes* 1.1)

In other words, the civil law or, better yet, *a* civil law is a body of law that a political community (what Gaius calls a *civitas*, which means a collectivity of citizens) establishes for and over itself. Only the members of that community, which is to say its citizens, have *a priori* access to its legal actions. The foundation of Gaius' claim is expressed by the reflexive and distributive pronouns "each" and "for itself": the term "civil law" denotes those bodies of law that each political community makes for itself.

The term *civitas* has two valences of relevance to any effort to understand how this framework was actualized in the organization of the empire. First, *civitas* meant "citizenship" (it is an abstraction from *civis*, "citizen," and must mean "the quality that these individuals share that makes them all citizens"). Second, *civitas* might by common metonymy also refer to a political community, to a collectivity of citizens, and by further metonymy to the city (or city-state) that those citizens inhabited. Hence, it might be useful to consider the implications of Gaius' definition along two lines: how did one's legal status – one's citizenship – affect the body of law that one was expected to use and observe, and, second, what was the relationship between legal system and territoriality?

Let us consider first the correlation between citizenship and law. An understanding similar to that of Gaius is clearly visible in the narrative of Livy, writing under Augustus, but describing (as he thought) Roman practice in the organization of subjugated communities already in the late fourth century BC. Consider the narrative Livy provides of the aftermath of a Roman war with the Hernici in 306 BC:

> Cornelius was left behind in Samnium. Marcius returned to the city in triumph over the Hernici and an equestrian statue in the forum was decreed, which was placed before the temple of Castor. To three polities of the Hernici – the Aletrinati, Verulani and Ferentinati [who had sided with Rome in the war] – because they preferred this to Roman citizenship, it was permitted that their laws should be returned to them and rights of intermarriage granted, which for a time they alone of the Hernici possessed. To the Anagnini, who had borne arms against Rome, was given citizenship without the vote: their rights of assembly and intermarriage were taken away and their magistrates forbidden any responsibility other than sacred ones. (Livy, 9.43.22–4; see also Livy, 9.9.6)

Observe that the favored peoples were allowed to remain independent, which is to say, they did not become Roman, and in consequence they were allowed to use their own systems of law. Such is likewise the reading of this exchange provided by another actor in the narrative, the Aequi, from whom the Romans demanded satisfaction a short while later:

> The Aequi responded that the demand was patently an attempt to force them under threat of war to suffer themselves to become Roman: the Hernici had shown how greatly this was to be desired, when, granted the choice, they had preferred their own laws to Roman citizenship. To those to whom the opportunity of choosing what they wanted was not granted, citizenship would of necessity be *pro poena*, as a punishment. (Livy, 9.45.6–8)

It is of course quite likely that Livy's narrative has been shaped by anachronism in ways we can no longer detect. It is therefore crucial that the same correlation between system of law and citizenship underlies the very earliest law on provincial jurisdiction for which we posses extensive testimony contemporaneous with its operation, namely, the *lex Rupilia*, the Rupilian law on the administration of Roman Sicily:

> The Sicilians are subjects of law as follows: actions of a citizen with a fellow citizen are tried at home, according to their own laws. To adjudicate actions of a Sicilian with a Sicilian not of the same citizen body, the praetor [that is, the Roman governor] should appoint a judge by lot, in accordance with the decree of Publius Rupilius, which he fixed on the recommendation of the [commission of] ten legates [sent to advise him at the formal organization of the province], which decree the Sicilians call the Rupilian Law. To adjudicate suits brought by an individual against a community, or by a community against an individual, the senate of another *civitas* should be assigned, granting the possibility that a *civitas* might be rejected by each side. When a Roman citizen sues a Sicilian, a Sicilian is assigned to adjudicate; when a Sicilian sues a Roman citizen, a Roman citizen is assigned. In all other matters judges are accustomed to be selected from among the Roman citizens resident in the assize district. Between farmers and collectors of the grain tithe, judgments are rendered according to the grain law which they call the Hieronican. (Cicero, *Verr.* 2.2.32)

The legal landscape of Roman Sicily is tessellated into jurisdictions, in each of which a different system of civil law is understood to obtain – that is, to use the terms employed by Gaius, a body of law generated by, and governing relations among, a political community whose membership is regulated and tracked by the polity itself. What is more, in Roman eyes, political belonging consisted nearly wholly in consent to a society's normative order: it had been this fundamental conviction that permitted early Roman society to give away the franchise on a scale – and in contexts – wholly without compare among democratic states of the ancient Mediterranean.[5]

This understanding of the relationship between juridical status, the legal articulation of communal membership, and system of law gave rise to policies directed toward the maintenance of purely local legal orders. Here, it is crucial to recognize that this was not a practice peculiar to Rome, nor was the allowance that subject communities should use their own laws in any way a concession. Rather, international law in Greek and Roman antiquity drew a clear distinction between the independence of communities (meaning their freedom of action in foreign affairs) and autonomy, which meant nothing more and nothing less than the right to use one's own laws. Within such a framework, a community could lose its independence but retain the use of its own laws without any dissonance. In modern terms, one might say their conception of sovereignty was not unitary but divisible.

To situate this ancient conceptual framework distinguishing sovereignty and autonomy within a modern framework for understanding the practice of empires, one might say that being an empire (and not a national state), Rome governed through the cultivation and management of difference – and not, that is, through the universalization of some national culture (or body of law), with all that entailed. A very great deal of Roman administrative law was thus directed toward controlling geographic aspects of social and economic conduct, most notably in forbidding forms of sociality (especially marriage) and rights of contract between individuals and groups across boundaries established by Roman agents. At a minimal level, Rome's aim was no doubt to prevent the realization of solidarity among conquered populations.

---

5. On consent to law in Roman conceptions of political belonging see Clifford Ando, "Law and the landscape of empire," in Stéphane Benoist and Anne Daguey-Gagey, eds, *Figures d'empire, fragments de mémoire: Pouvoirs, pratiques et discours, images et représentations, et identités sociales et religieuses dans le monde romain impérial. Ier s. av J.-C.–Ve s. ap. J.-C.* (Paris: Presses Universitaires de Septentrion, 2011), 25–47, and Ando, *Law, Language and Empire in the Roman Tradition* (Philadelphia: University of Pennsylvania Press, 2011), 3–4.

Within such a framework, the insistence that local communities should sustain discrepant systems of law (and so remain disjoined, one from another) suited provincials and Romans alike. In this way, the empire remained tessellated into as many communities as once were conquered, while the nominal persistence of pre-existing institutions in those myriad localities, under purely local leadership, was taken to conduce both a particular local and a singular imperial order. Hence the general principle declared by the emperor Trajan to Pliny when the latter was governor of Bithynia-Pontus in the early second century AD: "it is always safest, I think, for the law of any given citizen community to be observed" within its jurisdiction (Pliny, *Ep.* 10.113). Trajan clearly intended that it was "safest" for Rome so to act, but the right to be judged by one's own laws was nonetheless eagerly sought by provincials.

To return momentarily to the narrative of the rise of Severus in Chapter 2 and the point emphasized there, namely, that communities regularly sent embassies with gifts to congratulate emperors on their accession or latest victory: one of the benefits to communities in so acting, despite the cost, was that interaction with the emperor offered the opportunity to seek his continued support for such privileges. For example, the letter of Severus and Caracalla to Aphrodisias from 198 closes with thanks to the people of the city for their loyalty and affirms the commitment of the emperors to the city's ongoing use of "its existing constitution and its own laws."[6]

Three final observations regarding the legal culture of the early Roman empire deserve consideration before we turn to the historical situation immediately before and after the Antonine Constitution.

First, no evaluative framework, whether moral or ontological, is ever offered in a Roman text to adjudge between distinct bodies of civil law, because one adheres more closely to some transcendent norm or is authorized by a source of such; nor is any robust interest expressed in texts before the Antonine Constitution in their positive law content. The operative assumption seems to have been that local social orders are best secured by adherence to locally generated norms; and, as a corollary, Rome had neither an epistemic basis nor any deontological obligation to override those.

The second observation amounts in part to a caveat on the first: restricting access to Roman legal actions to Roman citizens did

6. J. Reynolds, *Aphrodisias and Rome* (London: Society for the Promotion of Roman Studies, 1982), no. 18, on which see p. 39).

amount in the context of empire to sustaining relations not simply of difference, but of hierarchical difference. Numerous Romans, including senators and emperors in their capacities as rulers and authors of laws, expressed very considerable misgivings about allowing aliens to use Roman actions: hence, for example, the clauses in a law on jurisdiction attributed to the emperor Augustus himself restricting distinctly Roman forms of procedure to the city of Rome, or the interdictions in that law and others forbidding aliens access to Roman courts or Roman legal actions.[7]

The final observation regarding Gaius' framework is as follows. In the landscape of empire as he describes it, the varied systems of civil law are conceived of as parallel or, perhaps, non-hierarchical, and as operating in non-overlapping spheres that are in the first instance defined in terms of territoriality. But parallelism is obviously not an adequate metaphor. This is so for a number of reasons, all of them effects of empire – each likewise affecting the nature of the pluralism that we observe at the end of the second century AD.

The first reason to discount parallelism as an appropriate model for the pluralist regime of the early and high Roman empire is as follows: a principal effect of empire within the Mediterranean world of the first century BC and first two centuries AD was greatly heightened human mobility, resulting in minority populations within civic communities of unprecedented number and prominence. What is more, because some of those individuals held Roman citizenship, Roman legal norms could be invoked in local contexts, with varied effects, including the wholesale removal of a given case to a Roman court. The most extensive documents arising from such cases are late republican and triumviral grants of legal privilege, in which favored provincials are granted by Roman dynasts the right to use their local court, or that of a neighboring city, or that of the Roman governor, according to their whim and perceived advantage.[8]

---

7. On the Augustan law on jurisdiction see Gaius, *Inst.* 4.103–5 and *lex Flavia municipalis* ch. 91, together with Ando, "Law and the landscape of empire," 28, and Ando, "Three revolutions in government," in Lucian Reinfandt, Stephan Prochazka and Sven Tost, eds, *Official Epistolography and the Languages of Power* (Vienna: Verlag der Österreichischen Akademie der Wissenschaften, 2012).

8. The two most important texts are the *Senatus consultum de Asclepiade*, RDGE 22, and the dossier of Seleukos of Rhosus, which was recently re-edited in Andrea Raggi, "The epigraphic dossier of Seleucus of Rhosus: A revised edition," *ZPE* 147 (2004), 123–38 = *SEG* 54, 1625. For a legal-historical perspective on the triumviral grants see Clifford Ando, "Pluralisme juridique et l'intégration de l'empire," in Stéphane Benoist, Ségolène Demougin and Gerda de Kleijn, eds, *Impact of Empire X* (Leiden: Brill, 2012).

A second reason to discount parallelism is that Roman interest was perceived and understood normatively to trump *both* local autonomy *and* the Romans' own commitment to the restriction of Roman law to Roman citizens. One finds a statement of principle to this effect in a schematic account given by Cicero of the legislative powers that remained to autonomous communities within the empire:

> When the Roman people enacted a law, if it was the sort of thing that it seemed it might be permitted to allied or free peoples to decide for themselves – by consulting not our interests but their own – which law they wished to use: it in that case, it might seem appropriate to inquire whether or not they bound themselves to the law. But when the matter concerned our common affairs, our empire, our wars, our victory, or our safety: in those cases, our ancestors did not want those people to have a choice. (Cicero, *Balb.* 22)

Clearly, the principle that these communities could craft and employ their own laws extended only so far as Roman interest permitted, where Roman interest was defined by the Romans themselves. In practice, one witnesses Roman interference in local systems of law earliest, most systematically and nearly exclusively in criminal law, where Roman interest in social order and its desire (largely) to monopolize the use of social violence virtually required Rome to penetrate more deeply into local affairs than it might otherwise have done. One gets a fine sense of the extent of Roman involvement in an edict of Gaius Petronius Mamertinus, prefect of Egypt from AD 133 to 137. It lists the crimes that the prefect's court would investigate, in Greek terms that exactly translate fundamental categories of Roman criminal law (*SB* XII 10929 = *P Yale* II.162). As a corollary, Roman interference in practice in non-Roman private law was nearly non-existent, issues essential to imperial governance not being at stake.

This systematic pressure on local courts notwithstanding, the legal pluralism of the empire as a whole could still have developed into a merely hierarchical system, in which the upper and lower systems operated by and large according to utterly distinct and locally generated principles. Such systems might usefully be characterized as pluralist not simply for the obvious reason that there co-exist within the same territorial space multiple norms, and multiple sources of norms, but because there existed within many fields of law around the empire no requirement of subordination, no regular external coordination, nor perhaps even rules of recognition. Indeed, the situation called into being by Roman theory comes very close to what a modern legal theorist might call institutional or even systemic pluralism.[9]

But in the perspective of practice, this is not what we see. Or, one might say, systemic pluralism, if it ever came into being, did not turn out to be sustainable. Rather, the fit or relationship between legal orders – which was in theory so narrowly hierarchical that to the Romans, at least, one could legitimately characterize it as parallel – was gradually transformed, such that the various local legal orders of the empire at large, which had previously existed in a purely hierarchical relation with Roman institutions, were gradually reoriented in fractal subordination to them.

This came about in spite of the Romans' own commitment to principles that conduced at least to an institutional pluralism. The next section describes two major pressures for change in the decades leading up to the Antonine Constitution: first, the widespread use of a Roman law of procedure in provincial contexts, and second, the recursive pressure on local institutions effected by the possibility of appeal to Roman courts.

The spread of Roman law before the Antonine Constitution

In focusing in this section on less direct modes by which Roman law spread, namely, through legal procedure and appeals to Roman courts after a local decision, I deliberately set aside the problem raised both explicitly and implicitly above, namely, that individuals granted citizenship prior to the Antonine Constitution will have found themselves serving two masters, as it were: entitled and betimes obliged to use Roman legal forms, and also at times constrained by the laws of the jurisdiction in which they lived. This difficulty is famously acknowledged in an inscribed copy of a citizenship grant from the reign of Marcus Aurelius preserved in North Africa, where it is said that the grant of citizenship to Aurelius Julianus and his family occurs *salvo iure gentis*, "with local law preserved" or, perhaps, "without prejudice to local law" (*IAM* 94). Although it is possible now to conjecture with some confidence the

9. On the classification of pluralist legal regimes see Nico Krisch, *Beyond Constitutionalism: The Pluralist Structure of Postnational Law* (New York: Oxford University Press, 2010).

problems newly enfranchised Roman citizens would have encountered and the solutions Roman authorities envisaged, case law is,
alas, lacking.[10]

The relevance of procedure to a broader history of legal change
might be described as follows. One of the most important and
widely acknowledged duties of Roman officials in the provinces was
holding a circuit court. That is to say, an essential obligation for the
Roman governor of any given province was to supervise court hearings on a schedule that took him from city to city in a circuit around
the province.[11] What is more, the judicial activity of Septimius
Severus (on which see above, p. 45) was in fact wholly typical: an
absolutely essential component of common expectations with regard
to the emperor was that he would be personally accessible to his
subjects, to ensure the rule of law to all comers.[12] That said, we
should not allow the person of the emperor to distort our perspective: the evidence may concentrate on him, but only an infinitesi-
mally small percentage of cases is likely to have reached him. Such
testimony as we have for the case load in local courts, and even at
Rome, suggests very heavy usage indeed.[13]

In the hearings conducted or supervised by Roman officials, it lay
nearly wholly within the discretion of the Roman magistrate to select
the legal framework he would apply or, for that matter, to choose
whether to investigate and issue a decision himself or to assign the
matter to others. As we have already seen, there were reasons both
principled (elaborated above in a reading of Gaius) and pragmatic
(elaborated in a reading of Trajan) why the Romans would tend to

10. See esp. Jane F. Gardner, "Making citizens: The operation of the *lex Irnitana*," in
Lukas de Blois, ed., *Administration, Prosopography and Appointment Policies in the
Roman Empire: Proceedings of the First Workshop of the International Network Impact
of Empire (Roman Empire, 27 B.C.–A.D. 406), Leiden, June 28–July 1, 2000* (Amsterdam: Gieben, 2001), 215–29.
11. Graham P. Burton, "Proconsuls, assizes and the administration of justice under the
empire," *JRS* 65 (1975), 92–106 remains unsurpassed as a brief study.
12. Fergus Millar, "Emperors at work," *JRS* 57 (1967), 9–19 = Millar, *Rome, the Greek
World, and the East*, vol. 2: *Government, Society, and Culture in the Roman Empire*, eds
Hannah M. Cotton and Guy M. Rogers (Chapel Hill: University of North Carolina
Press, 2003), 3–22; Millar, *The Emperor in the Roman World*, 2nd edition (Ithaca:
Cornell University Press, 1992), 203–52, 507–49.
13. For example, Dio as consul held jurisdiction and found 3,000 cases involving
adultery prosecutions alone awaiting him when he entered office (77[76].16.4). See
also Clifford Ando, *Imperial Ideology and Provincial Loyalty in the Roman Empire*
(Berkeley: University of California Press, 2000), 376–7 and Ando, "The administration
of the provinces," in David S. Potter, ed., *A Companion to the Roman Empire* (Oxford:
Blackwell, 2006), 177–92 at 190.

apply local law. But there are also reasons to think that the turn to Roman courts, and the use of Roman procedure, if not substantive Roman law, in those courts, must have affected people's perception of legal institutions and the rule of law, and even their conduct.

As regards procedure, one might recall first the very rapid development by Roman authorities in the provinces of a two-stage process, whose structure mimicked that of the so-called formulary system as it was practiced at Rome.[14] That is to say, a Roman magistrate, having heard the essentials of the case, though he had the authority to render a decision, instead delegated that authority to another, delivering jurisdiction in the matter to a judge or jury along with a statement of the issues to be decided. Consider for example two responses of Severus and Caracalla from their visit to Egypt in 199/200:

> Imperator Caesar Lucius Septimius Severus Pius Pertinax Augustus Arabicus Adiabenicus Parthicus Maximus and Imperator Caesar Marcus Aurelius Antoninus Pius Augustus to Varus son of Damasaeus: If you can claim the assistance due to immature age, the governor of the province will decide the suit for release. Posted in Alexandria.

> To Procunda daughter of Hermaeus through Epagathon, freedperson. If you can claim the assistance due to immature age, the governor of the province will decide the suit for fraud. Posted in Alexandria. (*POxy.* 1020; trans. A. S. Hunt)

Observe that Severus and Caracalla do not decide either case (though of course emperors often did just that). Rather, they reduce each case to a single question, and in all of these cases these happen to be questions of fact: in each case, whether the plaintiff is eligible for specific consideration due to age. The outcome of the case is entailed by the answer to that question. But the question, however simple it might seem, is not resolved by the emperors: rather, the case is delivered to another tribunal, with another judge, who has been given a formula for adjudicating the case at hand.

It is important to note that it lay fully in the power of the Roman magistrate to decide what system of law to apply. In remarks aimed at provincial magistrates, the jurist Julian, writing in the second quarter of the second century AD, provided a hierarchy of sources of

---

14. Among early texts attesting such a procedure, one should certainly cite the *lex de provinciis praetoriis* of 101/100 BC (*RS* 12, col. 4, ll. 31–9 at 35; cf. col. 5, l. 26) and the *lex Gabinia de insula Delo* of 58 BC (*RS* 22, ll. 31–5).

norms they should consult in settling local disputes (the text derives
from the eighty-fourth book of his *Digest*, where he probably dealt
with attempts by citizens of municipalities to use Roman courts to
escape local liturgies): "Regarding cases where we do not follow
[local] written law, the practice established by customs and usage
should be preserved. And if this is in some way insufficient, then one
must adhere to whatever is most analogous to it and follows from it.
If even this is obscure, then the law observed by the city of Rome
should be applied" (Julian, *Digest* bk. 84 frag. 819 Lenel = *Dig.*
1.3.32.*pr.*). Julian was not authorized to fix a requirement in this
regard: the text should be read as describing the position of a single
jurist, albeit a highly powerful and influential jurist, as he reflected
on the work of Roman magistrates in provincial contexts.

One knows that not only emperors, but also governors of
provinces, continued to delegate power of judgment to others – and
hence to employ a distinctively Roman procedure – in the high
empire from the frequent references to such actions among the
jurists. Consider, for example, the following commonsensical observation by the remarkable jurist Callistratus, whose career spanned
the reigns of Severus and Caracalla:

> In general, when the emperor sends cases back to the governors
> of provinces with a rescript to the effect that "[The appellant] can
> approach the person in charge of the province," to which is some-
> times added, "he will judge what is within his sphere of responsi-
> bility," no necessity is laid upon the proconsul or the legate to
> undertake the hearing himself, even if the phrase "he will judge what
> is within his sphere of responsibility" is not present: rather, he ought
> to judge whether he should conduct the hearing himself or assign a
> judge.[15]

Callistratus' sample rescripts – invented no doubt for their brevity –
are nonetheless a salutary reminder that Roman officials could and
frequently did refer appeals back to lower-level officials without any
response. A remarkable papyrus of the mid-third century – AD 245,
to be precise – discovered by the middle Euphrates and generated by
Semitic villagers newly become residents of the empire, reveals them
to have traveled across the desert to seek a possessory interdict (an
injunction against any change in ownership of property until a court

---

15. Callistratus, *De cognitionibus* bk. 1 fr. 1 Lenel = *Dig.* 1.18.9; see also Julian, *Dig.*
bk. 1 fr. 5 Lenel = *Dig.* 1.18.8.

decision can be announced) from a Roman official with supervisory powers over the entire east: after months of waiting, he did himself receive their petition and gave the response, "(Claudius) Ariston [the local centurion] will hear your case." Below that he scrawled, "I have read." This was not what Vorodes son of Sumisbarachos and his friends had hoped for from Roman justice.[16]

Allow me to emphasize once again that the use of Roman procedure did not entail the use of Roman substantive law. Again, one could cite a wide range of normative claims by jurists and emperors – the affirmation of Trajan to Pliny being a case in point – as well as records of particular cases preserved on papyrus, in which in one respect or another Roman procedure was followed but local law or local custom provided the substantive law framework. Perhaps the most famous example is a petition from AD 186, from the reign of Commodus, rehearsing a dispute between one Dionysia and her father over property, rights of marriage and divorce, and myriad other issues (*POxy.* 237). At several stages, a Roman magistrate concedes that, the parties being Egyptian, local Egyptian rather than Roman law should provide the norms. The hearing is postponed to allow the relevant Egyptian law to be discovered (or invented). At a later hearing, the text is read aloud, only later to be set aside by a judge who wished to reach a different conclusion! Despite the outcome in that one case, there is ample reason to believe that the system often operated precisely to steer cases to judges and arbitrators with local expertise and, indeed, a number of such experts are known from the honors granted to them by grateful localities.[17]

That said, Roman cultural and legal forms could and did influence local practice – could and did bring about cultural change – even when one did not use Roman substantive law. As proof, one might adduce documents produced before as well as during the third century. Consider, for example, the *Tabula Contrebiensis*, an inscription preserving the record of a case in which a Roman magistrate listened to plaintiff and defendant communities before writing a formula charging a third party to adjudicate: the formula contained

---

16. The formal publication of *P.Euphrates* by Denis Feissel and Jacques Gascou is a monument of scholarship: "Documents d'archives romains inédits du Moyen Euphrate (IIIe s. après J.C.)," *Journal des Savants* 1995, 65–119; (with J. Teixidor) 1997, 3–57; and 2000, 157–208. See also Bernard H. Stolte, "The impact of Roman law in Egypt and the Near East in the third century A.D.: The documentary evidence," in de Blois, *Administration, Prosopography*, 167–79.
17. Fournier, *Tutelle*, 25–40.

a full statement of the relevant legal issues as well as a stipulation regarding the legal framework to be employed (HD000668).[18] In other words, a Roman procedure was employed in order to empower autonomous Spanish communities to settle a dispute according to local norms. But every formal aspect of the text – the protocols, the dating formula, the medium, the language – as well as the constituents of the procedure – the formula, the delegation of jurisdiction, the legal fiction – exists in stunning contrast to the notional autonomy of the Spanish communities as well as the nomenclature of the Spaniards at its close. The cultural prestige of Roman power must have endowed this ensemble – the legal ritual itself, as well as the textual form taken by the record – with enduring legitimacy.

When we turn to the Christian martyr acts of the third century in Chapter 6, we shall have occasion once again to consider the cultural influence of Roman technologies for memory production.

Roman norms, of positive law *stricto sensu* as well as those of a less formal nature, also influenced local cultures and institutions of justice by virtue of the superordinate position occupied by Roman tribunals, even when such influence was not explicitly prescribed. Let me give four brief examples from the late second and early third century to illustrate how this occurred.

An inscription from Nicomedia, assigned by James H. Oliver to the reign of Hadrian but dated by Julien Fournier to the Antonine period, preserves an imperial edict that makes reference to circumstances under which the governor's court will accept appeals regarding decisions previously taken at the local level (Oliver, no. 94 = *TAM* IV 1, 3). (The condition of the text does not allow its full sense to be coherently reconstructed.) What is relevant at this juncture is the apparent rationale for allowing those appeals: "If the Council unfairly ..." Although the context is very specific (albeit unknown), the local authorities are put on notice that their conduct should conform to Roman standards of justice – whatever these were and however they were to be known.

The desire of Roman authorities to force conformity to Roman norms was made explicit in an edict issued by Antoninus Pius as governor of the province of Asia. The text is summarized (and

---

18. J. S. Richardson, "The *Tabula Contrebiensis*: Roman law in Spain in the early first century B.C.," *JRS* 73 (1983), 33–41; P. Birks, A. Rodger and J. S. Richardson, "Further aspects of the *Tabula Contrebiensis*," *JRS* 74 (1984), 45–73.

related material discussed) in the second book of a work *On public tribunals* by the Severan jurist Marcian:

> There is indeed extant a chapter of the rules that the deified [Antoninus] Pius issued under his edict when he was governor of the province of Asia, to the effect that irenarchs [local peace-keepers], when they had arrested robbers, should question them about their associates and those who harbored them, make transcripts of the interrogations, seal them, and send them to the attention of the magistrate.
>
> Therefore, those who are sent [to court] with a report [of their interrogation] must be given a hearing from the beginning although they were sent with documentary evidence or even brought by the irenarchs. The deified Pius and other emperors have written in rescripts to this effect: that even in the case of those who are listed as wanted, if anyone appears to prosecute one [of these], the defendants should not be treated as condemned but as though a charge were being laid afresh. Accordingly, when someone carries out an examination, the irenarch should be ordered to attend and to go through what he wrote. If he does this painstakingly and faithfully, he should be commended; if with insufficient skill and not with thorough reasoning, [the judge] simply notes that the irenarch has rendered an inadequate report; but if [the judge] finds that his interrogation was in any way malicious, or that he reported things that were not said as if they had been said, he should impose an exemplary punishment, to prevent anyone else trying anything of the kind afterward.[19]

In this case, the standards of Roman courts are imposed upon local policing directly, because the Roman court is the court of record for criminal cases. Moreover, what is ordained is not simply some set of abstract principles, which might be realized from locality to locality in different ways, but a set of practices, by which certain rules of evidence and techniques of knowledge production are enjoined on non-Roman communities.

Roman norms also came to affect not simply the running of local institutions for the administration of justice but even individual social and economic conduct by virtue of the possibility of appealing local decisions to Roman tribunals. This option was not universally available: not only did it require considerable energy and initiative on the part of appellants, but the Romans themselves instituted

---

19. Marcian, *De iudiciis publicis* bk. 2 fr. 204 Lenel = *Dig.* 48.3.6.1 (trans. O. Robinson).

various requirements aimed at discouraging an excess of appeals, whether cash deposits or thresholds regarding the value of the property at issue or the seriousness of punishment at stake.[20] What is more, of the tens of thousands of responses that the emperors and their legal departments must have delivered, a tiny handful survive – and crucially and sadly, many of those survive in extracts that select the substantive law content of the emperor's utterance and from which the details of the cases at hand have been systematically eliminated. Our ability to write a robust history of law in the provinces suffers accordingly.

That said, a famous and complex inscription at Athens preserves a series of responses by Marcus Aurelius to appeals from that city in what seems their original form. In two cases, Marcus turned back the appeal on the grounds that the appellant had presented documentation that was in one respect or another faulty or insufficient.

> Since he has presented neither the records of the Panhellenes nor the finding that was published, he shall plead his case before my Quintilii ... (Oliver, no. 184, plaque 2, ll. 24–6)

> I have already announced that the appeals of Epigonus and Athenodorus had been set aside with notations that they were incompletely prepared. (Oliver, no. 184, plaque 2, ll. 52–3)

In my view, such cases exerted pressure on future litigants, as well as non-Roman institutions, to conform their conduct *outside* Roman tribunals and prior to Roman action to the formal standards observed *within* Roman tribunals, whenever there existed the potential that a given case might be appealed to a Roman official.

We should also take note of the specifications made by Marcus Aurelius in the blanket clause that closes the omnibus rescript from Athens. In it, he establishes the procedure to be followed in all relevant cases in which he has rendered no decision, indeed, to which he has made no reply at all.

> If any other applications for trial that have depended on this session of the court have occurred about which I have made no statement, in lieu of a decision, they shall have been set aside to be examined before the special judge – even when a case is not on appeal – with exactly the same procedure with which they were going to be

20. James H. Oliver, "Greek applications for Roman trials," *American Journal of Philology* 100 (1979), 543–58; Fournier, *Tutelle*, 514–24.

examined; as to whose they may be, Ingenuus will write to me. (Oliver, no. 184, plaque 2, ll. 53–6)

The command operates by means of a fiction – cases not heard by Marcus are to be judged according to exactly the same procedure as they would have been if he had in fact heard them – that ordains an exact equivalence at the level of procedure between the court supervised by Marcus and the court established by him to hold jurisdiction in his stead.

There thus existed within the empire a varied and complex range of pressures urging standardization or homogenization around or, if you will, accommodation to Roman norms. What is more, these intensified visibly across the second century and into the third, from the reign of Hadrian to the reign of Severus, even prior to Caracalla's grant of universal citizenship. To that act and its aftermath we now turn.

Citizenship and law in the aftermath of the Antonine Constitution

Given the traditional doubts within the discipline regarding the social-historical effects of the Antonine Constitution, it is perhaps worth emphasizing that *over the long term* it effected a transformation in the legal landscape of the empire. This claim can be made with greater certainty today than a century ago in part because documentary records now available reveal its effects in a way imperceptible before, and in part because contemporary understandings of historical legal change are more nuanced.

We might begin by observing that the self-same logic that justified and sustained the legal pluralism of the early empire now urged the universalization of metropolitan law: I refer of course to the correlation between citizenship and legal system visible in Roman sources from the mid-Republic to Gaius. We can see this logic at work in a mid-third century rhetorical handbook attributed to one Menander Rhetor. As he observes, it had once been traditional in speeches of praise for cities to laud a city's adherence to the rule of law and its ability to sustain its autonomy, but such praise can no longer be made specific to a city:

[A further point about the political system] is that it is best for a city to be ruled in accordance with its own will, not against its will, and for it to observe the laws with exactness but not to need laws. This last section of praise, however, is virtually useless today, since all Roman cities are regulated by one <and the same *politeia.*>

(Menander Rhetor, Treatise 1, p. 360.10–16 Spengel; trans. after Russell and Wilson)

Nowadays the topic of laws is of no use, since we conduct public affairs by the common laws of the Romans (*tous koinous tôn Rhômaiôn nomous*). (Menander Rhetor Treatise 1, p. 363.4–14 Spengel; trans. after Russell and Wilson)

The two assertions, which map closely onto each other, are made with different vocabulary: the one employs *politeia*, a term that can mean constitutional order but also citizenship (Latin *civitas*); the other, *nomous*, meaning "laws." Menander thus suggests, as closely as one might in Greek, a correlation between political order and legal system mapping the one we have observed in Latin Roman sources.

The connection between change in citizenship and change in legal framework is also raised in papers filed in court. So, for example, in a sadly damaged text from Oxyrhynchus in Egypt, a petition from November 14, 223 (preserved in two copies on the same papyrus), the petitioners write:

(line 27) ...] happened to be ... the law of the Roma[ns ...
(line 28) ...] we are (Roman) citizens, declares that all [...] the slave[s ...[21]

The term that is translated "we are Roman citizens" (*politeuometha*) is a verb derived from the same root as Menander's *politeia*, and means in this form something like, "we live under such-and-such a form of government." But in this context, following so closely on the phrase "law of the Romans," it clearly amounts to an assertion of fact that indicates why the law of the Romans conditions the declaration that follows. (In both Menander's text and in the Oxyrhynchus papyrus, we are witnessing a change in Greek political vocabulary, such that they map more closely the Latinate framework that now structures life in the Greek east.)

The need these petitioners felt to assert the fact of their change in legal status, and also the causal connection between that change and the legal framework they employ a full decade after the Antonine Constitution, point to a further problem, namely, that change takes time. People struggled for many years to understand, to map, and to effect the changes that the Antonine Constitution had set in motion. This much is visible even at the level of nomenclature and identity.

21. *POxy.* 4961, ll. 27–8/75–6; trans. J. David Thomas.

As was already discussed in Chapter 3, the proper legal form of a Roman citizen's name had three parts. Greek names often had two, one's name proper and a patronymic, which is to say, the name of one's father in the genitive. The latter had no necessary place in the Roman form of one's name and, as we have seen, the individuals granted citizenship by Caracalla were supposed to take (and many did take) Roman names. But some clearly felt an anxiety that the stability of their identities was at risk, and so indicated in legal documents both their new name and their old one. Consider for example the start of another text from Oxyrhynchus, from AD 216/17:

> Aurelius Aeluriôn, in office as *kosmêtês*,[22] town councilor of Athribis, before he obtained Roman citizenship Aeluriôn son of Zoïlus, of the tribe Neokosmios and the deme Althaeus. (*POxy.* 1458)

Some four years had passed, and Aurelius Aeluriôn still yoked his new identity explicitly to the old. Undoubtedly one strong reason for this was that Roman nomenclature as it was expressed in Greek granted no easy means for naming one's father. The change set in motion by Caracalla urged one to efface the name of one's father – to cease to claim one's place in the world through biological kinship – in favor of a purely jural kinship with emperor and empire.

Two further aspects of the legal history of the empire after Caracalla deserve mention in this survey. Broadly understood, they indicate countervailing trends of influence and change. First, although Roman authorities wisely and inevitably allowed all manner of pre-Roman forms of conduct to persist in individual cases where relations had been established before Caracalla, across the third century they insisted in more and more strident tones on adherence to Roman norms. Second, certain non-Roman customs were, by virtue of their status after 212 as customs of Romans, redescribed as Roman in legal literatures. I consider these issues in turn.

The easy way that scholars speak of a homogeneous "Greco-Roman culture" or the ready assumptions they make of widespread bilingualism notwithstanding, Roman law differed in important ways from nearly all the other legal systems known from antiquity on topics of relevance to wide swaths of the population, notably in family law and inheritance (including rights of women to divorce, law of dowry, rules of legitimacy, and division of estates). One could

---

22. The term *kosmêtês* means "director" but what Aurelius Aeluriôn directs is not specified.

not simply disallow all existing marriages and contracts among those who were not Roman on the day before the Constitution. Indeed, ancient literature offers a number of negative judgments on the prudence and feasibility of effecting social change across too many fronts too rapidly. To the verdict of Dio on Pertinax (see p. 211) one might add the sage words attributed to the emperor Arcadius (reigned 383–408) in Mark the Deacon's life of Porphyry, bishop of Gaza, in response to a request from the bishop to authorize the use of force in converting pagans to Christianity:

> I know that that city is idolatrous, but it well-disposed toward the paying of taxes and contributes much. If then we afflict them suddenly with fear, they will take flight and will lose much revenue. But if it seems appropriate, good, we shall wear them down bit by bit, taking away honors from those mad for idols, and the other political offices, and we will command their temples to be shut and to give oracles no more. For when they are worn down, being altogther constrained, they will acknowledge the truth. For change that is exceedingly sudden is hard for subjects to bear. (Mark the Deacon, *Life of Porphyry* 41)

As it happens, these are issues on which there might well have existed considerable institutional memory, and there must have existed tried and tested methods for effecting a gradual reorientation to Roman norms. For not only did the Romans grant citizenship widely on *ad hoc* grounds, they had in fact given citizenship systematically to those who in certain classes of community had held a local magistracy. An immense and sophisticated body of law had clearly developed already by the end of the first century AD (and continued to develop thereafter) to guide and govern the transformation of non-Romans into Romans, with all the effects on relations of husbands and wives, fathers and sons, and masters, slaves and ex-slaves that the transformation entailed.[23] Of equal importance in the aftermath, Roman lawyers had developed a number of procedural work-arounds by which to admit alien persons and things to Roman courts, and the same operations were available to naturalize foreign legal forms. Most prominent among these were fiction, analogy and substitution.[24] We have already witnessed the operation of one such fiction in the rescript of Marcus Aurelius: these were likely now deployed on a massive scale.

23. Again, see for now Gardner, "Making citizens."
24. Ando, *Law, Language and Empire*, chapters 1–2.

Alas, the great bulk of records available to us from the third century survive in collections edited later in antiquity so as to extract from any given document a decision-making rule that might be applied to analogous cases. Hence, we are rarely in a position to assess in detail how specific problems were treated, nor to identify significant patterns. What is broadly visible on the part of Roman authorities is just this tendency to grandfather in existing relations while simultaneously insisting that in the future, only marriages (say) conducted *iure Romano*, in accordance with Roman law, will be honored. This body of case law (such as it is) was clearly generated by petitions from below, as people sought to have their particular situation or their local custom recognized as legitimate – or at least permitted as an exception – by a Roman court.

When we turn to the jurisprudence generated in the aftermath of the Antonine Constitution, we confront a deeply frustrating embarrassment of riches. Two things stand out immediately. First, the literature is immense. Second, as Fergus Millar has observed most clearly, a remarkable percentage of that literature was produced (often but not wholly in Latin) by men originating in the Greek-speaking east. This in itself amounts to a social-historical fact of immense importance.[25] It is very hard to explain how this generation could have come to prominence without a long history of education and institutional development in provincial contexts, nor why at this moment they turned to such massive efforts at systematization were it not for the need to make Roman law intelligible and useful to a political community of unprecedented size and diversity.

The situation is frustrating because, like the third-century responses to petitions, the overwhelming majority of Severan jurisprudence survives in codifications made under Justinian, when the Antonine Constitution lay some three hundred years in the past. Such comments as jurists might once have made about the pluralist landscape of the empire before Caracalla, or about the massive work of integration that must have occurred in the decades after, were systematically excised as irrelevant to the ongoing life of the law.

Nonetheless, it is possible to envisage a route whereby, contrary to some idealization of the Romanness of Roman law, local customs would be recognized not simply as local custom or prior law, but

---

25. Fergus Millar, "The Greek east and Roman law: The dossier of M. Cn. Licinius Rufinus," *JRS* 89 (1999), 90–108 = Millar, *Rome, the Greek World, and the East*, 2:435–64.

as Roman law by Roman courts. At this juncture it is important to recognize that the Antonine Constitution had foreclosed the very means for validating local practice that had been used in the trial of Dionysia, and likewise affirmed by Trajan: namely, the citation of local law. For the extension of Roman citizenship – and the eradication of alien communities as autonomous political entities – had necessarily also invalidated local codes of law.

That said, local practice remained local practice. Was there not some means by which it could be recognized and sustained in the now-Roman courts of local jurisdiction, to say nothing of courts supervised by Roman magistrates? As it happens, Roman legal theorists had long-standing debates regarding the normative status of custom, both positive and negative – what a modern lawyer might call custom and desuetude, following the Latin terminology *consuetudo* and *desuetudo*. As one might expect, exponents of these theories argued that statute law could not cover all social conventions that a court might be called upon to regulate, and hence that custom, too, should be understood as a form of law. Next, proponents of these theories argued that even statutes on the books might become invalid through sheer lack of adherence, rather than explicit repeal. There is, however, no evidence from the classical period that any court in fact took the further step of regulating adherence to custom, and precious little evidence for the actualization of doctrines of desuetude, either. Nonetheless, these doctrines were a bombshell, waiting to be exploded.

The situation of the empire after the Antonine Constitution was ripe for the exploitation of such theories. And while it is difficult to find explicit citations of those theories, the effects visible in extracts from jurisprudence after Caracalla are fully in accord with their operation. Among other things, jurists in the decade after the Constitution refer overwhelmingly to local custom – using phrases like *mos regionis* – where an earlier jurist would have cited local law. But these local customs were now the customs of citizens. Who was to say they were not law? Consider, for example, an extract from book 4 of Ulpian's commentary on the civil law as articulated in the praetor's court. He there took up the problem of honoring non-civil-law forms of contract before the law:

> (pr) In the common private law of nations, some agreements give rise to actions, some to defenses.
> (2) But even if the matter does not fall under the head of another contract and yet a ground exists, Aristo [a jurist of the late first

century AD] in an apt reply to Celsus states that there is an obligation (*obligatio*). Where, for example, I gave a thing to you so that you may give another thing to me, or I gave so that you may do something, Aristo says this is a *synallagma* (a transaction or contract) and hence a civil obligation arises (*civilis obligatio*). And therefore I think that Julian was rightly reproved by Mauricianus in the following case. I gave Stichus to you so that you would manumit Pamphilus; you have manumitted; Stichus is then acquired by a third party with a better title. Julian writes that an *actio in factum* is to be given by the praetor. But Mauricianus says that a civil action for an uncertain amount, that is, *praescriptis verbis*, is available. For the contract described by Aristo with the word συνάλλαγμα (*synallagma*) has been made and hence this action arises. (Ulpian, *Ad edictum* bk. 4 fr. 242 Lenel = *Dig.* 2.14.7)

The problem before Ulpian is the need to provide a generic action for disputes arising from non-Roman forms of bilateral agreement: hence his invocation of the common private law of nations (*ius gentium*), and the preservation within the jurisprudential and textual tradition of the Greek term *synallagma*. In other words, the foreignness of the concept is marked through an insistent denotation of the foreignness of the term.

But what is striking is that the (enforceable) obligation arising from the non-Roman contract is itself said to be *civilis*, meaning in this context that it is "a civil-law obligation." Outside specifically legal contexts, the term *civilis*, however, simply means "citizenly": it means "civil-law" only insofar as the law of a citizen body is its *ius civile*. The Greek contract is a civil-law contract perforce because it was a contract between citizens. Such was the world Caracalla made.

CHAPTER 5

The empire and its neighbors: Maximinus to Philip

Ardashir's penetration of Roman territory in 230 was only the beginning. Across the next half century, Rome would reap what it had sown: foreign military forces would make a mockery of the frontiers, crossing the Rhine and Danube in violence, sailing the Hellespont and sacking the cities of Syria and the east.

To speak of reaping what one has sown might seem to invoke narrow models of agency and causation and concepts of balance and justice inapposite to long-term historical processes. I employ the term in two senses. First, some of the wars of this period did in fact fit those narrow models, at least in some accounts. For example, quite in contrast to Roman claims that the Sasanians aspired to rule some greater Persian empire – claims that cast Sasanian aggression as wars of conquest – Ardashir and his son Sapor seem to have described their wars with Rome as retaliation for Roman violations of one or another treaty (more on this below). In a somewhat different situation, but equally dialogic in its dynamics, there is good reason to believe that the Goths and Germans who poured across the Danube and Rhine and sailed the Black Sea chose their moments of attack in part in response to perceived moments of upheaval and weakness within the empire.

But I also wish to suggest a broader, more abstract model of historical action. In this model, the focus is not on this or that attack and its motivation, but on the question why Rome found foreign aggression in the third century so difficult to repel. To answer that question, we must look beyond the strengths or failings of any one general, army or campaign – though these should of course not be discounted. We should have regard, too, for long-term changes in the culture, economy, institutional capacity and infrastructural power of the societies with which Rome reckoned. On that topic, comparative evidence suggests that we should expect states sharing frontiers with Rome, and, indeed, societies well beyond those frontiers, to have developed gradually along a variety of axes in response to Rome. In part such changes resulted from conscious mimesis and cultural borrowing. In part they resulted from direct stimulus: Roman diplomatic practice treated all partners to bilateral interaction as if they possessed institutional structures homologous with Rome's, and no doubt prolonged exchanges of this kind provoked institutional development along lines consonant if not wholly harmonious with Roman expectations. But whatever the range of causes – and one can imagine many – the results, in short, are developments that enable borderland societies to resist the imperial power by becoming more like it.[1] And of course, in time, these developments may enable those societies to threaten the imperial power itself.

In speaking in such terms, I do not wish in any way to reject or diminish the purely contingent problems that commenced in 230 or so, when the empire experienced profound stress along many frontiers at once, on a more-or-less unprecedented scale. What is more, the long succession of those attacks caused a crisis of manpower that was, again, nearly unprecedented. Coming on the heels of the Antonine plague and the Severan civil wars, these made response and recovery phenomenally difficult.

Let me mention two further general themes of this and the subsequent narrative chapters. First, ongoing crises on multiple fronts brutally exposed and exacerbated the related military and political weaknesses of the empire's structures of governance. In brief, the empire desperately needed military leadership on multiple fronts at the same time – good generals, to say the least, with power of command stretching across provinces in order to coordinate action along an entire front. But because the system made every successful general into a potential emperor, overarching commands were perceived as dangerous to imperial self-interest. This is not to say that the constitutional and military system could not envision such a thing: numerous individuals had held special commands in earlier ages, often with explicitly overarching powers. But this had occurred under strong emperors, and they often gave such commands to their

---

1. See esp. Thomas J. Barfield, "The shadow empires: Imperial state formation along the Chinese–Nomad frontier," in S. Alcock, T. N. D'Altroy, K. D. Morrison and C. M. Sinopoli, eds, *Empires: Perspectives from Archaeology and History* (Cambridge: Cambridge University Press, 2001), 10–41. See also B. Shaw, "Autonomy and tribute: Mountain and plain in Mauretania Tingitana," in P. Baduel, ed., *Desert et montagne: Hommage à Jean Dresch. Revue de l'Occident Musulman et de la Méditerranée* 41–2 (1986), 66–89, and Clifford Ando, "Aliens, ambassadors and the integrity of the empire," *Law & History Review* 26 (2008), 491–519.

children or had at least had unquestionably sane and reasonably competent adult children of their own. In other words, the system, such as it was, had tolerated extraordinary commands when such could be balanced with the fatally underdetermined but still essential dynastic logic at its heart. Needless to say, the ability to strike such a balance rapidly collapsed as the legitimacy of successive candidates became less and less secure.

Second, the ongoing military and political crises caused an economic crisis. There remains a vigorous debate about the nature, extent and timing of this crisis. But the problem may be briefly stated. The Roman empire employed a precious-metal monetary system in which the value of coins was (as it seems) notionally tied simultaneously to the quantity of precious metal in them and the rate at which the central government would exchange bronze coins for silver, and silver for gold. Starting in the reign of Nero (with a brief upward tick under Pertinax and Julianus), the percentage of silver in the denarius had gradually been reduced.[2] Although scholars had once assumed that the debasement of coin must have triggered massive inflation, the two indicators of prices and precious metal content do not co-vary in the third century. In other words, the ability of people to detect, and the extent to which they cared about, the debasement of the coinage must have been less than was once assumed – no doubt in large measure because of the ongoing backing of the silver coin by the gold.

The fact that debasement did not trigger exactly proportional inflation does not mean it is not a sign of trouble. Debasement clearly testifies to a need on the part of the central government for money, which it could meet neither through exaction (legal or otherwise) nor through production of new coin.[3] But if inflation did not exactly co-vary with debasement, the need of the government for silver was nonetheless not without effects on regional and aggregate money supply. The central government had always used the occasion

2. Data summarized in D. R. Walker, *The Metrology of the Roman Silver Coinage*, vol. 3 (Oxford: British Archaeological Reports, 1978), 106–43.
3. On the productivity of the empire's silver mines in Spain, which had supplied a great bulk of the bullion in the early empire, see Jonathan Edmondson, "Mining in the later Roman empire and beyond: Continuity or disruption?" *JRS* 79 (1989), 84–102, summarizing the archaeological evidence at 91: "The conclusion to be drawn from the archaeological evidence is traditional, but seems consistent: namely that the apogee of large-scale mining of gold, silver and tin in the Iberian peninsula occurred during the first and second centuries A.D. Thereafter the mines do not seem to have operated on quite such the same scale; there was a decline in production."

of receipt of money to recast the metal as new coin. Payment of greater salaries and massive donatives of the late second and third centuries will have required removing silver from the central Mediterranean basin and directing it toward the army, and in times of social and military upheaval the patterns and rate of circulation of money will not have brought that coin back into circulation in the pacified provinces evenly and quickly. Although archaeological data now permit the loose assessment that levels of material and economic upheaval varied from region to region in the third century, narrowly economic data do not permit an assessment of discrepant rates of inflation across the empire, to say nothing of the specifics of cause from case to case. But there can be no doubt that the central government's difficulties with its expenditures had complex and deleterious effects.

Maximinus the Thracian (February/March 235–mid-April 238)

Gaius Julius Verus Maximinus was, it seems, the second equestrian to seize the throne. An exemplar of the universally hostile later tradition, the *Historia Augusta* goes to some length to explain that the reign of Maximinus was more ignoble than that of Macrinus because Maximinus was "the first from among the corps of soldiers to be proclaimed emperor while not yet a senator – without decree of the Senate" (SHA *Duo Maximini* 8.1). Whether purely because of Maximinus' rank, or because he arose from outside the ranks of the governing class, two separate challenges were made to Maximinus by consulars honored in the previous regime. In one case, we are told that the impetus was supplied by an eastern cohort of Osrhoenian archers angered at the death of their kinsman. In notable support of the ongoing importance of particular forms of social prestige, we are told that the archers sought out an ex-consul to be their candidate.[4] But both usurpers – if such they be – were rapidly dispatched, and effective resistance did not rise for another two years. Whatever hostility was felt at Rome was muted: Maximinus was voted the regular honors and co-opted into all priestly colleges within a month of his acclamation, on March 25, 235 (*CIL* 6.2001, 2009).

Perhaps because of genuine concern for the conduct of war, or from dislike of the aristocratic culture of Rome, or because of his greater comfort with the legions whose support had elevated him –

4. Herodian, 7.1.5–11; SHA *Duo Maximini* 10.1–11.6.

or all three – Maximinus did not travel to Rome. Instead, he remained on the German front through the winter of 235/6. Early in 236, perhaps on the anniversary of his own accession, Maximinus named his adult son Maximinus Caesar. The empire desperately needed intelligent leadership: while Maximinus lingered on the Danubian frontier, Ardashir struck again, laying waste to the province of Mesopotamia and devastating the cities of Nisibis and Carrhae – the very region, in other words, that Septimius Severus had seized in the 190s against all historic precedent. (That said, Ardashir did not retake the entire region: Roman troops survived for the time being at Singara and Hatra.) Maximinus, however, had apparently not elevated his son to provide stability to an attenuated command structure, but simply to establish a dynasty. He did not exploit the elevation of his son to create overarching commands along the Danube and Euphrates. Rather, the two simply campaigned together in Dacia before wintering at Sirmium (as it seems) in 236/7.[5] The summer of 237 was wasted in still further campaigning against the Dacians and Sarmatians.

Not that Maximinus was wholly unaware of the wider world. He sent communiqués to Rome, accompanied by enormous painted panels depicting his campaigns and his own central role in combat (Herodian, 7.2.8), and he continued to add victory *cognomina* to his titulature: *Germanicus* in 236 and *Dacicus Maximus* and *Sarmaticus Maximus* by 237. But every anecdote and, indeed, all evidence suggest a man utterly unwilling to confront – and perhaps unable to comprehend – those aspects of the world that were not susceptible to intimidation and resolution by the force of his own two hands. (That said, the late antique law codes preserve three rescripts published under his name – not an abundance, to be sure, but more than one might have expected.)

His gross irresponsibility as ruler notwithstanding, Maximinus did retain control of the machinery of government. Such is in any event clear from the hostility he aroused in Italy and Africa, hostility that seems to have been motivated by the extraordinary financial demands made by his agents and perhaps by the pressure that these placed on social relations at Rome writ large. It is notable that Maximinus is credited not simply with squeezing the rich: he also drew away monies intended for the grain supply, cash donations

---

5. Herodian describes Maximinus as wintering once at Sirmium, but it was already then and long after the site of choice for imperial commands in the region (7.2.9).

to the plebs, and festivals. Herodian observes with some candor that the poor are not generally inclined to side with the rich in their anger over imperial rapacity unless it affects them, too (Herodian, 7.3.5). Certainly when trouble for Maximinus at Rome did come, it seems to have found aristocracy and plebs united against him.

238: The year of seven emperors

The first stone of the avalanche fell in the spring of 238, perhaps as early as January but more probably in March.[6] A group of wealthy landowners in North Africa gathered and armed their rural clients in resistance to an imperial procurator based in Carthage who was zealous in pursuit of money and keen, we are told, for the eye of Maximinus. (Africa was both rich and at peace, which made it an easy object for plunder by its own government.) Confrontation spilled over into violence and the procurator lay dead. Perhaps in principled resistance to Maximinus, and certainly from terrified self-interest, the conspirators sought an emperor of their own in opposition to him: they acclaimed the elderly governor of the province, Marcus Antonius Gordianus Sempronianus Romanus. Stunningly, he accepted. The next two months were to expose the folly of his position, the weakness of the Senate, the imbecility of Maximinus and the fragility of armies on the move – the staggering idiocy, one might say, of the entire imperial system. Had it not involved enormous suffering, the situation might be named bathetic.

Gordian completed two actions as emperor, one harmless and the other decisive. He first traveled to the ancient seat of the province, Carthage: its ancientness and dignity would allow him, it was said, "to act exactly as if he were in Rome" (Herodian, 7.6.1). There he elevated his son as co-ruler (hence Gordian I and Gordian II), and he wrote to Rome. Publicly he promised a massive donative and sought the support of the Senate; privately, he urged the assassination of

6. The chronology of 238 is hopelessly confused. The separate chronologies of the literary sources cannot be reconciled with each other – each author no doubt relied on the information available at his position within the empire, but apart from all other factors, that information must have varied with political control. Nor does the evidence of titulature clarify the situation. The various chronologies proposed in the secondary literature rely on (often quite sensible) claims regarding plausibility and speed of communication. For a sane review of the evidence and possibilities see Michael Peachin, "Once more A.D. 238," *Athenaeum* 77 (1989), 594–604 and Peachin, *Roman Imperial Titulature and Chronology, A.D. 235–284* (Amsterdam: Gieben, 1990).

Maximinus' praetorian prefect, one Vitalianus.[7] The folly or desperate courage of Gordian was matched in Rome by the Senate, a corporate body that had not undertaken a courageous act in at least two hundred years. Vitalianus was murdered; the Senate acknowledged Gordian and his son, declared Maximinus and his son public enemies, and wrote to the governors of all the provinces, seeking their support. Herodian implies, perhaps correctly, that the courage of the Capitol was facilitated by the deliberate spreading of a rumor to the effect that Maximinus was already dead. Its bravery is otherwise hard to explain (Herodian, 7.6.3–9, 7.7.4–6).[8]

Alas, neither Gordian father and son nor the Senate had any troops under their direct command. For Gordian I and II this was fatal: a commander of senatorial rank in Numidia, one Capellianus (his full name does not survive), hearing of his revolt, led troops to Carthage. The city population was instantaneously routed and Gordian II killed; Gordian *père* hanged himself in his room. They had reigned three weeks.

When the news reached Rome, it felt like a thunderclap. Having declared its opposition to Maximinus, it could scarcely expect better from surrender than further resistance. Events now enter the domain of the burlesque. Absent any obvious candidate connected by blood or lieutenancy to a previous regime, the Senate chose two of its own: Marcus Clodius Pupienus Maximus and Domitius Caelius Calvinus Balbinus. Both were elderly, though how old is hard to tell: Pupienus was around 70 and Balbinus more than 60. Nor can their earlier careers be reconstructed with certainty: abhorring a vacuum, the *Historia Augusta* now begins to fabricate information in earnest.[9] But according to Herodian, the populace rioted and demanded an emperor from Gordian's family.

7. Perhaps Publius Aelius Vitalianus, a procurator in Mauretania Caesariensis who erected a milestone on behalf of Maximinus and his son (*HD*017516).
8. It no doubt helped that Senate and people seem to have acted thus far in unison. One motivation that can probably be discounted if not wholly set aside is senatorial anger with Maximinus over some loss of senatorial prestige: not only is he not accused (as Elagabalus was) of appointing lower-status persons to high office, but such data as we have suggest a striking continuity in governing personnel across the last years of Severus Alexander, the reign of Maximinus and into the reign of Gordian: see K. Dietz, *Senatus contra Principem: Untersuchungen zur senatorischen Opposition gegen Kaiser Maximinus Thrax* (Munich: Beck, 1980).
9. Pupienus had governed a German province and Asia and was ordinary consul in 234. About all that is absolutely secure regarding Balbinus is a minor priesthood and his second consulate as ordinary consul together with Caracalla in 213.

There was a young boy, the child of Gordian's daughter, with the same name as his grandfather. Sending some from among those with them, [Balbinus and Pupienus] ordered that the child be brought back. They found him playing in the yard at home: placing him on their shoulders, they carried him through the middle of the crowd, showing him off and saying that this was a descendent of Gordian and addressing him by that name. (Herodian, 7.10.7–8)

Gordian was either twelve or thirteen years old.

The three emperors in Rome now prepared to meet the two Maximini, who had long since set out for Italy. Against the expert and experienced soldiers of Maximinus, Pupienus and Balbinus raised a band of raw recruits from the youth of Italy. While Gordian and Balbinus remained in Rome with a garrison, Pupienus marched north, eventually encamping at Ravenna, while select senators scattered to the cities of the north to organize local resistance. Luckily for them – or at least for Gordian – the fragility of their situation was easily matched by rashness on the part on Maximinus. According to Herodian, he had departed Sirmium for Italy with such haste that his march was actually slower because of the lack of customary advance notice regarding the collection of supplies (Herodian, 7.8.10–11). Counting on the cooperation of populations along the way, he encountered difficulty as soon as he reached Italy: the population of Emona had abandoned their city, and Maximinus' army went hungry (Herodian, 8.1.4–5; SHA *Maximini* 21.5). Aquileia therefore assumed even greater importance for the provisioning of his army, but its population closed their gates against him. They were led by the evidently redoubtable Tullius Menophilus, the senator dispatched there for just this purpose (Herodian, 8.2; SHA *Maximini* 22.1). Maximinus was then unwilling, or perhaps unable, to advance through hostile country while leaving a large, prosperous city at his back. He laid siege to Aquileia, but was of course also unprepared for this operation. His army lost confidence in him in proportion with its hunger. After four weeks, upset with their conditions, his soldiers murdered both Maximini and reconciled with Pupienus at Ravenna and with Gordian, Balbinus and the Senate at Rome (Herodian, 8.5.3, 8–9; 8.6.4; SHA *Maximini* 23.2).

The pressure on their government was immense. Needless to say, extant narratives for the year concentrate overwhelmingly on the struggle for the throne. Nonetheless, scraps of information in contemporary and later sources, and inference from subsequent events, make clear that the frontiers were breached again in 238 along at least two fronts: bands of Carpi and Goths were ranging across the Danube just west of the Black Sea, even as others sailed the Sea itself; and Ardashir had renewed his assault on Hatra and the east. News from both regions appears to have reached Rome before the summer was out: according to the *Historia Augusta*, it was agreed that Balbinus should take charge in Germany, Pupienus in the east, while Gordian remained in Rome (SHA *Maximus et Balbinus* 13.5). What is more, they were terribly short of money: pay and donatives were owed on a massive scale, but coin had been short already under Maximinus. Their immediate solution was the reintro- duction of a Caracallan experiment in a deeply debased double denarius, the so-called antoninianus. (Fiscal policy during Gordian's sole rule continued this trend, resulting in a terrific debasement of the silver coinage.) We cannot know what role the new coin in particular played in angering the army: no matter. Quarreling between Pupienus and Balbinus made the situation worse, and in a riot of seemingly remarkable brutality, the Praetorians seized the men and degraded and murdered them before mutilating their bodies (Herodian, 8.8).

"Since they could find no one else at that moment," the mur- derers then seized the Caesar Gordian and acclaimed him Augustus (Herodian, 8.8.7). A boy on the threshold of puberty was now sole ruler of the Roman world.

Something of the insanity of this year is well captured in a famous dedication on an altar from Aigeai, in Cilicia. It was carved in at least three stages, by three different hands, labeled below (A), (B), and (C).

> (A) To Imperator Caesar Marcus Antonius Gordian, pious and fortunate Augustus, holding the tribunician power, and to the gods the Gordians, the ancestors of Imperator Gordian Augustus, and to the gods the Augusti;
>
> To Alexander and Severus and Antoninus and Domna
>
> (B) and to the gods the Augusti;
>
> (C) and to Asclepius
> and to Hygeia
> and to the gods the Augusti. (*SEG* 32.1312)

The text in the second line was carved over an earlier erasure. The underlying text may have read "To Pupienus and Balbinus and the gods the Augusti." The names of Pupienus and Balbinus were often erased, though no official condemnation of memory is recorded. The choice of Aigeai makes sense nonetheless: best not to tie oneself to any one ruler; better to rest one's hopes on the dead.

The arrival of Sapor (240–72)

The reign of Gordian III presents a number of challenges to narrative (though none so serious as arise with the fragmentation of empire in the next generation). Among other things, though the temptation is great to focalize the narrative on the person of the emperor, Gordian III is perhaps even more unlikely than Severus Alexander to have exercised any real agency or influenced the crafting of policy, even regarding appointments. As a related matter, the actual focus of ancient narrative on the person of the emperor makes the reconstruction of action away from his person, by the persons actually in charge by the Danube or in the east, very difficult.

That said, the dominant personality of the reign of Gordian and perhaps prime driver of Roman policy from his accession in 240 until his death in 272 was Sapor I, son of Ardashir. As an interlocutor, antagonist and rival to Rome, Sapor exhibited dynamism and strategic intelligence, and achieved success, whose only rivals in Roman experience were those of Hannibal of Carthage. What is more, Sapor also displayed a remarkable capacity to regroup and reform after setbacks, one that had no parallel in Roman wars in the east to that date. Although (as we shall see in Chapter 7) his final years witnessed a number of setbacks along his western frontier, these came largely at the hands of Odaenathus of Palmyra, whose own success proved evanescent.

Sapor's rivalry with the great kings of the past, western and eastern, extends to one further domain beyond military glory relevant to this book. Like his father Ardashir, Sapor arranged for a series of monumental relief sculptures depicting in iconographic form his greatest successes. But beyond that, he wrote a statement of his deeds – an ideological and formal cousin to the *Res Gestae* of Augustus – which, like the Augustan text, he ordered inscribed in the languages of empire as he knew them: (Middle) Persian, Parthian and Greek. Beyond mere historical details and a valuable non-Roman perspective on particular incidents – and confirmation that Ardashir and Sapor had much more on their minds than contests with Rome – the *Res Gestae Divi Saporis* sheds light on one crucial question of Roman–Sasanian relations: did Ardashir and Sapor conceive the desire and announce a program to reclaim the borders of the Persian Kings of Kings of the Achaemenid period? Did they, in other words, aspire to extend the borders of the Sasanian empire to the Mediterranean coast? The answer, as David Potter above all has shown, is negative. To a point, the currency of this rumor in the early years of Ardashir and its failure to die over the next generation testify to the persistence of error and anachronism in the Greco-Roman historical tradition with regard to the east. But it also testifies to the profound anxiety that a newly dynamic eastern empire raised in the Roman governing class: if the Sasanians truly intended to retake greater Syria and Palestine, the threat they posed was existential. Such was the fear inspired by Ardashir and Sapor, and perhaps it would not have displeased them.

The eastern campaign of Gordian III

Not surprisingly, Gordian ruled effectively largely to the extent that authority was delivered into the hands of competent subordinates. As with Severus Alexander, one imagines, too, that such stability as there was rested on a consensus in the governing class, to which people might buy in for varied reasons. Curiously, Gordian faced an almost immediate threat from Africa Proconsularis, the province that had elevated his grandfather and uncle: the leader was the governor sent by his own administration, one Sabinianus (SHA *Gordiani* 23.4), whose movement ended (as before) when the governor in command of Mauretania, a temporary official of equestrian rank named Faltonius Restitutianus, acted swiftly to quash it.[10] Its failure to produce ripple effects similar to those provoked by Gordian III's grandfather undoubtedly has multiple causes, but one surely was a fairly pervasive unwillingness among the governing class to wreak further havoc. Gordian I had succeeded (on behalf of his grandson, it turned out) in part because large numbers of persons elsewhere were convinced their own lot would be improved by a change in ruler, in spite of all the risks associated with usurpation. No one accepted

10. The third legion, which was stationed in Africa, was disbanded early in the reign of Gordian III, either because it was complicit in his (grand?)father's death or because it was somehow complicit in this revolt, but no certainty is possible on this issue. On Faltonius see *HD*011843 and 033379.

those risks when Sabinianus rose against Gordian III.

One of those competent subordinates was Tullius Menophilus, the senator who had held Aquileia against Maximinus. He was sent to Lower Moesia to hold the Danubian front against the Carpi and the Goths. So far as we can tell, he performed his job quite adequately, combining diplomatic bribery (to fracture alliances among Rome's enemies) with holding actions until he could win advantage, before acting militarily in 240/1. He was then removed under circumstances that remain obscure – the *Historia Augusta* reports that Gordian himself campaigned in Moesia, quite possibly in 241 (SHA *Gordiani* 26.4) – but in the end, all we know is that Menophilus' name was erased from several inscriptions: the punishment suggests that some conflict with imperial authority must have been involved in his downfall.

The second such subordinate, and far the more important, was Gaius Furius Sabinius Aquila Timesitheus, an equestrian official whose career had begun with a minor post in Spain twenty years earlier and had rapidly advanced through a succession of offices notionally associated with the emperor's private property (*ILS* 1330). The intertwining of the emperor's property with that of the state mirrored other forms of ideological obfuscation in the structures of law and finance under the Principate, many of which had ceased to have real meaning as the politics of monarchy changed from Augustus on. That history need not be traced here. What needs to be said is simply that as the size of the emperor's private property grew, the officials supervising those properties acquired immense importance in the politics of provincial governance, often rivaling and clashing with governors (they also regularly exercised jurisdiction), while the bureaucracy controlling the "private accounts" of the imperial household acquired great power – and produced some men of real competence – within the overall structure of imperial government. Similar power blocs are visible at other periods – the secretariats in charge of legal correspondence; the office in charge of the emperor's chambers; and so forth – and of course many coexisted and competed with one another. The connection between Timesitheus and Gordian was publicly cemented by Gordian's marriage – at 16 – to the former's daughter Furia in 241 (SHA *Gordiani* 23.5–6).

By this time, the situation in the east was dire. Ardashir's last act before his death in April 240 had been the taking of Hatra, which had held out, with Roman assistance, despite a series of Sasanian attacks that commenced in 238.[11] Ardashir was succeeded by Sapor: the date is supplied by a contemporary autobiography by none other than Mani, the prophet and founder of a religious movement whose influence would reach to every corner of the Roman empire (*Cologne Mani Codex* 18 = Gardner-Lieu 50).

The Romans appear to have viewed the Sasanian attack on Hatra as an act of aggression and, what is more, to have understood it in light of their ongoing belief that Ardashir and Sapor wished to (re)conquer formerly Persian territories from the Cilician Gates to Gaza, if not beyond. War was duly declared, accompanied by religious ceremonies that invoked earlier wars between Europe and Asia, petty squabbles that had rapidly become, in the delusional mirror of Hellenic historical reflection, existential battles for the soul of the west.[12] Timesitheus as praetorian prefect seems to have been sent ahead by sea, with Gordian following by land. Timesitheus had on his staff two brothers who hailed from Arabia: the elder, Julius Priscus, had like Timesitheus ascended principally through offices in the administration of the emperor's properties. The career of the younger brother, Julius Philippus – or Philip, as he is known in English – before 241 is not known.

The actual war with Persia went stunningly well, until it went very badly. It is possible, even likely, that the war began already in 242, in a campaign that commenced before Gordian arrived in the east. If so, it was Timesitheus who expelled Sapor's forces from Roman territory, and it would be to this campaign that the victory of "Gordian" over Sapor at Rhesaina mentioned by the fourth-century Antiochene historian Ammianus should be attributed.[13] What does seem to be clear is that Timesitheus raised Julius Priscus to the praetorian prefecture (alongside himself) at some point in 242.[14] But it is also possible that the literary tradition is correct in nearly unanimously placing Gordian at the head of the expedition, in which case it commenced only in 243 when the emperor joined the eastern

11. For the attack in 238, see above, p. 108. For the Roman presence at Hatra, see Dodgeon-Lieu 1.4.5. On the fall of Hatra see Maurice Sartre, *D'Alexandre à Zénobie* (Paris: Fayard, 2001), 962–6.
12. Louis Robert, "Deux concours grecs à Rome," *CR Acad. Inscr.* 1970, 7–27 at 13–17 = Robert, *Choix d'écrits* (Paris: Les Belles Lettres, 2007), chapter VIII, 247–66 at 253–8.
13. Ammianus, 23.5.17, on which see David S. Potter, *Prophecy and History in the Crisis of the Roman Empire: A Historical Commentary on the Thirteenth Sibylline Oracle* (Oxford: Clarendon Press, 1990), 194.
14. Potter, *Prophecy*, 213–15.

army and supplemented its forces with others he had gathered on his march.[15]

Either way, by 243 the Romans had achieved remarkable success, re-traversing (as will become apparent, one cannot say "recapturing") all the territory the Sasanians had taken in the campaigns of 238–41. Unfortunately, in that same year, deep in Persian territory on the route to Ctesiphon, Timesitheus took ill and died, with Philip promoted by his brother Priscus to replace their patron, so that the brothers together exercised the prefecture (SHA *Gordiani* 28.1). For reasons unknown – the death of Timesitheus cannot have helped – that winter found Gordian on campaign deep in Sasanian territory well into the rainy season. He got as far as Meshike, where his army suffered a spectacular defeat before Sapor. Gordian apparently survived and led his army in retreat back up the Euphrates to the region known as Zaitha. There Gordian was slain, if he was not dead already: if he was murdered, it was done by Philip, or at Philip's instigation, or by troops in anger, panic and fear.

We will turn momentarily to the resolution of the war by Gordian's successor Philip, and the politics of his selection. The remarkable aftermath of Gordian's death in the historical record deserves some scrutiny in its own right.[16]

First, a monument was raised to Gordian's memory *in situ*, but his body was returned to Rome in honor, and he was showered with praise by Philip. Second, though some Latin sources denounce Philip as Gordian's murderer in no uncertain terms, Philip's memory was not condemned after his death. Third, the Latin sources in particular evince no knowledge of the terrible defeat that led to Gordian's death. We may conclude from these facts that Philip's decision to hang his legitimacy in part on the legitimacy of his predecessor demanded in turn that Gordian's campaign be deemed a success, and the state of communication in the empire was such that the news spread by the emperor (particularly from a position outside the empire, whence his monopoly over communications was that much greater) created first impressions that were very hard to overcome, if ever evidence to the contrary in fact circulated.

---

15. Outside grounds of practicality within reconstructions of the campaigns, the major evidence supporting a campaign by Timesitheus in 242 is an Apocalypse of Elijah that may have described a war against Persia led by Timesitheus and Philip the prefects: see Potter, *Prophecy*, 194 n. 21 and Dodgeon-Lieu 357 n. 15.

16. The sources may be canvassed in Dodgeon-Lieu 2.2.1; they are assessed by Potter, *Prophecy*, 201–11.

Figure 10 A detail from a narrative relief of Sapor at Bishapur. Sapor's horse tramples Gordian III, while Philip the Arab surrenders (Photograph: Matthew Canepa, reproduced with permission)

The view from the east was altogether different. Sapor commemorated these events in his autobiographical inscription at Naqsh-e Rustam and depicted them in monumental form several times over (see Figures 10 and 14):

> Immediately as I entered into kingship over the nations, Gordian Caesar gathered a force from all the Roman empire and the Gothic and German nations and advanced into Assyria against the race of the Assyrians and us. At the borders of Assyria at Meshike there was a great all-out war. And Gofrdian Caesar was killed and I destroyed the army of the Romans and the Romans chose Philip Caesar. And Philip the Caesar came to a parley and gave us five hundred thousand dinars [= 500,000 Roman *aurei*] for their lives and became tributary to us, and because of this we have named M[e]shike "Peroz-Sapor" ("Victorious is Sapor"). (*Res Gestae Divi Saporis* 6–8 [Greek text])[17]

17. On the appropriate translation of the Greek term *denarôn* see J. Guey, "Deniers (d'or) et denier d'or (de compte) anciens," *Syria* 38 (1961), 261–74. Agreeing with Guey, as part of a broader consideration of whether Philip made a one-time payment or agreed to pay an annual tribute, is Thomas Pekáry, "Le tribut aux Perses et les finances de Philippe l'Arab," *Syria* 38 (1961), 275–83.

To the election of Philip, his surrender, retreat and reign, we now turn.

Philip the Arab and the jubilee (244–9)

The announcement of Philip's succession to Gordian must have raised eyebrows around the empire. It is scarcely more intelligible in hindsight. Philip's career lacked the distinction of his brother's, who was also the senior. (Priscus' subsequent career cannot be narrated in detail, but one can at least affirm that he was not conspicuously incompetent, while Philip appears to have been incapable of decisive action.) There remained, too, numerous consulars who had been close to Gordian and involved in the revolt against Maximinus. The confusion is usefully condensed by David Potter: "Like Macrinus, and like Maximinus as well, Philip was not the most important man in the state when he took the throne."[18] Perhaps the best explanation is that offered by Potter in another context, namely, that Philip's obscurity was a distinct recommendation. In the event of an assassination not directly connected with a usurpation, "the men who held most power were not inclined to select a ruler from among themselves" (Potter, *Prophecy*, 211): further examples (all later) might be Tacitus and Diocletian in the third century and Jovian in the fourth.

Philip's first three acts were to strike a treaty with Sapor; designate his son, also named Philip, his successor (by means of an appointment as Caesar); and name his brother Priscus to a super-arching command over the entire east, as *(Cor)rector totius orientis*, a title that means "Official in charge of straightening out the entire east" (*ILS* 9005, a dedication to the "brother and uncle of our Lords, praetorian prefect and *rector Orientis*"; see also *IGRom.* 3.1201–2). Priscus seems to have had the unenviable task of collecting the tribute to Sapor from the provinces of the east, a task made all the more difficult by the fact that Sapor was to be paid in gold. (The rulers of Iran may have learned a lingering lesson about the debasement of Roman silver coin when they accepted payment from Macrinus.) Documentary evidence reveals Priscus also to have functioned as one might expect a deputy emperor to have done, which means, *inter alia*, that he attended judicial proceedings and heard appeals: it was Priscus who disappointed the appeal from Vorodes

18. David S. Potter, *The Roman Empire at Bay, AD 180–395* (London: Routledge, 2004), 36.

son of Sumisbarachos and his friends in Chapter 4 (pp. 88–9).

In pursuit of money, both immediate and long-term, Priscus also seems to have instituted a remarkably ambitious set of reforms in Egypt (as well as an emergency levy). The reforms were two-pronged: first, unused land was to be identified, surveyed and placed under cultivation through sale; and second, personnel were lined up – largely through the imposition of liturgies – to actualize that process and reap its rewards.[19] The policy seems to have failed because the population of Egypt was not robust enough to make it profitable. In the event, when revolt against Philip came in the east, as surely it would, we are told that its support was motivated by the heavy financial exactions of Philip's regime (Zosimus, 1.20.2).

Philip then hastened to Rome: perhaps he had absorbed a lesson from the fall of Maximinus not to neglect the capital city. He was there by summer 244 and remained there long enough to commence the year as ordinary consul for 245. The time would come when legitimate rulership did not have to be performed and acknowledged at Rome, but not yet. There Philip supervised an elaborate state funeral for Gordian, expecting, no doubt, that honor given his predecessor would rebound to his credit, too.

The events that followed are sufficiently complex and poorly attested to defy chronological ordering. I therefore restrict myself to four issues: relations with Sapor; the collapse of the Danubian frontier; the millennium of Rome – and, of course, Philip's death.

Under circumstances wholly obscure to us, Philip repudiated his treaty with Sapor. That said, the Romans had a long history of striking treaties to save armies in tight spots, only to repudiate them through means of specious legality.[20] The Byzantine chronicler Zonaras, relying on a Greek source of the period (very likely Dexippus of Athens), attributes agency in the matter to Philip, admittedly in a single sentence (Zonaras, 12.19). A contemporary oracle, written after the events it describes but purporting to predict them, announces that the respite created by Philip's peace with Sapor will be short-lived and appears to describe Roman action in 245/6, itself followed by a Sasanian reaction:

19. P. J. Parsons, "Philippus Arabs and Egypt," *JRS* 57 (1967), 134–41.
20. The most famous example is surely the aftermath of the battle of the Caudine Forks: the Roman Senate repudiated the agreement on the grounds that the elected magistrate had lacked authority to strike it, but of course by that time the Roman army was safe. The denunciation placed by Livy in the mouth of the Samnite general is apt: "You always cloak deceit under the guise of law" (Livy, 9.11).

> When they (Philip father and son) will rule in wars and become lawgivers, there will briefly be an end to war, but not for long; when the wolf shall swear oaths to the dogs of gleaming teeth against the flock he will ravage, harming the wool-fleeced sheep, and he will break the oaths and then there will be the lawless strife of arrogant kings. (Thirteenth Sibylline Oracle, ll. 25–32, trans. David Potter, quoted with permission)

The account provided by Sapor is brief and to the point, and, as far as concerns Roman duplicity, wholly consonant with the Roman sources:

> And (Philip) Caesar lied again and acted unjustly towards Armenia. We rose up against the nation of the Romans and annihilated a force of 60,000 Romans at Barbalissos. (*Res Gestae Divi Saporis* 9 [Greek text])

Sapor's reference to Armenia raises questions that deserve a response, even if their answers are largely matters for speculation. Zonaras suggests that Philip ceded Armenia and Mesopotamia to Sapor, an act impossible in the terms Zonaras employs, as Armenia was technically an independent kingdom and contemporary evidence shows Priscus to have served as governor of Mesopotamia immediately after Philip's accession (*IGRom.* 3.1202). That said, we have emphasized, first, that the right to name and crown the kings of buffer states was a traditional area of contestation between Rome and Iran; and second, that Ardashir and Sapor continued for many years to confront lingering hostility from loyalists to the Arsacid house at the borders of their empire. It seems that from Sapor's point of view, Sasanian control over Armenia was a *sine qua non* of ongoing peace.

Philip's motivations were very likely different: whatever the uncertainties of war, they may well have been preferable to the unhappiness that payment or, rather, the gathering of tribute caused. An emperor can demand monies in support of war. No emperor can demand monies on the same scale to pay for peace, in a base display of weakness, and expect to live.

As in the east, so in the north Philip named a close relative, his father-in-law, one Severianus, to an overarching command (Zosimus, 1.19.2). Though we do not possess epigraphic testimony as to his title, Philip himself referred to his father-in-law's position when rejecting an appeal to a legal judgment given by him. The ruling specifies that no appeal to a provincial governor or the praetor would be permitted "against the judgment of he who was then judging *vice Caesaris*, in the place of Caesar": "for against the judgment of he who conducts hearings *vice Caesaris*, only the *princeps* himself makes restitution."[21]

As in the east, so in the north Philip appears to have stopped the payment of tribute to the Goths that had become systematic under Gordian.[22] The price that he accepted in recompense was war, a risk that appears at least momentarily to have broken in Philip's favor. The Carpi crossed the Danube in 245. In response, Philip himself campaigned in the north in 245/6 and declared a major victory: he assumed the names Carpicus and Germanicus Maximus (in both cases the title is known from provincial texts: *P. London* 3.951; *IGRom.* 4.635, while a *Victoria Carpica* was announced on the coinage); and he triumphed in Rome in late summer 247. It was very likely on that occasion that Philip elevated his son, now perhaps 9 years old, from Caesar to Augustus.

The evidence that Philip's gamble paid at least a short-term dividend is twofold, both speaking to issues beyond mere economics. First, there is enormously widespread evidence for the refurbishment of roads during Philip's reign. As a formal matter, the maintaining of roads was usually the responsibility of the communities along the road, but like virtually all construction projects, it might be financed in part through tax relief. What is more, like virtually all infrastructural maintenance, some prodding from the center was likely to have been necessary to make it happen.[23] (Skeptics of Philip's ability to coordinate such action should recall the evidence for the ambitious if misguided reforms undertaken by Priscus in Egypt.) The second

---

21. *Cod. Iust.* 2.26.3. On the concept of governing (and judging) *vice Caesaris*, see Michael Peachin, *Iudex vice Caesaris: Deputy Emperors and the Administration of Justice during the Principate* (Stuttgart: Steiner, 1996).

22. The source for all those who claim this is Jordanes, *Getica* 89, who may have had a source (of whatever reliability) for this information, or he (or his source) inferred it – but it should be noted that his text at this point is a tissue of falsehoods and inaccuracies, jumbled together with the occasional fact: "For when Philip was ruling the Romans, who alone before Constantine was a Christian, together with his son, also named Philip, in the second year of whose reign Rome celebrated its millennium, the Goths were tranformed from friends into enemies by the withdrawal on the part of Philip of their subsidy, which act they received poorly." See Ernst Stein, "Iulius. 386. Philippus," *RE* X.1 (1918), cols 755–70 at col. 762 and Pekáry, "Tribut," 279.

23. Stein, "Iulius (Philippus)," col. 766 cites milestones as of 1918 from Dalmatia, Upper Pannonia, Lower Pannonia, Noricum, Upper Moesia, Asia, Cappadocia, Africa Proconsularis, Numidia, Mauretania Caesariensis, Sardinia, Gallia Narbonensis, Aquitania, Upper Germany and Britannia.

piece of evidence for renewed financial confidence in the central administration under Philip derives from an evident choice on his part to spend money extravagantly at the capital: the millennial anniversary of the city of Rome fell during Philip's reign, and he apparently threw the City an enormous and expensive party, from April 21 to 23, 248.[24]

Whether these were in fact partially financed by monies that would otherwise have been drained away through transfer payments from center to periphery can be debated, though perhaps not excluded. In any event, in 248, as it seems, parties aggrieved by Philip's financial policies erupted in anger in both east and west. In the east, a usurper named Jotapianus ranged widely in Syria before being suppressed (apparently) by Julius Priscus or, possibly, killed by his own soldiers (Aurelius Victor, *Caes.* 29.2; Zosimus, 1.20.2). There was also rioting in Alexandria: though we do not know the cause and cannot specify the date, it is not hard to believe that the well-attested squeezing of Egypt for funds by Julius Priscus spurred a violent reaction.[25]

In the west, the Goths, no longer subsidized, swept across the border into Lower Moesia. Seemingly triggered by this fracturing of the Danubian border, the Carpi resumed their raids and placed Dacia under assault. Some local troops, their state aggravated, perhaps, by an imperial policy that had made an assault likely but left them without appropriate support after Philip's departure, sought to resolve their grievances by now standard means: they acclaimed their commander, Tiberius Claudius Marinus Pacatianus (Zosimus, 1.20.2). He was not wholly a flash in the pan: he minted coins at Viminacium for some months. It is a sign of his own ambition, and the capacity of even a ruler so weak as Philip to set the ideological horizons of contemporary politics, that one of Pacatianus' coins is dedicated "To eternal Rome, in its thousand and first year."[26] He was nonetheless killed by his own troops only months into the insurrection, under circumstances no longer recoverable.

24. Alas, no record survives of the form taken by the celebration, though the fact of the celebration is widely observed in later literary sources and Philip advertised it widely on his coinage. See *RIC* Philip nos 12–24, SAECULARES AUGG, and 25, SAECULUM NOVUM (both mint of Rome), as well as no. 85 from the mint of Antioch and nos 106–8 and 111 from an uncertain eastern mint.
25. Parsons, "Philippus," 140.
26. Death: Zosimus, 1.21.2. Coins: *RIC* Pacatianus nos 1–7. No. 6 bears the legend ROMAE AETERNAE AN MILL ET PRIMO.

Philip reacted not by going himself, as might have been prudent, but by sending a local boy made good: Gaius Messius Quintus Decius Valerinus.[27] Born in a village named Budalia in the vicinity of Sirmium, Decius had governed both Lower Moesia and Lower Germany under Alexander Severus, as well as Hispania Citerior under Maximinus. He would seem superbly qualified.

According to Zosimus, Decius was acclaimed by the soldiers of Lower Moesia because, in addition to all their prior grievances, they now had to make their own emperor to avoid punishment at the hands of the one they had just betrayed (Zosimus, 1.21.3; see also Zonaras, 12.20). The acclamation must have taken place by June. Philip, who appears to have tried to avoid just this action, now departed Rome for a civil combat with its northern armies. The armies met at Beroea, where, in early September 249, Philip was killed. His son presumably died with him; Philip's brother Julius Priscus, who had seemed the far more dynamic and capable figure, disappears from the historical record.

Before we depart the reign of Philip and deplore too swiftly his personal weaknesses, we should remark upon his principal experiment. This was the creation of two super-regional commands, the one along the Danube, the other in the east. This was clearly an attempt to address a number of structural weaknesses at once. Those weaknesses included, first, the fact that the emperor could be in only one place at a time, but, second, the rapidly collapsing mechanisms for consolidating the legitimacy of one's rule meant that the emperor could scarcely afford to deliver extensive military authority into anyone else's hands. And yet, third, emperors had to do just this, because the nature of the threat to the frontiers now required coordinated action on a super-provincial scale. The nature of the Gothic and Sasanian victories over the next few years will demonstrate this conclusively.

The appointments of Priscus and Severianus were clearly responses to some perception of the threat now facing the empire and the incapacity of its command structure to meet that threat. Philip's use of his relatives was his attempt to mitigate the threat inherent in surrendering military authority to another. It smacks, of course, of the dynastic politics that led him (and others) to crown

27. The epigraphic evidence for Decius' final name attests both "Valerinus" and "Valerianus." I follow A. R. Birley (and others) in regarding the former as correct (*Brill's New Pauly* vol. 4 [2004] s.v. Decius II 1, p. 154).

their children of whatever age, and naturally such choices often led to disaster: there was no reason to believe that Severianus in particular was up to the job.

Of course, the form taken by Philip's solution was hardly innovative: grants of super-regional power of command to relatives had commenced under Augustus. But the context in which Philip acted was different, and if the precedent was obvious, it had not been taken up by anyone in nearly a century. Variations on it were needed and would soon be crafted, but it would be fully two generations before conditions of personality and talent and the world at large would allow one to succeed.

CHAPTER 6

Religion

In stark contrast with events in the political and military spheres, religious life in the third century is attested by a nearly incomprehensible quantity of evidence. Indeed, one event in the domain of religion – the publication and enactment of an edict by the emperor Decius enjoining sacrifice on all residents of the empire – is without doubt the single best-attested event in the third century and quite possibly one of the best-attested actions of government in all of antiquity. In the face of such riches, a survey in a single chapter must be selective. A volume like this one – which is to say, a volume within a chronologically ordered series – has as its first responsibility the description and analysis of change: in this case, to establish a framework of understanding that might carry one from the settled pluralism of the early empire to the Constantinian revolution, in such a way that the Constantinian revolution (and its aftershocks under Julian and Theodosius) appears less revolutionary.

To be more precise, what this chapter will not do – what in brief compass one could not do – is describe the full range of religious phenomena, or even of change, if by that is intended a listing of sites where this or that god is worshipped in the third century but not in the second, or a table of newly attested identifications between some indigenous god and a Greek or Roman one, or the construction or refurbishment of temples in their geographic dispersal, important though these things are within some interpretive frameworks. Nor, frankly, will I be able to discuss all important changes that work to differentiate a third-century context from those earlier and later. I exclude several as insufficiently connected to the larger, interrelated arguments that bind this chapter to the volume as a whole. For example, the imagery of sacrifice virtually disappears from ancient relief sculpture in this period, and though this is clearly an interesting and quite possibly an important development, it lies outside the network of concerns central to this chapter.[1] Nor will I devote special attention to the rise in the Sasanian east, and arrival in the Roman west, of the cult founded by the new prophet Mani, which provoked both intense fascination and intense hostility among the governing classes of Rome.[2]

Instead, I concentrate on such changes in the sociology of religion and the construction of religious identities as might be described as effects of empire. Such changes might be visible within ancient evidence as changes in the material culture of cult, or the representation of deity, or articulated in texts in theological, doctrinal or eschatological terms. But those are not generally the terms in which I shall speak. The job of the historian of religion is not merely to rehearse or to echo the self-understandings of the religionist. Rather, I wish to describe how and when it became possible for ancients to speak of plural "religions" – not least paganism and Christianity, as well as Judaism and Manichaeism – and to understand them as historically autonomous cultural formations and thus in competition in the first place.

To speak in somewhat different terms, the great revolution of the high Roman empire in the religious domain is not its conversion to Christianity, but its conversion to an understanding of religion in which conversion was meaningful. This was accomplished, I suggest, through a tentative but ultimately abortive decoupling of the religious and political components of identity. This chapter seeks to make that claim intelligible as a lens upon religion in third-century Rome.

Religious pluralism in classical Roman thought

Roman religious thought, and Roman government policy in respect to religion in the empire at large, were founded upon two distinctions that were taken as axiomatic. The first operated to separate those aspects of religious life that lay within the discretion of the individual (where the individual was almost always conceived as existing within various sorts of non-state communal structures:

1. Jaś Elsner, "Sacrifice in late Roman art," in Chris Faraone and Fred Naiden, eds, *Greek and Roman Animal Sacrifice: Ancient Victims, Modern Observers* (Cambridge: Cambridge University Press, 2012).
2. The best entry into the history of Manichaeism in the Roman period is provided by Iain Gardner and Samuel N. C. Lieu, eds, *Manichaean Texts from the Roman Empire* (Cambridge: Cambridge University Press, 2004).

family, ethnic group, club, guild, cult association, etc.) from those aspects that were entailed by that individual's political affiliation, which is to say, by citizenship. (The emergence of this public–private distinction is an historical problem of great importance, but it lies well outside the chronological parameters of this inquiry.) As was stressed in studying Caracalla's edict on citizenship, it is crucial to understand that the Latin term "public" means "of and for the citizen body." By contrast, the English term "public" can mean something as banal as "out in the open" or, by exclusion, "outside the private sphere." But in Latin, the public had a powerful normative and communal component: membership in a political community brought specific obligations in many domains, including religious life. (In addition, in Latin language and Roman thought, it was the *private* that was created through acts of exclusion: the public was conceived as historically and ontologically primary.)

This brings us to the second, closely related distinction central to Roman religious thought. Political boundaries were understood to map religious boundaries, more or less exactly. (That said, political boundaries were not the only ones the Roman recognized in their religious lives.) The most concise expression of this distinction is provided in a speech of Cicero: "Every political community (or community of citizens) has its own *religio*, as we have ours" (Cicero, *Flac.* 69). Here it is crucial to recall the oft-repeated warning not to be misled by the etymological descent of modern "religion" from Latin *religio*: the Latin term could describe a set of cultic practices or a disposition or both, but none of those was understood as exclusive, such that possession or experience of one *religio* meant that one could not experience or participate in another. (I deliberately do not use the term "belong" in reference to a *religio* when speaking of the classical period.)

The enduring power and historical importance of this vocabulary should not be underestimated, nor those of its correlate: namely, classical society's failure over the long term to develop alternative vocabularies and concepts for discussing (and experiencing) religious and political belonging. The two most common apparatus by far described the religionist as a member of a philosophical school (*hairesis*; *secta*) or as a member of a political community (employing *politeia/politeuesthai*). Hence, just as the assertion that one was "Roman" made a claim both of citizenship and of religious affiliation, so, by implication, the assertion that one was a Christian might be employed to reject all standard forms of social and political attachment. Consider, for example, the account provided by the Christian community at Lyons of the deportment under interrogation of one Sanctus:

> He resisted the tortures with such constancy that he did not speak his own name or his community or the city whence he came, nor whether he was slave or free, but to all questions he answered in the Roman tongue, "I am a Christian." (Eusebius, *Hist. eccl.* 5.1.20)

Sanctus names only his status as Christian precisely because he understood that identity not simply to trump, but even to efface all other forms of social belonging: familial, social and jural-political. Indeed, the divorce he effects between the political and the religious is itself a new and experimental claim, one ultimately rejected by the third-century church and abandoned altogether in the fourth century. The aside to the effect that Sanctus spoke in Latin is of course in part mere precision, but it is also useful insofar as Greek ethnics did not carry the same implications in the legal sphere that certain ethnics ("Roman" and "Latin" in particular) did in Latin.

The non-existence of a conceptual or linguistic apparatus for distinguishing "religions" in the modern sense of the term means that Roman vocabularies for discussing the varieties of religion under the empire reveal substantially different priorities than would a modern vocabulary of religion. In a classical Roman text, a Roman magistrate, Marcus Valerius Messalla, writes to the Greek community of Teos regarding the piety of the Roman people:

> That we have wholly and constantly attached the highest importance to piety toward the gods one can estimate particularly from the goodwill that we have experienced on this account from the divine. Not only that, but for many other reasons we are convinced that our own high respect for the godhead has become manifest to everyone. (*SIG* 601 = *RDGE* 34, ll. 11–17)

Outside the one plural, "gods," Messalla otherwise employs radically underdetermined singulars: "the divine," "the godhead." Similarly underdetermined language was used by the senator Manilius Fuscus in his capacity as head of the Roman priestly college of Quindecemviri, the Board of Fifteen for the Performance of Rites, in an address to the Senate regarding the performance of the Secular Games under Severus in 203 (the text is fragmentary):

> Amidst the happiness and rejoicing of the human race, it is appropriate for you to give thanks for present goods and to take care for

> hope for the future, Conscript Fathers, such that ... you command rites to be performed at common expense, with all due worship and veneration of the immortal gods (*omnique cultu adque veneratione immortalium* <16 letters missing>) ... for the security and eternity of the empire, and that you should frequent the most sacred places for the giving and rendering of thanks, so that the immortal gods (*dii immortales*) should give to our descendents those things that our own ancestors founded and which, along with the things they took from even earlier generations, they delivered to our own age.[3]

In this formulation what is important is an attitude of piety and its realization in worship in some aggregate, *not* the absolute sameness of the acts performed everywhere, *nor* the identity of those "immortal gods" from whom favor is requested and to whom thanks is delivered.

We witness the gradual intrusion of an alternative conception, organized around the identity of particular gods (each potentially the object of its own religion), in a Christian text of the first half of the third century, in words attributed by the author to a fictive pagan:

> Thus we see through all empires, provinces and cities that each people has its own sacred rites and worships its municipal gods: the Eleusinians worship Ceres, the Phrygians the Mother of the Gods, the Epidaurians Aesculapius, the Chaldaeans Belus, the Syrians Astarte, the Taurians Diana, the Gauls Mercury; the Romans, all gods. (Minucius Felix, *Octavius* 6.1)

In writing about religion, classical Roman texts evince a stunning – and as it happens, widely shared – lack of interest in the identity of gods. (This would not be true at the level of ritual action: then, of course, a very specific god or set of gods is named as the recipient of each gesture.) What is more, the central terms in Cicero's panoptic view make no judgment about correctness, nor does he show any interest in the question of whether groups do or should share gods (or whether some gods might not really be gods at all). Rather, his interest lies in the universal nature of religion itself, defined as a set of social conventions and ethical imperatives, but the fact of their variance – *civitas* by *civitas* – does not rise to the level of an ontological distinction (such that each is a "religion" with a reality, origin

---

3. *Commentarium ludorum Septimiorum* 1.21–5 in G. B. Pighi, *De ludis saecularibus populi Romani Quiritium libri sex*, 2nd edition (Amsterdam: Schippers, 1965), 142.

and authorization distinct from the others) or exclusionist ideology.[4]

In so describing the *religious* pluralism of the empire, Cicero's formulation bears a distinct resemblance to the account given by Gaius of the empire's *legal* pluralism (above, p. 78). Indeed, the descriptions rely on identical grammatical operands, a distributive ("each," "every") and a reflexive ("for itself"). The similarity points to a further issue: the interest of the imperial center ran deeper than an acknowledgement of the mere existence of pluralism. (That said, in comparative historical terms, the fact that an empire should content itself with the mere observation of pluralism is a notable fact in its own right.) It was not simply that each locality was understood to have its own *religio*. It was also held that ongoing religious life at the local level conduced to both local social order and an overarching imperial order, too.

We can witness these related beliefs in operation simultaneously in a wide variety of third-century texts, in which emperors grant requests by localities for privileges of various kinds – normally, of course, the mere continuance of those granted by earlier emperors, on the grounds that the emperors wish to support local religious life in some form. For example, when Aphrodisias congratulated Caracalla on his accession to joint rule with his father Severus, the city also asked that its privileges and autonomy be continued. Caracalla granted that request because the citizens of Aphrodisias were all the more attached to the empire "because of the god(dess) who protects your city," namely Aphrodite.[5] But one did not need to share a god with Rome, or even to worship a recognizably Greek or Roman god, to receive such gestures: the village of Baetocaece, which superintended a famous temple of Baal, received in the mid-250s a Latin letter from the emperors Valerian and Gallienus confirming the privileges of the village and its temple (*IGRom.* 3.1020).

But one can see expressions of the local and specific nature of religious life, and of the value of local religious life to the Roman emperor, no matter the locality, in contexts other than the granting of privileges. For example, when the Aezanitae wrote to Septimius Severus to congratulate him on his victory over Niger and to observe the appointment of Caracalla as Caesar – and sent a gold statue of

---

4. By "exclusionist ideology," I refer to a system of thought according to which membership in one religious community was taken to require non-membership in others.
5. J. Reynolds, *Aphrodisias and Rome* (London: Society for the Promotion of Roman Studies, 1982), no. 18.

Victory as their crown gold – Severus wrote a polite reply that he allowed might be deposited "among their local gods" (*ILS* 8805 = Oliver, no. 213 ll. 24–5). Again, in a decree of Caracalla from 215, preserved on the same papyrus as the citizenship decree, the emperor expelled from Alexandria Egyptian peasants who had migrated from the countryside to the city without employment-related justification. But he issued a broad exemption for Egyptians who came to the city for the festival of Serapis or other festivals, bringing animals for sacrifice (*Sel.Pap.* no. 215; Oliver, no. 262).

Finally, it is essential to observe that religious regulations generated in some local community or in Rome were binding only on the community that generated them. As evidence for this, one might adduce the famous correspondence between Pliny and Trajan regarding the scruple involved in a request by the city of Nicomedia to move the city's temple of the Mother of the Gods. Pliny hesitated to approve the request, he wrote, because the temple had no *lex*, no statutes governing such an eventuality; it lacked such statutes, Pliny surmised, because the "the method of consecration" (*morem dedicationis*) practiced in Nicomedia was "different from that practiced among us." Trajan responded that Pliny could be "without fear of violating religious scruple," "as the soil of an alien city cannot receive consecration as it is performed according to our law" (Pliny, *Ep.* 10.49–50: *cum solum peregrinae civitatis capax non sit dedicationis, quae fit nostro iure*). The crucial language is legal: Nicomedia being a non-Roman city, it is not governed by Roman law – and, to adopt Cicero's language, being a non-Roman city, it has its own *religio*. Trajan implicitly absolves the city of any obligation to employ a "method of consecration" that accords with Roman law, even as he reassures Pliny that Pliny himself will incur no scruple if he approves an act that would be (religiously) illegal and inappropriate at Rome.

Effects of empire

The landscape in which Caracalla intervened – in which the devotees of Mani were shortly to proselytize, and Christians ran afoul of the law (and each other) – was far more fluid than this characterization in terms of norms might seem to allow. Before we turn to Caracalla and the new religious dynamic that the edict of universal citizenship helped to enable, we should consider briefly some patterns of change in the sociology of religion in the period, especially such as shaped the emergent patterns of religious conflict in the second half of the third century.

That said, for all that this brief section focuses on the fluidity or, perhaps, the loosening of prior certainties in cultic life in the private domain, we should not forget the very different meanings of public and private in the Roman period. In traditional understanding, one's religious life apart from obligations at the civic level was just that: separate from, not superordinate to, the religious entailments of political belonging. It is not that religion was private and civic life was public, nor that one's religious life as a citizen was expected to determine one's private conduct. The distinction worked rather to insulate the two spheres from each other in ways that were conducive to social order in a heterogeneous society, even when the nature of its heterogeneity – the important axes of difference – shifted profoundly over the course of centuries. It was a conceptual system developed in the context of empire, and to a point very well suited to it. That said, precisely because political belonging brought religious entailments, it was emphatically *not* true of Greco-Roman polytheism that "each group worships certain gods in whom it believes," as the Christian Dionysius of Alexandria maintained, with the implication that one was also free to reject all others (Eusebius, *Hist. eccl.* 7.11.8). To describe the foundation of the system as having anything to do with the choice of gods is, as we have seen, to mischaracterize it completely (but in a very Christian way).[6] This is a problem to which we shall return.

Across the period of the first three centuries, the signal social-historical developments within the empire are nearly all connected with human mobility. The great connectivity of the Mediterranean as a domain unto itself, and the bridges of pacified space brought into being by the empire, greatly reduced the risks (and transaction costs) associated with the movement of both persons and goods. The results of importance here were several: one was a vast growth in the number of cities with significant immigrant populations. As a consequence, the significant conurbations of the high Roman empire were heterogeneous along multiple axes – ethnicity, language, dress, to name but three – to a degree wholly unprecedented in the ancient world.

6. Please observe that the Roman official questioning Dionysius, one Aemilianus, invites him to worship Christ if he wants: Aemilianus does not care a whit about Dionysius' religious commitments in his (Roman) private life (Eusebius, *Hist. eccl.* 7.11.9: "Who is stopping you from worshipping this one [Christ], too, if he is god, along with those who are gods by nature?"

Migrant individuals and groups naturally brought their gods with them. What is more, they spread first where transportation was easiest. The phenomenon has been documented multiple times: material and documentary remains reveal cults to have spread around the Mediterranean first along shipping lines, then up rivers to major cities, and only then along roads and, lastly, into the countryside. One consequence of this phenomenon was the presentation of new religious choices to the pre-existing populations. A further result was the articulation of a specifically religious component to identity, as religion became one among several cultural forms (dress and cuisine being two more) that united the members of those immigrant communities in contradistinction to the populations among whom they resided. (I do not claim that this phenomenon was new under Rome, merely that it was likely greater in scale than ever before.) At times, these cultic identities served to link immigrant populations with each other or with some notional homeland, such that the population might meaningfully be described as a diaspora. In such cases – the Tyrian merchants of Puteoli and Rome are a notable example – ties both cultic and economic often bound the homeland to the migrant group.[7]

The function of religion in echoing and hence reinforcing the social bonds within immigrant populations might be compared very loosely to the rise of distinctive cultic commitments within military units, which were also communities distinct from the populations alongside which they betimes resided. In both cases, there is no evidence that cultic ties were conceived as exclusionary; but none-

---

7. On migrant communities in the Roman empire see Nicole Belayche and Simon C. Mimouni, eds, *Les communautés religieuses dans le monde gréco-romain: Essais de définition* (Turnhout: Brepols, 2003); Lellia Cracco Ruggini, "Nuclei immigrati e forze indigene in tre grandi centri commerciali dell'impero," in J. H. D'Arms and E. C. Kopf, eds, *The Seaborne Commerce of Ancient Rome*, Memoirs of the American Academy in Rome, 36 (Rome: American Academy in Rome, 1980), 55–76; Ramsay MacMullen, "The unromanized in Rome," in Shaye J. D. Cohen and Ernest S. Frerichs, eds, *Diasporas in Antiquity*, Brown Judaic Studies, 288 (Atlanta: Scholars Press, 1993), 47–64; Nicole Belayche, "Les immigrés orientaux à Rome et en Campanie: Fidélité aux *patria* et intégration sociale," in André Laronde and Jean Leclant, eds, *La Méditerranée d'une rive à l'autre: Culture classique et cultures périphériques* (Paris: Diffusion de Boccard, 2007), 243–60; R. Compatangelo-Soussignan and Christian-Georges Schwentzel, eds, *Étrangers dans la cité romaine. "Habiter une autre patrie": Des incolae de la République aux peuples fédérés du Bas-Empire* (Rennes: Presses Universitaires de Rennes, 2007); and K. Verboven, "Resident aliens and translocal merchant *collegia* in the Roman empire," in Olivier Hekster and Ted Kaizer, eds, *Frontiers in the Roman World* (Leiden: Brill, 2011), 335–48.

theless, they could have served to reinforce other social bonds that worked to unite the group in contradistinction to outsiders.[8]

Of course, it is true of religion in general – not merely in respect to immigrant groups – that it tends to map and hence to justify all manner of social distinctions. Whatever else religions might be, they are also ideological formations, and as such they work to justify varied forms of social differentiation and particular distributions of wealth and power, often by locating authorization for those structures in some non-human or transcendent domain. The dominant modern theories of religion in the ancient Mediterranean – theories of religion as "embedded," or of "polis-religion" or "the civic compromise" – all share this view.[9] On their understanding, the fundamental structures of civic cult in particular were homologous with the normative structures of social and political power, and indeed were not understood autonomously from them.

As we have seen in very general terms, imperial rule set in motion social and demographic change on a massive scale. Such change must have placed enormous stress on the ability of purely civic cult to map, explain and justify the dynamics of social life. This gap, between some ritual, verbal and gestural language of cult in its efforts to emplace the world, and the social-material realities of life in the increasingly variegated landscape of empire, set in motion a variety of dynamic processes. Any number of such processes,

---

8. On the legion as total institution, see Ramsay MacMullen, "The legion as a society," *Historia* 33 (1984), 440–56, reprinted in MacMullen, *Changes in the Roman Empire* (Princeton: Princeton University Press, 1990), 225–35, and Nigel Pollard, "The Roman army as 'total institution' in the Near East? Dura-Europos as a case study," in David Kennedy, ed., *The Roman Army in the East* (Ann Arbor: Journal of Roman Archaeology, 1996), 211–27. It would be almost impossible today to survey even the bibliography on religion and the Roman army: one might begin with Oliver Stoll, "The religions of the armies," in Paul Erdkamp, ed., *A Companion to the Roman Army* (Oxford: Blackwell, 2007), 451–76; see also Eric Birley, "The religion of the Roman army, 1895–1977," *ANRW* 2.16.2 (1978), 1506–41; J. Helgeland, "Roman army religion," *ANRW* 2.16.2 (1978), 1470–505; and Ian P. Haynes, "Religion in the Roman army: Unifying aspects and regional trends," in Hubert Cancik and Jörg Rüpke, eds, *Römische Reichsreligion und Provinzialreligion* (Tübingen: Mohr Siebeck, 1997), 113–26.

9. For surveys of modern theories of ancient religion see Andreas Bendlin, "Looking beyond the civic compromise: Religious pluralism in late republican Rome," in Edward Bispham and Christopher Smith, eds, *Religion in Archaic and Republican Rome and Italy* (Edinburgh: Edinburgh University Press, 2000), 115–35; B. Nongbri, "Dislodging 'embedded' religion: A brief note on a scholarly trope," *Numen* 55 (2008), 440–60; and Clifford Ando, *Religion et gouvernement dans l'empire romain* (Paris: Éditions du Cerf, 2012).

however important, must here be set aside as too loosely connected with the overall themes of this chapter. One important example is the development of competition among cultic and oracular centers, and technologies and ritual practices for asserting the supremacy of one's local shrine or god over against some other(s): hence, not only did worshippers acclaim their god in comparative terms – as best or highest, for example – but communicative technologies were adopted to record and publicize those claims within the larger communicative and cultic community of the empire.[10]

This faltering in the ability of civic cult to account for the complexity of the world that empire had brought into being is also visible in the enormous explosion in extra-familial but non-political religious groups: cult associations often enough organized around gods themselves understood as immigrant or epiphanic rather than resident – Isis, say, or Jupiter Dolichenus or Mithras or Christ. In some of these, whether from explicitly rejectionist motives or not, we sometimes witness periods (usually early) in which the conduct of the religious community upends various social norms. So, for example, the communal records from the early third century of the cult association for Jupiter Dolichenus on the Aventine in Rome reveal a hierarchy of membership internal to the cult in which slaves appear alongside the free and freed, and Greek, Roman and Semitic names commingle.

Patron	Patrons	Patron
Aurelius Magnesius	Aurelius Sarapiacus	Aur(elius) Asclepiodotus
Lamrpias <sic>	Gem(inus) Felix	M(arcus) Aur(elius) Eutyces
Patron	Vi(bius) Eutycianus	Aturmarurius
Mem(mius) Leo	Cor(nelius) Crescentianus	Titus Annius Nicevitus
…	…	…[11]

But a slightly later text from the same community displays a different, and more traditionally Roman, set of priorities:

10. Angelos Chaniotis, "Megatheism: The search for the almighty god and the competition of cults," in Stephen Mitchell and Peter van Nuffelen, eds, *One God: Pagan Monotheism in the Roman Empire* (Cambridge: Cambridge University Press, 2010), 112–40.
11. *HD020859* = Monika Hörig and Elmar Schwertheim, eds, *Corpus cultus Iovis Dolicheni (CCID)* (Leiden: Brill, 1987), no. 373 = Mary Beard, John North and Simon Price, *Religions of Rome*, vol. 2 (Cambridge: Cambridge University Press, 1998), no. 12.3a.

By order of Jupiter Optimus Maximus Dolichenus Eternal, for the
preservation of the firmament and for the pre-eminent divinity, in-
vincible provider, Lucius Tettius Hermes, Roman knight, candidate
and patron of this place, for the welfare of himself, his wife Aurelia
Restituta, his daughter ... and for the welfare of the priests and
candidates and worshippers of this place, he presented a marble
plaque with its setting and columns.

  Jupiter Optimus Maximus Dolichenus chose the following to
serve him: Marcus Aurelius Oenopio Onesimus, called Acacius, as
recorded ...[12]

In this second text, the individual who held the highest rank and
presumably also the greatest wealth *outside* the cultic context was
granted, undoubtedly by virtue of that rank and wealth, a place of
extreme prominence *within* the cult. In addition, he was allowed to
assert the priority to him of traditional social relations over cultic
ones: family first, cult community second. What is more, the list of
officers that follows is no longer displayed in tabular form, with
ranks and persons all mixed up: the list is in prose and organized
hierarchically. And all this was commanded by the god himself.[13]

  The cult community of Jupiter Dolichenus on the Aventine was
not unusual. In virtually all cultic communities whose structures and
membership we can trace at this level, the revolutionary or emanci-
patory potential of religion – or, perhaps, the revolutionary potential
that many religionists like to claim on behalf of their religion – failed
of its promise. Instead, they came to mimic or echo, and thus to
support, the systems of social differentiation at work in the population at large. In the case of the one cultic community that developed
a translocal system of coordination and governance, this characterization holds especially true: not simply the diocesan structure of
the church at large, but the protocols and parliamentary rules of
Christian councils mimicked those of the Roman state and its local
offspring. Hence the form taken by the third-century martyr acts is
nothing more and nothing less than an exacting copy of a Roman
record of a judicial proceeding, of the sort Antoninus Pius ordered
local officials to keep when interrogating suspects (p. 91), or that
was transcribed and posted at Dmeir (p. 61). The clear implication

---

12. *ILS* 4316 = Hörig and Schwertheim, *Corpus cultus Iovis Dolicheni*, no. 381 = Beard
et al., *Religions*, vol. 2, no. 12.3b.
13. We can see similar forces at work in cult communities of Isis, where by the third
century prominent Romans occupy major priesthoods – all, of course, *iudicio maiestatis
eius*, "by the judgment of her majesty" (*AE* 1998, 876, from AD 251).

is that the Christian community possessed no mechanism, no resource, for the authentication and validation of historical memory of such an event more potent than the form granted to the culture at large by the workings of imperial government, whose own insistence on exactitude in knowledge production had been trumpeted by Antoninus Pius and by others elsewhere.[14]

Where the cult of Dolichenus is concerned, at a formal level – in respect of medium, language and layout – the various forms taken by the rosters of the cult look like nothing so much as the member-ship records of Roman priestly colleges or the albums of curial orders.

Religion in a world of universal citizenship: The decree of Decius

Such tentative, ultimately abortive upendings of traditional forms of social differentiation within religious life existed in complex histori-cal relation to changes in the normative structures of politics and political belonging. Far the most important of the latter was, of course, Caracalla's decision to grant citizenship to all free residents of the empire. Recall that Caracalla made that grant in order to enable a more effective, more universal display of piety in thanks-giving, whose form was notionally to be a procession to the temples by "all my people" (p. 54). There is, however, no evidence of any substantive requirement, let alone enforcement mechanism, by which individual or even communal participation in the Caracallan thanksgiving was compelled or verified.

A substantive requirement and enforcement mechanism is, however, exactly what was laid down in late 249 by the new emperor, Decius. His act was no doubt inspired in part by the religious cast given the age by the millennium of Rome, though whether Decius saw himself as continuing from Philip by way of commencing the new era with an act of piety, or as reacting to millennial anxieties aroused by that event, is not clear.[15] (The broad

14. This summarizes an argument laid out at greater length, made in reference to both the Christian martyr acts and the so-called *Acta Alexandrinorum*, in Clifford Ando, *Imperial Ideology and Provincial Loyalty in the Roman Empire* (Berkeley: University of California Press, 2000), 117–30 and *passim*.
15. On the possibility that the millennium aroused anxieties around the empire see David S. Potter, *Prophecy and History in the Crisis of the Roman Empire: A Historical Commentary on the Thirteenth Sibylline Oracle* (Oxford: Clarendon Press, 1990), 39 and 258.

cultural significance of the millennium should at any rate not be in doubt: recall that the usurper Pacatianus in Moesia advertised on his coins that his reign had commenced in the year 1001: see p. 119.) What is clear is that by fall 249 at the latest Decius ordered all residents of the empire to sacrifice to the gods for the eternity of the empire, and further that he required some, perhaps all, persons to obtain a certificate of compliance with the order.[16]

A remarkable number of certificates of compliance with the Decian edict survive, and they reveal some aspects, at least, of this moment with stunning clarity (Figure 11):[17]

> To the officials in charge of the sacrifices, from Aurelius Sakis of the village of Theoxenis, with his children Aion and Heras, temporarily residents in the village Theadelphia. We have always been constant in sacrificing to the gods, and now too, in your presence, in accordance with the regulations, we have sacrificed and poured libations and tasted the offerings, and we ask you to certify this for us below. May you continue to prosper.
>
> (2nd hand) We, Aurelius Serenus and Aurelius Hermas, saw you sacrificing.
>
> (1st hand) The 1st year of the Emperor Caesar Gaius Messius Quintus Traianus Decius Pius Felix Augustus, Pauni 23. (*PMich.* inv. 262; trans. from APIS)

The mechanics by which the residents of the empire were known and catalogued and their compliance assessed is of course an historical problem of the highest order, somewhat to the side of the history

16. Regarding the date, observe that Eusebius implies that the order to sacrifice arrived in Alexandria on the heels of the announcement of Decius' succession to Philip (*Hist. eccl.* 6.41.9–10). As many have observed, in part because some Christians declined to comply (though many did), the Decian edict is one of the best-documented events in the history of ancient government. But the decree of its documentation is also due to the remarkable punctiliousness of Roman government: the so-called Decian *libelli*, like Roman tax or census returns, would exist apart from the furor the edict caused among Christians. For a sane and judicious summary of the event itself and its aftermath see Graeme Clarke, "Third-century Christianity," *CAH*[2] XII 589–671 at 625–37. See also the Guide to Further Reading.

17. John R. Knipfing, "The *libelli* of the Decian persecution," *Harvard Theological Review* 16 (1923), 345–90 remains the best starting point for consideration of the certificates. He catalogues forty-one texts. A number have been discovered since, including *POxy.* 2990 and 3929; *PSI* VII 778; and *SB* 9084.

Figure 11 A certificate of compliance with the Decian edict on sacrifice, *PMich.* inv. 262 (Digitally reproduced with the permission of the Papyrology Collection, Graduate Library, University of Michigan)

of religion.[18] It will be taken up in Chapter 8, "Government and governmentality."

What needs emphasis here is the apparent lack of interest on the part of imperial officials in the identity of the gods to whom any one individual sacrificed – or, perhaps one should say, the lack of interest on the part of the imperial government in the identity of the gods addressed in any given locality. Aurelius Sakis, for example, declares only his constancy in sacrificing to unnamed "gods," and the same wholly generic plural is employed again and again in the Decian certificates. Because some number of Christians, seeking the instant entry to heaven that contemporary doctrine insisted was the reward for martyrdom, refused to comply with this base-line requirement, we possess a number of narratives detailing the negotiations between Roman and local officials and Christians over the minimal act that might satisfy the edict. One of the most detailed and precise such narratives concerns Pionius, bishop of Smyrna. Some way into his conversation with the provincial governor occurs the following exchange:

> The proconsul said: "Sacrifice."
> [Pionius] replied: "No, for I must pray to (the) god."
> He said: "We worship all gods and heaven and all gods who are in heaven. I suppose you hearken to the air? Sacrifice to it."
> He replied: "I do not hearken to the air but to the one that made the air and heaven and everything in them."
> The proconsul said: "Tell me, who made them?"
> He answered: "It is not possible to say."
> The proconsul said: "Obviously it was (the) god, the very Zeus who is in heaven. For he is king of all the gods." (*Acta Pionii* 19[19])

To employ a Roman term, what was wanted was a demonstration of *religio*, a demonstration of an appropriate disposition: what we might term the narrow theological content of the act was remarkably negotiable. Pionius' initial reply to the proconsul, employing the simple noun "god," must have baffled, even in an era when Christians were everywhere and the fundamentals of their beliefs

---

18. For now, I observe simply that the use of census records in the enforcement of the edicts on sacrifice is deduced from Eusebius, *Hist. eccl.* 6.41.11, quoting Dionysius of Alexandria, on which see W. H. C. Frend, *Martyrdom and Persecution in the Early Church: A Study of a Conflict from the Maccabees to Donatus* (Oxford: Blackwell, 1965), 407–8.

19. See also *Acta Cononis* 4.3–4 and Louis Robert, *Le martyre de Pionios prêtre de Smyrne* (Washington, DC: Dumbarton Oaks, 1994), 109–10.

were widely known to all within the empire. The proconsul's response may have been condescending, but it illustrates a phenomenon widely attested in the third century: the Romans wanted little more than confirmation that one was religious. If that meant allowing Pionius to sacrifice to the air, so be it. This proconsul, at least, did not care if the object of Pionius' worship was a god: he wanted Pionius to be the sort of person who had religious commitments, and he wanted Pionius to express those commitments in support of emperor and empire.

The perplexity and frustration of Roman officials in the face of Christian intransigence is manifested particularly in their frequent exasperated but remarkable refusals to punish. Not only do Christian texts record numerous occasions when an absolute refusal to comply was nonetheless followed by dismissal from the tribunal, but even in those localities and on those occasions when some Christian was punished, the government made no attempt to round up the community as a whole. For example, on several occasions during the imprisonment, interrogation, death and burial of Cyprian, bishop of Carthage, the Christians of Carthage – indeed, we are told, the whole of the Christian community – gathered to witness and celebrate his example, and to demand that they themselves be punished.

> [The proconsul Galerius Maximus] read the decision from a tablet: "It is decided that Thascius Cyprian should die by the sword." Cyprian the bishop said: "Thanks be to god." After his sentence the community of brothers said: "Let us be beheaded with him."

None was seized.

> So Cyprian died and his body was laid out nearby to satisfy the curiosity of the gentiles. At night, however, his body was taken away and conducted in prayer and with great pomp by the light of candles and torches to the cemetery of Macrobius Candidianus, which lies near the fishponds on the Mappalian Way, and there it was buried. (Acta Cypriani 4–6)

A reader of Christian martyr acts might be reminded of an earlier event, also in Carthage, namely, the death in the reign of Severus of the Christians Perpetua and Felicitas and their companions. They were visited in jail on numerous occasions by members of the Christian community and conducted rites there (see, e.g., Passio Perpetuae 3.7, 6.7 and 9.1). Had government officials been interested in capturing many Christians, then in 203, or in 258 when

Cyprian died, they could simply have closed the doors of the prison with the Christians inside or arrested those who accompanied the cortège of Cyprian. But no such act is ever attested.[20] Indeed, even in the city of Rome, where one might have thought conservatism and imperial scrutiny would heighten tensions, the authorities under Decius conducted a handful of executions but simply released from custody without any punishment whatsoever many confessed Christians (Cyprian, *Ep.* 49 and 54.2).

One effect of the Decian edict was to bring unwonted attention and pressure to bear upon Christians around the empire, and it was rapidly numbered by them among the so-called persecutions. No doubt it was the first such event that was nearly universal in scope. But despite occasional shifts in scholarly fashion and even judgment in the matter, it seems to me in no way whatsoever credible as an act directed at Christians, for three reasons above all: first, despite the huge volume of contemporaneous documentation, there is not a shred of evidence that such was its purpose. One cannot simply deduce intent from effects, to say nothing of doing so exclusively from the perception of effects by one affected party among many.

Second, the edict of Decius is wholly intelligible on its own terms, in line with a wide range of religious actions stretching back to the Roman Republic and continuing through the gesture of Caracalla (see pp. 54–7). Not for naught did the community of Cosa in Italy fund a public dedication to Decius as "Restorer of Rites and Freedom" (*HD007089*). Third, the interpretation of the edict as designed to persecute the Christians fails – indeed, fails abysmally – the same test that Dio's construal of Caracalla's edict does. Just as Caracalla had no need to give away citizenship merely to raise taxes, so the Roman government could have moved against the Christians on the basis of existing law: it had in the past and it would soon do so again. Indeed, the jurist and one-time praetorian prefect Ulpian was able in the 210s to collect and cite numerous imperial rescripts attesting the range of punishments emperors had sanctioned for the crime of being Christian.[21]

---

20. The sanest history of the persecutions remains Frend, *Martyrdom and Persecution.* A more recent assessment dedicated specifically to the third century – and also very well done – is that of Clarke, "Third-century Christianity."

21. Ulpian, *De officio proconsulis* bk. 7 fr. 2191 Lenel = Lactantius, *Div. inst.* 5.11.19, a mere testimonium from Lactantius regarding the content of Ulpian's text. For an illustration of its likely form, see Ulpian, *De officio proconsulis* bk. 7 fr. 2192 Lenel, a survey of legal actions against fortune-tellers of various kinds.

Ulpian's collection of evidence raises one further issue that deserves attention in this context, and that is the local nature of both religious life and government action. A rescript is a fancy name for a reply: Ulpian's collection might thus be said to testify above all to the overriding importance of local initiative in Christian persecution until the 250s. The imperial government became involved in order to confirm the content of positive law, and of course the central government enjoined its own supervision of any legal matter carrying the death penalty (on this see pp. 144 and 91). But the initiative and energy in persecutions prior to Decius seem always to have been local. This remained true even in the generation before Decius, a period of perhaps three and a half decades during which very, very few attacks on Christians are attested at all. One purely local event, attested in the city of Rome in 235 and seemingly nowhere else, resulted only in the exile of the pope and a presbyter to Sardinia. (Indeed, the pope, Pontianus, seems long to have remained hopeful that even exile to Sardinia might be deemed too severe, and only resigned his office once he found himself on the island.[22]) Another, also in 235, seems to have been confined to Cappadocia, where a particularly malevolent governor was provoked to action by a series of earthquakes and local casting-about for a scapegoat.[23]

As regards Christian persecution, the immediate aftermath to the reign of Decius looks not so different from before: a handful of purely local actions dot the historical record. This situation changes dramatically for the worse in 257, during the joint reign of Valerian and Gallienus. It was in the context of following through on some order of theirs that Dionysius of Alexandria conversed with the governor of Egypt and offered his observation that every community of any kind worships the gods in which it believes (see above, p. 129). The immediate upshot of that conversation was not the execution of Dionysius, nor exile to Sardinia, but banishment to Cephro in Libya. The laxity of the prefect of Egypt notwithstanding, it is clear that the edict was generated from the center and was intended to apply to the empire as a whole, and that in some provinces, at least, its enforcement was strict and suffering wide-

22. See the list of bishops of Rome in the Codex Calendar of 3452: *MGH Chronica Minora* 1 p. 74 l. 37–p. 75 l. 3.
23. The evidence is contained in a letter of Firmilian, bishop of Caesarea, preserved in the corpus of Cyprian: see Cyprian, *Ep*. 75.10.

spread.[24] It also seems clear that the edict did not initially target Christianity as such, but Christians, in this sense: it did not enjoin the prosecution and punishment of Christians *per se* but commanded that they should be made to perform the common rites of empire in addition to whatever observance they made in private. In other words, Christians could be Christian, so long as they also conducted themselves as proper Romans.

As regards the themes of this chapter, the persecution under Valerian and Gallienus is notable on two grounds. First, as under Decius, the emperors did not command the discovery and punishment of Christians as ends in themselves, but the performance of a religious act. (We will consider momentarily the nature of that act.) Second, though there is every reason to believe that the emperors knew in 257 what the effect of Decius' edict had been and so could have – must have – understood that their very similar action amounted to an attack on the Christians (and perhaps others), some Christians at the time did not understand it to be motivated narrowly by a desire to attack them or, perhaps, chose to depict the edict in such terms. Cyprian the bishop of Carthage, for example, responded to the proconsul's request that he should sacrifice with the claim that Christians pray day and night for the preservation of the emperors (*Acta Cypriani* 1.2). It may well be that he imagined, as Tertullian had done – albeit sarcastically – that the heart of the issue was political loyalty and that this issue could be disaggregated, as being political, from the problem of religion.[25] He was wrong.

The future of religious history

In ancient history, one should not rely overly much on highly particularized evidence to reveal a general trend, or a local paraphrase or single witness to a text to reveal its original wording. Nonetheless, the documentation for the martyrdom of Cyprian from 257/8, which

---

24. The principal accounts include Eusebius, *Hist. eccl.* 7.12 for the east; *Liber Pontificalis* 25, for Rome; the *Passio Montani et Lucii* for Carthage/Africa Proconsularis; and the *Passio Mariani et Iacobi* for Numidia (commencing in Cirta and ending in Lambaesis).

25. Cyprian would not have been naïve in so believing, nor in believing that this position might be efficacious: the explicit rationale for the few religious interdictions to survive from the Roman period is generally that the illegal act affected *publica quies imperiumque populi Romani* (the public peace and power of the Roman people). The rationale thus privileged the overriding importance of the citizen community.

purports to use the transcribed proceedings generated by the government itself, reveals fascinating developments upon the language apparently used by Decius in his edict of 249/50. In the earlier case, as we have seen, citizens (perhaps residents) of the empire appear to have been ordered to sacrifice "to the gods" for the safety of the emperor and empire. In 257 the wording was different:

> The proconsul Paternus spoke to the bishop Cyprian in his chambers: "The most sacred emperors Valerian and Gallienus have considered it appropriate to send letters to me in which they order that those who do not cultivate Roman *religio* should acknowledge Roman rites (*eos qui Romanam religionem non colunt debere Romanas caerimonias recognoscere*)." (*Acta Cypriani* 1.1)

Leaving the meaning of *recognoscere* ("acknowledge") to one side, the language of this text suggests that two crucial changes had taken place or were underway. First, the act that the citizens were required to perform, and the disposition they were expected to hold, are explicitly described as Roman. They were normatively Roman insofar as they were entailments of citizenship; and they were definitionally Roman, it seems, in reaction to some other. The previously unarticulated potential of "Roman" to indicate both a juridical status and a religious affiliation discussed in Chapter 3 in connection with the Antonine Constitution is here very nearly actualized.

Again, neither *religio* nor *caerimonias*, "rites" (one among many terms for such), has here definitively come to mean something like our "religion." Nonetheless, it is clear that Roman self-understandings, and Roman conceptions of the constituents of culture, were under stress – were undergoing redefinition – as a result of the vast work of self-differentiation underway in the Christian community. In all manner of cultural contexts, boundary-drawing on the part of one community – or, one might say, efforts by one group to define itself *as* a distinct community – spur contrapuntal efforts by the culture from which it draws back: as a result, each must perforce exist simultaneously in relations of close homology and utter alterity to the other.[26]

What became of earlier concessions that every locality had its own

---

26. Two suggestive works on boundary-drawing of this kind in the ancient world are Daniel Boyarin, *Border Lines: The Partition of Judaeo-Christianity* (Philadelphia: University of Pennsylvania Press, 2004) and Thomas N. Sizgorich, *Violence and Belief in Late Antiquity: Militant Devotion in Christianity and Islam* (Philadelphia: University of Pennsylvania Press, 2009).

religio? How far did Rome go in requiring the local practice of some specifically Roman religion? If we bracket the emergent conflict with Christianity, what does the future history of paganism hold, within the storylines we have laid down thus far?

Evidence before Decius illustrates a number of possibilities, ranging from the assertion of radical separation at the level of law (the position of Trajan in his response to Pliny, above, p. 128) or the grand recognition of the validity but also the otherness of alternative *religiones* with their many unnamed and unspecified gods (the upthrust of the remarks by Valerius Messala and Manilius Fuscus, above, pp. 125 and 125–6) to an insistence on some minimal Roman content. The requirement imposed on Roman colonies and municipalities well into the third century was that they should pay cult to the Capitoline triad and the deified emperors, with nearly everything else up to be determined by local authorities.[27] In some places not reconstituted as Roman communities, the aftermath of the Antonine Constitution witnessed an efflorescence not of cult to the Capitoline triad but simply to Jupiter Capitolinus–Zeus Kapitolios (see, e.g., *BGU* II 362, page 3 ll. 1–9 and page 5 ll. 1–17, from Arsinoë). An extreme outlier would be the ritual life of a Roman military unit, for which we have the evidence of a detailed ritual calendar from the reign of Severus Alexander, belonging to a single unit stationed at Dura Europos, an outpost at the very eastern frontier of empire. The liturgical year of the unit was extraordinarily Roman, even as other evidence – material, epigraphic and artistic – suggests that the private religious lives of the soldiers were fully as eclectic and cosmopolitan as those of the residents of any metropolis.[28]

---

27. The *divi* (deified emperors) in municipal religious life: see *HD018575* = Girard-Sens part IV, no. 8, a charter from Lauriacum in Austria in the reign of Caracalla. For the earlier evidence see John Scheid, "Aspects religieux de la municipalisation: Quelques réflexions générales," in M. Dondin-Payre and M.-T. Raepsaet-Charlier, eds, *Cités, municipes, colonies: Les processus de municipalisation en Gaule et en Germanie sous le haut empire romain* (Paris: Publications de la Sorbonne, 1999), 381–423; Jörg Rüpke, "Religion in the *lex Ursonensis*," in C. Ando and J. Rüpke, eds, *Religion and Law in Classical and Christian Rome* (Stuttgart: Steiner, 2006), 34–46; Clifford Ando, *The Matter of the Gods* (Berkeley: University of California Press, 2008), 95–119; and Ando, "Exporting Roman religion," in Jörg Rüpke, ed., *A Companion to Roman Religion* (Oxford: Blackwell, 2007), 429–45.
28. R. O. Fink, A. S. Hoey and W. F. Snyder, "The *Feriale Duranum*," *YClS* 7 (1940), 1–222. The religious life of third-century Dura is the subject of a huge bibliography but there has been no synthetic treatment beyond a very brief essay by C. Bradford Welles, "The gods of Dura-Europos," in R. Stiehl and H. E. Stier, eds, *Beiträge zur alten Geschichte und deren Nachleben: Festschrift für Fritz Altheim*, vol. 2 (Berlin: De Gruyter,

Such evidence as we have – and it is not consistent in quality or level of detail – suggests widespread variation in the *form* taken by local implementations of the ritual requirement under Decius and, where we can tell, under Valerian and Gallienus as well. This is in contrast to the Decian certificates of compliance, where the wording is bland to an extreme and largely homogeneous. At the level of language, the specification was sometimes added that one must worship not simply "the gods" but those gods that preserve the empire (Eusebius, *Hist. eccl.* 7.11.6–7). The ritual was occasionally rendered the more Roman by its being conducted at the local Capitolium (this is firmly attested at Carthage, which, however, was a Roman colony, and its practice was no doubt the more Roman because of that[29]); it may at times have been conducted on an altar dedicated to the emperors;[30] and local officials must normally have encircled the altar with statuettes of local gods as well as of the emperors, living and deified. At the final stages of any persecution that did not descend to mob violence, a Roman official would have had to be present in order to approve any serious penalty, especially capital ones, and then the tribunal would have been marked with *fasces*, the staves that symbolized Roman magisterial authority.[31]

This seems a remarkably low level of homogeneity, of top-down control, particularly for a ritual requirement enjoined by the emperor himself and explicitly tied to the juridical condition of Romanness. Elsewhere in relations between the metropole and the very near periphery we witness tentative signs of greater penetration by metropolitan authorities and norms into local life. In a famous exchange of correspondence of the year 295, for example, the town council of Cumae instituted a new priest for the cult of Magna Mater and, for reasons unspecified, sought approval for this decision

1969), 50–65, together with Ted Kaizer, "Language and religion in Dura-Europos," in Hannah Cotton, Robert G. Hoyland, Jonathan J. Price and David J. Wasserstein, eds, *From Hellenism to Islam: Cultural and Linguistic Change in the Roman Near East* (Cambridge: Cambridge University Press, 2009), 235–53, and Kaizer, "Patterns of worship in Dura-Europos: A case study of religious life in the classical Levant outside the main cult centres," in C. Bonnet, V. Pirenne-Delforge and D. Praet, eds, *Les religions orientales dans le monde grec et romain cent ans après Cumont, 1906–2006: Bilan historique et historiographique* (Brussels: Belgisch Historisch Instituut te Rome, 2009), 153–72.

29. On the Capitolium at Carthage see Cyprian, *De lapsis* 8 and 24 and *Ep.* 49.13.3.

30. For altars to the emperor in the Greek world see A. Benjamin and A. E. Raubitschek, "Arae Augusti," *Hesperia* 28 (1959), 65–85.

31. *Fasces*: see *Acta Pionii* 10.4, implying that they would be displayed when a Roman official was present at the punishment, and Robert, *Martyre de Pionios, ad loc.*

from the college of Quindecemviri at Rome, which granted its approval and certified this return letter.[32] But this is virtually the only such document asserting Roman control over local religious life from a Roman authority other than the emperor, until, of course, the bishop of Rome began (largely on the basis of falsified documentary evidence) to claim primacy over the Catholic church in the west.[33]

The rule was rather the persistence of local *religiones*, centered on local institutions and locally recognized deities, subject to the ongoing ebb and flow of historical cultural change. As testimony, we might examine a very much later account of pagan religious practice, partly descriptive and partly normative, by the orator Libanius of Antioch, who wrote late in the fourth century AD just as the tide of anti-pagan violence and legislation was reaching its crescendo:

> If the security of the empire rests on the sacrifices performed there, then we must believe sacrifice everywhere to be profitable. Indeed, just as the gods in Rome give greater things, so those in the fields and the other villages give lesser things. (Libanius, *Or.* 30.33; trans. A. F. Norman, with modifications)

The circumstances of its composition notwithstanding, Libanius' text offers a vision of religious practice as distributed: "there" is Rome, and "everywhere" else – in all the fields and villages of the empire (and the world) – one finds religious practice homologous with that of Rome, but not identical to it, either. It can exist in support of Rome, because it echoes Rome.[34] To that extent, one might say that Libanius understood high imperial paganism in terms kindred to those in which I described the evolution of local law: religion in Antioch is not the same as in Rome, nor is it different, either, such that they are either the same "religion" or different ones. Rather, the understanding of them, and very likely their practice, had evolved such that each existed in a relation of fractal reduplication with the other.

32. *ILS* 4175 = Beard et al., *Religions*, vol. 2, no. 10.4b.
33. What is more, as Thomas Keith has remarked to me, the request for the approval of the Quindecemviri appears to have originated at Cumae, in which case the correspondence may illustrate a perverse continuance of local autonomy, though on this one occasion the locality was choosing to subordinate itself to the metropole.
34. One is reminded, of course, of Caracalla's desire that his people should approach shrines, or that Egyptians not otherwise permitted in Alexandria should be allowed to sacrifice there.

CHAPTER 7

Failure and fragmentation: From the accession of Decius to the death of Gallienus

During the quarter century that commences with the accession of Decius in 249, the Roman empire came close to collapse as a political formation. That it did not requires substantial and specific explanation. The Conclusion to this volume will offer one such. It is the task of the two remaining narrative chapters, 7 and 9, to describe the errors, events and catastrophes that brought the empire to the point of ruin and then brought it back.

Alas, the same features that make the period analytically fascinating also render it nearly impossible to narrate. In short, enemies along two fronts penetrated the frontiers at will, sacking cities in the very heart of the empire and pillaging to the gates of Rome. As the capacity of the central government to justify itself collapsed – or, in other words, as the central government ceased to be perceived as effective in defense of the state – the political elites in various regions broke away and established themselves as autonomous or semi-autonomous polities. Nor were these wholly stable. There were thus many years when military action was taking place on three or more fronts, by several individuals who styled themselves emperor or who had self-deputized themselves in the service of one or another emperor – and of course, at any given moment, one Roman army might launch itself against another.

The fragmentation of political authority, compounded by military chaos, presents formal problems that are not easily solved. A year-by-year account, for example, would produce gibberish, as a dozen separate strands would have to be rehearsed each year, as far as that year carried any given story, only to break off until the next year. Naturally, all historians of Rome, and many historians of empire, confront such problems. In the Roman tradition, perhaps the most beautiful and certainly the most enduring solutions are those of Tacitus and Gibbon, each of whom deviated regularly and substantially from the form that he notionally practiced, in the former case the annal and in the latter sequential narrative.

A conventional means for rehearsing the tale of these years is to select a sequence of rulers – Decius to Gallus to Valerian to Gallienus to Claudius, and so forth – whose actions are made central, while all others are labeled usurpers or pretenders or rulers of something other than Rome. If this practice had to be justified, one might cite some factor like control over the city of Rome or recognition by the Senate that distinguished the lead characters in one's scheme, nor would such be without historical importance. But in point of fact, the practice of selection has always been both politicized and teleological. The standard genealogy of imperial power was constructed in antiquity largely by counting backwards, as it were, from Diocletian in 284: who died or was killed, such that Diocletian became emperor? And whose death had made way for him? And so on. These institutional and political factors naturally combine, institutions and institutional knowledge-production never being apolitical. A further endorsement of the standard genealogy derives from the late antique law codes, which might seem to testify to the actual practice of individuals in conducting themselves as emperors – and may do just that. That said, the late ancient codes of law certainly testify to the operation of both practical and political factors in the recognition of certain individuals as legitimate adjudicators of the law, such that their decisions are held dispositive in future legal actions.

Nor was the work of memory production performed only at the end: as we have already seen, an important component of the legitimation of power in the ancient present was the construction of the past. Every would-be emperor connected himself to some predecessor, through adoption or titulature or what have you, fully as assiduously as he built bridges to the future by promotion of his offspring.

In consequence, in rehearsing the history of the third century as we do, we follow rather uncritically in the footsteps of a series of Latin summaries produced in the mid-fourth century and later by Aurelius Victor, Eutropius and the *Historia Augusta*, the structure of whose narratives was overdetermined by political imperatives, both the ones I have just mentioned regarding the legitimating power of the past, and their inverse, namely, the suppression of memory that goes hand in hand with the delegitimization of certain rulers and would-be rulers as mere usurpers (or worse). Far the most intelligent of those authors whose narratives of the third century (mostly) survive is the author of the *Historia Augusta*. He made just these issues of legitimacy, memory and political power the subject of a fictitious debate, recalled at the opening of a book dedicated to four failed candidates for the throne:

> For you know, my dear Bassus, how great an argument we recently had with that lover of history Marcus Fonteius, when he asserted that Firmus, who had seized Egypt in the time of Aurelian, was not an emperor but merely a mini-bandit. Rufius Celsus and Ceionius Julianus and Fabius Sossianus and I argued against him, maintaining that Firmus had worn the purple and called himself Augustus on the coins he struck, and Archontius Severus even brought out certain coins of his and proved, moreover, from Greek and Egyptian books that in his edicts he had called himself *Imperator* (*autokratôr*).
>
> For his part, Fonteius had only the counter-argument that Aurelian wrote in one of his edicts not that he had killed a usurper (*tyrannus*) but that he had rid the state of a mini-bandit – as though a *princeps* of such renown might have called such a fly-by-night figure a usurper, or as though mighty emperors did not always name as bandits those whom they killed when attempting to seize the purple. (SHA *Firmus* 2.1–2)

Three features of the conversation merit attention. First, there is simply the fact that there existed no means to settle the question of whether Firmus had in fact been an emperor of the Roman world. (His having "ruled" only in Egypt evidently did not rule out the possibility that he was actually an emperor, which shows how drastically foreshortened horizons of expectation with regard to imperial power had become.) Second, the very limited means available to historians to assess claims to legitimacy reflect hugely important realities of political life for contemporaries: how were the residents of Egypt to know who the emperor was? The simple fact of the matter was that Firmus in Egypt, like Pacatianus in Moesia or Jotapianus in northern Syria, had minted coins, commanded soldiers, issued edicts and – who knows? – almost undoubtedly supervised the settlement of legal disputes. The material, practical and ceremonial mechanisms for behaving like an emperor were available to many: legitimacy in the exercise of social and political power was, to an extent nearly incomprehensible today, actively built up through the faltering construction of a social consensus.

Third, the *Historia Augusta* highlights the active role played by a would-be emperor's historical successors in the formation of memory. But we should observe two further ramifications of this contest over naming. On the one hand, it draws attention to the need of emperors to control not only the construal of the past but also that of the present: to name someone even an illegitimate emperor – a *tyrannus* – was to open debate regarding one's own legitimacy, by allowing that the issue was contestable. One sees the same argument played out in other periods in Roman history using different terminology: the condescension with which an emperor avows an intent to concentrate on foreign policy, against public enemies of the Roman state, while ignoring mere private enemies of his person, is another symptom of this dynamic.[1] Finally, the reference to edicts points to a difficulty regularly observed in ancient sources but little discussed by them as a general problem, namely, the terribly vulnerable position of even large communities in the empire when caught between contesting candidates for the throne. To return to two cases already noted, it is doubtful that, had they been left to their own devices, either Byzantium or Aquileia would have wished to contest the legitimacy of Severus or Maximinus, but the one found itself on the wrong side of history when Severus won, while the other waited out the collapsing legitimacy of its besieger (pp. 36, 107). Nor was alignment during war the only issue: a city that made the mistake of merely obeying, or decreeing congratulations to, a usurper might find itself having to give even more crown gold to the ultimate victor. In this way, too, the instability of third-century politics brought the empire to feed upon itself.

Death on the frontier: Decius (249–51)

To judge from the rapid appearance of reaction at the local level, the edict enjoining universal sacrifice must have been nearly the first act of Decius as emperor following the death of Philip in 249. The fundamental conservativism visible in that act was matched by a noteworthy historical consciousness, for Decius also ordered the production of a remarkable series of commemorative coins. These revived portraits of prior consecrated emperors – namely, those that the institutions of the state had deemed worthy of posthumous honor. Included in the series were Augustus, Vespasian, Titus, Nerva, Trajan, Hadrian, Antoninus Pius, Marcus Aurelius, Commodus,

---

1. This was often done using plays on the terms *hostis* and *inimicus*, though no historically stable contrast in their application to private and public enemies is in fact observable.

Severus and Severus Alexander (absent were Claudius and Pertinax, as well as the more recent Gordians I, II and III) (Figures 12 and 13).[2] In part, the series was a means by which Decius advanced a claim about his own competence – upon his accession, he also took an additional name, Trajan. But it was also of a piece with the reactionary revivalism of the edict on sacrifice: as we have seen, the consecrated emperors as a collective were among a tiny number of Roman gods respect for whom in official contexts was enjoined upon colonies and municipalities around the empire (p. 143).

If one were to examine the reign of Decius in search of notable achievements or trends beyond the edict on sacrifice and an appalling record of military failure, one would have to cite his success in stabilizing the domestic political situation in the east: Philip the Arab's brother Julius Priscus disappears from the historical record, seemingly without disturbance, and it may be that the revolt of Jotapianus lingered into the reign of Decius before coming to naught. How this occurred, and what role Decius played in the process, are unknown. One might also place Decius in the vanguard of a cohort of individuals from the Danubian provinces, connected by ethnicity and political disposition as well as interpersonal contact, who rose to prominence in the army and occupied the throne in a rough sequence that commences (to a point) with Decius and includes Claudius, Aurelian, Probus, Diocletian and Maximian. We have seen that Philip may have sent Decius to Moesia because of his ties to the region; Decius himself advertised his origins on a set of coins vaunting both Dacia and Pannonia.[3]

That said, things began to fall apart at some point in 250, and the cataclysms that erupted in both north and east laid the ground for a substantial diminution in imperial power and the fragmentation of imperial government for a generation. Neither sequence of events can be reconstructed with any security. As Decius himself traveled from Rome to the Illyrian front, there to die in 251, only to be succeeded by another general operating along the Danube, I will describe events in the European theater of operations through the reign of Valerian first, before I return to events in the east in 251 and beyond. Indeed, as we shall see, events in the east took the course they did very largely in reaction to the emperor's absence.

In 250, during Decius' second consulate, Marcus Ratinius [–]

---

2. *RIC* Decius nos 77–100.
3. Pannonia and Dacia on the coins of Decius: *RIC* Decius nos 5, 12, 13, 14, 20–6, etc.

(a)

(b)

(c)

(d)

(e)

(f)

Figure 12 The consecrated emperors according to Decius: (a) Augustus, (b) Vespasian, (c) Titus, (d) Nerva, (e) Trajan and (f) Hadrian (Images drawn from the collection of the American Numismatic Society and reproduced with permission of the ANS)

(a)   (b)

(c)   (d)

Figure 13 The consecrated emperors according to Decius: (a) Antoninus Pius,
(b) Commodus, (c) Septimius Severus and (d) Severus Alexander; Marcus Aurelius
was part of the series but is not represented here (Images drawn from the collection
of the American Numismatic Society and reproduced with permission of the ANS)

Saturninus, a legionary of the First Italian Legion, the Decianic,
stationed in the Chersonese, left a dedication in the kingdom of
Bosporus, in modern Ukraine (*HD050583*). It may be, as David
Potter suggests, that Saturninus had been dispatched to learn more
of the massive population movements then taking place across
the Ukrainian steppe, resulting in pressure all along Rome's
central European border.[4] If so, whatever information was sent by
Saturninus is likely to have arrived alongside the news that the
border had collapsed.

4. David Potter, *The Roman Empire at Bay*, AD *180–395* (London: Routledge, 2004),
244 n. 121.

Who these peoples were who poured across the Danube in 250 and soon sailed the Black Sea – and ultimately passed the Hellespont – cannot now be recovered. The point is an important one and deserves some emphasis. To begin with, we might ask what we mean when we ask what the identity was of those who invaded across the Danube. Often enough, the search for the identity of such peoples is itself based on a delusion, that population groups of this kind will have stable identities that one can trace across the centuries: we want these "Goths" to be the Goths who defeated Valens at Adrianople in 378, for example. That answer would make the one group more important; it might seem to make history more coherent. But such quests are rarely so innocent in their effects. In form, at least, they resemble the efforts made in an earlier age to identify specific population groups in antiquity as the direct ancestors of modern European nations. Those efforts and their projects have been largely discredited and set aside, though not wholly. Further caution is always warranted.

What is more, even if we have successfully emancipated ourselves from the ideological motives that impelled those efforts to locate in antiquity the roots of some European present, we nonetheless rely in very large measure on ancient sources produced under their own very similar cultural constraints: those of classical ethnography, which sought ever to employ the names and taxonomies of the tradition's earliest exemplars, and hence crippled their accounts with persistent anachronism; or those of historiography in the so-called barbarian kingdoms, which in their own way sought to provide stable histories and historical identities for the peoples then constructing themselves as Mediterranean polities.[5] The other major source of information available to us, namely, the residual evidence of the material culture of the peoples in question, provides little information for the third century beyond establishing the negative conclusion that the Gothic populations who invaded the empire in the late fourth century were different from, and probably not related to, those who invaded in the middle of the third.[6]

The situation is not altogether hopeless, of course. It is very likely that the bulk of the information about the Gothic invasions of the third century derives from a contemporary eyewitness, the historian

5. On ethnography of the Roman period see Greg Woolf, *Tales of the Barbarians: Ethnography and Empire in the Roman West* (Oxford: Blackwell, 2011).
6. Peter Heather and John Matthews, *The Goths in the Fourth Century* (Liverpool: Liverpool University Press, 1991), 51–101.

Dexippus of Athens. Furthermore, it may well be that his attribution of specific actions and campaigns to different tribal groups does in fact bear some relation to the political and social articulation of the populations in question. In any event, we are hardly in a position to second-guess him, and the account that follows will offer no correction to the tradition in this regard. What is more, nearly any available global term for describing these groups as a whole – Germanic, Gothic, Skythian – can be indicted for both distortion and anachronism, but the state of our knowledge leaves little choice but to speak in global terms. This warning will have to suffice as a caveat to the reader.

Decius left Rome for the Danubian provinces in 250. He must have announced victories of some kind: he is given the victory titles of both Germanicus and Dacicus Maximus that very year (the former only on a milestone in Tunisia, *AE* 1942/3, 55; the latter only on milestones in one Spanish province, *CIL* II 4949 = *Hispania Epigraphica* record no. 10486). But the invading forces were clearly not cowed and did not go away. The next year, probably in spring 251, Decius may have suffered a great defeat at Beroea,[7] while the city of Philippopolis in Thrace, which had been under siege, was sacked and its population taken in slavery (Dexippus, *FGrH* 100 F 26). Decius' political position was weakened, and two usurpers declared for the throne, one in Rome (the wholly obscure Julius Valens [Licinianus]), the other the governor of Thrace, Titus Julius Priscus, who may simply have felt that the risks involved in defending Thrace could not succeed, or would not be rewarded to his liking, with Decius on the throne.[8]

According to Dexippus, Decius fell upon the Goths as they were retreating from Roman territory with the booty and captives taken at Philippopolis. The Goths appear to have formed themselves into

---

7. The major source for this defeat, Jordanes, *Get.* 102–3, contains an unnerving combination of details found nowhere else and sheer improbabilities. That said, the thirteenth Sibylline Oracle may also refer to a major defeat by Decius before his death: see David S. Potter, *Prophecy and History in the Crisis of the Roman Empire: A Historical Commentary on the Thirteenth Sibylline Oracle* (Oxford: Clarendon Press, 1990), 280.

8. It must be said that we actually have no idea at exactly what moment, and hence under what conditions, Valens and Priscus acted. Aurelius Victor, for example, connects Valens' usurpation only with Decius' absence from Rome (*Caes.* 29.2–3). I do not believe the assertion of Jordanes to the effect that Priscus allied with the Goths and permitted the sack of Philippopolis: it reads like a doublet with the genuine action of Trebonianus Gallus.

three columns: Decius attacked the third in a swamp near Abrittus, himself at the head of his army, if Dexippus is to be believed. Decius' army was utterly destroyed. His body and that of his elder son Herennius were never found.

Trebonianus Gallus (251–3) and Aemilius Aemilianus (late summer to early fall 253)

Though defeated and in disarray, the forces concentrated on the Danube were the only ones in a position to name a successor to Decius: they knew before anyone else that he was dead, and they desperately needed a commander. They acclaimed as emperor the highest-ranking official on the spot, the governor of Lower Moesia, one Trebonianus Gallus. His son Volusianus, then around 20 years of age, was named Caesar. For his own sake, so that he could rush to Rome – and perhaps because no alternative was in fact possible – Gallus immediately struck a truce with the retreating Goths, who departed Roman territory with their booty and captives intact.[9]

Decius had died around June 1, 251 – an inscription from Rome is written as though he were alive on June 9; another names him *divus*, dead and consecrated, on the 24th of that month (*CIL* VI 31120 and 36760). Decius had had two sons: the elder, Herennius, had been named co-ruler and died with his father. The younger, Hostilianus, had remained in Rome at the rank of Caesar. Gallus sought to establish goodwill, and pre-empt suspicion of his own motives, by elevating Hostilianus to the rank of Augustus, as co-ruler, ahead of his own son (Aurelius Victor, *Caes.* 30.1; Zosimus, 1.25.1; cf. *AE* 1979, 302), but Hostilianus is last attested alive in early July. His death is attributed to plague by Aurelius Victor and the anonymous *Epitome de Caesaribus* and to Gallus by Zosimus: testimony, at the very least, to the epistemic uncertainties that inhere in a world without forensic science (Aurelius Victor, *Caes.* 30.2; *Epit. de Caes.* 30; Zosimus, 1.25.1). In the event, Gallus elevated Volusianus to the rank of Augustus by late summer (*ILS* 525), and the only recorded legal decisions of the reign are attributed to Gallus and his son, without Hostilianus.

Allowing marauding invaders to depart with all their booty was

---

9. We rely once again on the highly problematic narrative of Jordanes, *Get.* 106, though he tells us nothing that we might not have guessed (i.e. that there was a truce) while saying much that is fundamentally confused.

not an effective deterrent to future depradation, and trouble continued in 252, indeed, escalated (Zosimus, 1.27.1). That year groups Zosimus describes as "Goths, Boranoi, Burgundians and Carpi" passed the Hellespont in boats and attacked the coast of Asia Minor, whose wealthy cities had seen no military action other than civil war for more than a quarter of a millennium. Apart from the deployment of small local militias, government response was slackjawed helplessness, and some great civic centers – including, as it seems, the great temple of Artemis at Ephesus – were destroyed.[10] The sense that the central government had lost its way to some fundamental degree must have seemed confirmed in later years, when the boats returned and sailed at will.

Each of the varied sources for 253 describes its no doubt chaotic events in a few sentences at most.[11] The governor of Upper Moesia, one Aemilius Aemilianus, was acclaimed as emperor by his troops in late summer: it is clear that he had been directing the war against the Goths, though we have no idea whether merely in his own province or along the Danubian front more generally.[12] He seems even to have been successful (Zosimus, 1.28.1). Certainly the year 253 witnessed stunningly little Gothic activity in the empire's interior. Once acclaimed, Aemilianus set out for Italy. Gallus, like Philip before him, was finally stirred to action by a domestic threat to his person. The tradition suggests that Gallus had wits and time enough to summon a force from Gaul, under the command of Publius Licinius Valerianus. The timing is not impossible, and certainly the story aided Valerian in later describing his action as motivated solely by a concern for justice, and so evincing a sense of piety and loyalty that received further testimonial when, as it seems, Valerian consecrated Gallus after his arrival in Rome. But if Gallus had the wits to call for aid, he lacked the smarts to wait for it: Gallus and Volusianus met Aemilian in northern Italy, at either Interamna or Forum Flamini, where they were killed by their own troops. Whether the indolence of Gallus had lost their loyalty, or they feared to meet Aemilian's

10. Potter, *Prophecy*, 311–14.
11. On the Latin side, see Aurelius Victor, *Caes.* 31 and Eutropius, 9.5. On the Greek, here including Jordanes as part of the reception of Dexippus, see Zosimus, 1.28, Zonaras, 12.21 and Jordanes, *Get.* 105.
12. The likelihood that his command was *de facto* if not also *de iure* overarching is perhaps increased by the fact of his acclamation by several legions: I Italica, IV Flavia, VII Claudia and XI Claudia (R. Hanslik, "Vibius. 58," *RE* VIII.A.2 (1958), cols 1984–94 at 1992).

more tested legions, or both, is beyond recall. "They were killed at Interamna, having completed not even two years' rule; they achieved nothing notable whatsoever" (Eutropius, 9.4).

Virtually the only fact related about Aemilian as emperor is the duration of his reign: eight-eight days, according to one source, and three months in others.[13] As Eutropius quipped: "most obscurely born, Aemilian ruled obscurely" (Eutropius, 9.6). (The extraordinary brevity of reigns in this period is the object of some fascination in the later historical tradition: the fact that Gallus had reigned less than two years is also much remarked, though two years was comparatively long.) In any event, Valerian was acclaimed by his troops on his way to Italy – whenever it was that he had departed, with whatever motivation. He and Aemilian met near Spoletium, where history repeated itself. Aemilian was murdered by his troops, and rule passed to Valerian.

The western empire under Valerian and Gallienus (253–68)

Valerian had one surpassing qualification for rulership (perhaps his only one), namely, an adult son, Gallienus.[14] After the death of Aemilian, Valerian went immediately to Rome, arriving in late September, where he elevated Gallienus to joint rule – perhaps first to Caesar, but if so, to Augustus before October 22. The period of their joint rule presents something of a paradox: the existence of two emperors, both certainly more active than Philip or Gallus, neither as bumbling as Decius, should have permitted a certain repair, retrenchment or consolidation. Even bracketing the death of Valerian in 260, Gallienus ruled fairly firmly for fifteen years. But the best that can be said of their joint reigns may well be that they hindered rather than aided the further collapse of the Roman state, and that Gallienus in particular did so by recognizing the limitations of its power.

Valerian's reign ends in Persia, and so we must soon turn our attention to events in the east between 251 and his death in 260. But first let us hold our gaze a bit longer in Europe.

13. He also receives just about the shortest biography in *RE* of any emperor: *RE* I.1 (1893) s.v. Aemilius (24) cols 545–6. Eighty-eight days: the Codex Calendar of 354. Three months: everywhere else except Zonaras, who says "not four months."

14. In fact, Valerian had another son, named after himself, who must have been in some respect unsuitable for command: he serves largely as a representative of the family in Rome, serving as consul in 265, and is killed after Gallienus' death in 268.

Both Valerian and Gallienus departed Rome in 254, Valerian soon going east, Gallienus north. But the division of rule between them was not or, rather, could not be strictly geographic (cf. Zosimus, 1.30.1). Valerian is known to have been in Asia Minor in 254 and Antioch in 255 but appears in Germany in fall 256 before perhaps spending the late fall and winter of 256/7 in Rome.[15] He returned to the east in late 257 and his activities are centered there until his capture by Sapor in 260.[16] Part of the problem with any strict division, if such was intended, was of course that the European and Asian theaters were not wholly separate: the Gothic raiders that passed the Bosporus and ravaged Asia in 252 did so again in 256, 262 and 266, even as others moved at will through peninsular Greece in 267, and as we shall see, they drew the attention of the armies of the east. (The chronology is far less certain than this rehearsal of dates might suggest.)

Gallienus on the other hand remained firmly in the west for the great bulk of his reign. He appears to have based his command first along the Danube, in either Sirmium or Viminacium. Virtually no significant testimony to his actions there survives, though he and Valerian took the titles *Germanici maximi* before 254 was out (*CIL* XI 2914), and the coinage of the western mints boasts the legend *Victoria Germ(anica)* several times over the next few years.[17] Nor were the boasts meaningless: for a few years at least, the successes of the Gothic raiders at sea were not matched by similar successes on land. But Gallienus' troubles were multiplying: there are signs that Germanic tribes were putting serious pressure on the Rhine frontier in these years – perhaps partly in response to a perception of Roman weakness, and certainly in response to a revival and development in strength and ambition on their part – and it may well be that significant Roman manpower in the area had been drawn away by Gallus

15. The presence of Valerian in Rome is largely deduced from *Cod. Iust.* 6.42.15, though of course the protocols of laws are the parts of the text most subject to error in transmission. The transmitted text puts Valerian or Gallienus or both in Rome six days before the Ides of October, 256. Gallienus was ordinary consul for 257, and some believe he would have entered into office in Rome, and if Valerian were there in October, perhaps he would have remained in Rome for the occasion. There are also those who believe Valerian and Gallienus then issued their edict enjoining sacrifice upon the Christians while in Rome together – it was issued early in 257.
16. The data are available in L. Wickert, *RE* XIII.1 (1926) s.v. Licinius (Valerianus) (173), cols 488–95 at 491–2.
17. *RIC* Gallienus nos 27–35, 39–50, 61–3, etc. In addition to the material discussed in the Guide to Further Reading, see L. Wickert, *RE* XIII.1 (1926) s.v. Licinius (Egnatius) (84), cols 350–69.

in 252/3 to prepare for an expedition against Persia (Aurelius Victor, *Caes.* 32.1; see also below, p. 166). Not only Gallienus' propaganda over the next few years but the subsequent history of Gaul in his reign suggest that the locals perceived their need for protection to be great.

At some point before 257, perhaps in anticipation of transferring his own headquarters away from the Danube but certainly with an eye to dynastic stability, Gallienus elevated his elder son, also named Valerian, to the rank of Caesar.[18] By 257 Gallienus was head-quartered near the Rhine: the Danubian frontier was nominally under the control of Valerian II but real power and leadership rested with the governor of Pannonia, Ingenuus. Valerian II died soon thereafter, probably in early 258, probably along the Danube. Gallienus immediately elevated his younger son Saloninus to Caesar. Gallienus' presence in Gaul no doubt achieved something: it is not simply that he names himself "Restorer of the Gauls" on the coinage, but also that the frontier collapsed immediately upon his departure in 259, when he certainly took troops from the border zone and left a vacuum of authority if not of leadership.

Events over the next two years moved utterly beyond Gallienus' capacity to respond, and indeed, perhaps in some respects beyond the capacity of the system as he had received it. Without adhering to a strict chronology – such being in any event unrecoverable – we can say that the western empire was invaded by multiple parties: Alamanni and Franks came across the Rhine, with at least one group of Franks reaching the Spanish provinces; another Alamannic army passed the Alps and reached Milan; a Iuthungian raid crossed the Alps by an eastern route and reached the outskirts of Rome before turning back north; and fighting burst out all along the Danube. As Gallienus sought to stem the tide, the various legions on the Danube in 259 (where Gallienus was not) and the Rhine in 260 (when Gallienus had left it for the Danube), abhorring a vacuum of imperial authority, both acclaimed their commanders.

At a moment, then, when the empire desperately needed unified action and competent leadership, the political system failed in the basic task of retaining the loyalty of soldiers and commanders: and

---

18. Dietmar Kienast, *Römische Kaisertabelle: Grundzüge einer römischen Kaiser-chronologie* (Darmstadt: Wissenschaftliche Buchgesellschaft, 1990), ad loc. cites *CPR* I 176 as revealing Valerian II as Caesar in 255, but the papyrus should be dated to 257 (http://papyri.info/ddbdp/cpr;1;176).

more. Material, money and lives were wasted in the suppression of the revolts by Ingenuus and another commander, Regalianus, along the Danube, and the suffering of Italy at the hands of the Iuthungi and Alamanni might well have been lessened had Gallienus been able to direct his attention there sooner, arriving as he did only in summer 260 (Zonaras, 12.24). As it was, without the assistance of an immensely capable lieutenant, one Aureolus, Gallienus might have failed in all these tasks: it was Aureolus, in fact, whose skill defeated Ingenuus, and Aureolus again who defeated the usurpers from the east, Macrianus father and son.[19] To understand who they were and whence they arose, we await a turn to the east.

Postumus and the Gallic empire (260–74)

The political chaos on the Rhine that commenced after Gallienus' departure followed a predictable form to an unexpected conclusion. The governor of Lower Germany, Marcus Cassianius Latinius Postumus, defeated a Germanic raiding party as it returned across the Rhine with its booty.[20] Gallienus' deputy in the region, one Silvanus, who had the Caesar Saloninus in his charge at Cologne, demanded that Postumus surrender the booty to him. Postumus gave it to his troops instead; they acclaimed him emperor; and he marched on Cologne. Silvanus and Saloninus were promptly delivered up. And then ... nothing. Or, rather, Postumus chose *not* to march on Italy, and Gallienus lacked the will or resources to march on him. Gallienus was probably not up to it at the level of generalship, and Aureolus was fighting Macrianus. Gallienus did strike at Postumus after the defeat of Macrianus, but ineffectively, and the situation rapidly lapsed into stasis.

It is alas not possible to write a cogent political history of the state that Postumus ruled, the so-called Gallic empire. Having been excluded from the genealogy of legitimate power, his reign was likewise excluded from narration: Aurelius Victor reduces his ten-year rule to a single sentence, Eutropius to two.[21] That said, much can be gleaned from the evidence of inscriptions and coins about the form of government under his rule, and some lessons drawn from the

19. On the defeat of Ingenuus see Zonaras, 12.24. On Macrianus and his sons see below, p. 170. On Aureolus see W. Henze, "Aureolus," *RE* II.2 (1896), cols 2545–6.
20. Aurelius Victor, *Caes.* 33.8; Zosimus, 1.38.2; see also Zonaras, 12.24.
21. Aurelius Victor, *Caes.* 33.8; Eutropius, 9.9.1–2.

small but remarkably positive assessments that trickle down in the Latin tradition.[22] Three related points deserve emphasis here. First, Postumus clearly sought to establish a new state, on whatever justification, in the Roman empire beyond the Alps. For not only did he come rapidly to rule Gaul, Britain and northern Spain – and perhaps parts of Raetia – but he determinedly kept within those limits, despite several provocations from Gallienus.

Second, the nature of Postumus' ambitions, their height as well as their cultural and political horizons, were utterly Roman: this is apparent from his own titulature and that of his subordinates, as well as the legends, language and images of his coins.[23] Indeed, it is likewise apparent from the broader political culture that sustained him. As confirmation, we might cite the inscription first published in 1993 that revealed the reach of Postumus' influence into Raetia. The stone is re-used: it had recorded a dedication in honor of the Severan house for the safety of Severus Alexander.

> In honor of the divine [imperial] house, for the safety of Emperor Severus Alexander Augustus ...

> In honor of the divine [imperial] house. Dedicated to the holy goddess Victory, because of barbarians of the race of Semnones and Iuthungi slaughtered on the eighth and seventh days before the Kalends of May and routed by the soldiers of the province of Raetia and [those stationed] in the Germanies, and likewise many local peoples, as a result of which many thousands of Italian captives were freed. Marcus Simplicinius Genialis, distinguished equestrian, acting in the place of the governor, together with his army placed this freely and deservedly, being satisfied of their vows. Dedicated three days before the Ides of September in the year when our lord Emperor Postumus Augustus and Honoratianus were consuls. (*HD044953*)

---

22. Two fine works on the Gallic empire provide thorough and helpful surveys of the epigraphic and numismatic evidence: see Ingemar König, *Die gallischen Usurpatoren von Postumus bis Tetricus* (Munich: Beck, 1981); and J. F. Drinkwater, *The Gallic Empire: Separatism and Continuity in the North-Western Provinces of the Roman Empire, AD 260–274* (Stuttgart: Steiner, 1987).

23. An easily accessible and utterly typical example might be *ILS* 561: Postumus is there named "Emperor Caesar Marcus Cassianius Latinius Postumus, Pious, Blessed, Unconquered Augustus, *pontifex maximus*, Germanicus Maximus, holding the tribunician power, consul for the second time, proconsul." The next year he added the utterly conventional "father of the fatherland" (see, e.g., *HD019696*): one wonders whether it was clear what the referent for "fatherland" was.

The re-use of the altar from one reign to another, Roman to Gallic, reveals the exact reduplication of the opening formula; the continuation of the precise contemporary titulature of Roman social ranks (Genialis is *vir perfectissimus*, here translated as "distinguished"); the use of the language of Roman public law for Genialis' office (*agens v(ice) p(raesidis)*, "acting in the place of the governor"); and the continuation in Gaul of the office of consul and the use of consuls to name the year. The gratitude expressed in the dedication finds an echo in the summary offered by Eutropius:

> Then, with matters in a terrible state and the Roman empire nearly destroyed, Postumus, who had been born in Gaul in the humblest circumstances, assumed the purple and ruled for ten years, in such a way that he restored by his great virtue and moderation provinces that had been nearly consumed. (Eutropius, 9.9.1)

The language of restoration – we have seen that Decius was "restorer of rites" and Gallienus was "restorer of the Gauls," before he wasn't – is of course the language of Roman public praise for legitimate rulers. Its application to Postumus is striking.

Third, the essential Romanness of the so-called Gallic empire is visible despite its rapid co-optation of local elites into a surprisingly robust administrative apparatus. At the level of the soldiery, this is perhaps not surprising: a high percentage of legionaries now served in the area where they were recruited. The army that Postumus inherited will thus already have been composed predominantly of locals. But a very great number of the officials known from the reigns of Postumus and his successors appear on the basis of nomenclature to have had local roots. Unfortunately, we cannot say how many of these had begun their service under Gallienus. But the simple fact of the matter is that *de facto* autonomy from Rome did not spur the expression of any latent Gallic character or nationalist ambition in the forms of governmental power now visible to us.

Put in slightly different terms, there is no evidence that Postumus or any resident of his empire wished to overthrow Rome, or to be formally independent of Rome, or, for that matter, to fashion themselves by some means as somehow non-Roman.

Alas, Postumus was also a typical Roman emperor of the third century in that he suffered an attempted usurpation in 269, by one Laelianus, based at Moguntiacum. Postumus successfully put down the rebellion but then forbade his troops to plunder the city: outraged, they killed him.[24] The empire of Postumus had no better system to legitimate a new emperor than had Rome itself, and Postumus' immediate successor, Marius, was soon murdered and succeeded by Victorinus, who lasted perhaps two years. When Victorinus was slain, we are told by the *Historia Augusta* that his mother Victoria promoted the candidacy of one Tetricus, "a senator of the Roman people and governor of Gaul" (SHA *Tyr. Trig.* 24.1). The less colorful account of Eutropius makes Tetricus governor of Aquitania and describes him as acclaimed by the soldiery. Unsurprisingly, as the political situation in Gaul devolved toward burlesque, Tetricus "suffered many revolts by the soldiers" (Eutropius, 9.10.1).

The Roman empire of Gaul came to an end in 274, when the emperor Aurelian defeated Tetricus and reincorporated his territories into the whole.

Sapor and Rome

When we parted company with Sapor in the reign of Philip the Arab in 244, Philip had first struck a treaty with Sapor to preserve the army of Gordian III upon that emperor's death and later repudiated it (p. 116). We have also seen that Sapor boasted of his retaliation in his epigraphic autobiography:

> And (Philip) Caesar lied again and acted unjustly towards Armenia. We rose up against the nation of the Romans and annihilated a force of 60,000 Romans at Barbalissos. (*Res Gestae Divi Saporis* 9 [Greek text])

In point of fact, the battle in question occurred in 252, a half decade after Philip's action. But the intervening period seems to have done little to settle the east. Indeed, the military and political successes achieved by Sapor when he did return, and the upheaval he set in motion even when his actions fell short of success, suggest important failures on the part of Rome on at least two levels. First, the losses suffered by the army in the pointless expeditions of Severus Alexander and Gordian III were not restored, perhaps not at the level of manpower, certainly not in the skill and prestige of the command structure. The dynamic Julius Priscus may constitute an exception, but he was also part of the problem. Indeed, he brings us to the second level on which Rome failed in the east: the loss of prestige on

---

24. Eutropius, 9.9.1; Aurelius Victor, *Caes.* 33.8; Zosimus, 1.40.1.

the part of the army seems to have substantially undermined the willingness of locals to tolerate the exactions of Roman government, which were sharpened precisely by its failures. An account on this scale does not suffice even to enumerate the local insurrections and rebellions that littered the eastern Roman empire in this period. The revolt of Jotapianus was but one (p. 119); there were many more.

That said, the history of the east over the long term is largely shaped by Sapor's two great campaigns and the forms of local reaction that these provoked, in Emesa and above all in Palmyra, and it was Sapor's turning away from Rome that permitted the restoration and stabilization of Roman rule in the east.

The massive and stunningly successful campaign of Sapor in 252 is intimately associated in the historical tradition with the enigmatic figure of Mariades, a one-time member of the upper class of Antioch who is variously described as a traitor or usurper.[25] Mariades was certainly involved in some fashion in the sacking of Antioch, a staggering blow to the very heart of the empire. But he may have first provided inspiration for the single strategic move perhaps most responsible for Sapor's overall success: Sapor advanced his forces not, as was traditional before and after, west across the highlands of northern Mesopotamia, but up the Euphrates. (It was traditional for the Romans to invade by proceeding south, down the Euphrates: it was rather harder to move supplies for tens of thousands of men upstream.)

The details of Sapor's campaign upon reaching Roman territory are relatively unimportant: what is clear is that he found Roman troops massed in great number at Barbalissos and smashed them completely, after which he was able to divide his forces into two columns (and perhaps later divide them again) and move nearly at will through Roman territory. (Regarding the Roman troops that Sapor found assembled at Barbalissos: a gathering on such a scale can mean nothing other than preparations for a campaign, but nothing is known of any such.) To get some idea of the devastation wrought, one should read both Sapor's own account and the wrenching lamentation of an Antiochene source preserved in the thirteenth Sibylline Oracle. In the *Res Gestae Divi Saporis*, the passage continuing from the reference to Barbalissos above runs as follows:

---

25. Potter, *Prophecy*, 268–73 provides a summary and analysis of the accounts of the man and his actions; see also Dodgeon-Lieu 3.1.5.

(10) The province of Syria and the provinces and territories above it, all these we burned and laid waste and destroyed, and in that one campaign [we conquered] from the Roman state the [following] fortresses and cities:

(11) the city Anatha with its territory; Asporakan Birtha with its territory; the city Sura with its territory; the city Barbalissos with its territory; the city Hierapolis with its territory;

(12) the city Beroea with its territory; the city Chalcis with its territory; the city Apamea with its territory; the city Rephaneia with its territory; the city Zeugma with its territory; the city Ourima with its territory;

(13) the city Gindara with its territory; the city Larmenaz with its territory; the city Seleuceia with its territory; the city Antioch with its territory; the city Cyrrhus with its territory;

(14) another city Seleuceia with its territory; the city Alexandria with its territory; the city Nicopolis with its territory; the city Sinzara with its territory; the city Chamath with its territory;

(15) the city Aristeia with its territory; the city Dichor with its territory; the city Dolichê with its territory; the city Dura with its territory; the city Circesium with its territory; the city Germania with its territory;

(16) the city Batna with its territory; the city Chanar with its territory; and from Cappadocia, the city Satala with its territory; the city Doma with its territory;

(17) the city Artangilla with its territory; the city Suisa with its territory; the city Suda with its territory; the city Phreata with its territory. Altogether, 37 cities with their territories. (*Res Gestae Divi Saporis* 10–17 [Greek text])

To the reader in Naqsh-e Rustam, this must have seemed an awesome achievement. To the eastern Roman empire, it amounted to ruin. No source provides so immediate a sense of the material devastation as the anguished cry of the Sibylline Oracle, which lists many of the same cities as Sapor (the "fugitive from Rome" is Mariades):

Now for you, wretched Syria, I have lately been piteously lamenting; a blow will befall you from the arrow-shooting men, terrible, which you never thought would come to you. The fugitive from Rome will come, waving a great spear; crossing the Euphrates with many myriads, he will burn you, he will dispose all things evilly. Alas, Antioch, they will never call you a city when you have fallen under the spear in your folly; he will leave you entirely ruined and naked, houseless, uninhabited; anyone seeing you will suddenly break out weeping; and you will be a prize of war, Hierapolis, and you, Beroea; you will join with Chalcis mourning for your recently wounded children. Alas for as many as live by the steep peak of Casius and by Amanas, as many as the Lycus and Marsyas, as many as the silver-eddied Pyramus washes: they will leave ruin as far as the borders of Asia, stripping the cities, taking the statues of all and razing the temples down to the all-nourishing earth. (Thirteenth Sibylline Oracle, ll. 119–36; trans. David S. Potter)

What justification was there for Roman government, if it permitted such suffering? What alternative was there?

One notable omission among the cities listed by Sapor is Emesa. If Sapor did not encounter significant resistance moving within Roman territory, he certainly encountered trouble leaving Roman territory (and would again). A priest of Elagabal of the royal house of Emesa, one Uranius Antoninus – named in other sources Sampsigeramus, and still elsewhere described as calling upon Kronos – appears to have led a purely local militia in resisting Sapor, and in consequence Emesa was spared devastation.[26] For the next year and a half Uranius Antoninus acted the very Roman potentate: he employed the flamboyantly Roman name Lucius Julius Aurelius Sulpicius Uranius Severus Antoninus, and he minted coins at Antioch in a Roman denomination, with Latin legends and a very Roman portrait, with the god Elagabal on the reverse. There is no evidence that he had any ambition other than defense of his city and region and regional honor for what he did, and apparently the only symbolic and discursive apparatus through which such claims could be negotiated across cultures were purely Roman ones. Given the date at which his coinage ceases, it seems that with the news of Valerian's imminent arrival, Uranius retreated to his former station. Nothing else is known of him.

As we have seen, Aurelius Victor reported that the army gathered in the west under Valerian in 253 – with which he defeated Aemilian – had been assembled in preparation "for the imminent war" (p. 159). It is likely that he refers to an eastern campaign planned by Gallus in retaliation for Sapor's attack in 252/3. (Indeed, it may be that the force assembled at Barbalissos whose destruction Sabor at *Res Gestae Divi Saporis* 9 [p. 117] had also been mustered for this campaign.) Gallus' death and the subsequent upheaval caused a delay of some years before Roman strength in the area was fully renewed. Fortunately for them, so far as we can tell, Sapor paid only

---

26. The available sources are translated in Dodgeon-Lieu 3.2.2–3. For the coinage see *RIC* Uranius Antoninus.

intermittent attention to his western border between 253 and 257. What is clear is that Valerian wished to concentrate his forces in Syria for a counter-attack, and that he was continually distracted by the Gothic sea-raids on the coast of Asia, including a massive but undated raid that inflicted significant damage on Nicomedia (Zosimus, 1.35.1). We are told by the only significant literary source for this attack, Zosimus, that a unit of Valerian's army was infected by the plague when he led it against the Goths and that this diminished his effectiveness in the confrontation with Sapor (Zosimus, 1.36.1). Zosimus connects the story with Valerian's final expedition in 260, but Valerian had also declared a "Victoria Parthica" in 257 – the event is known only from his titulature and coinage. Whatever happened, the strategic outcomes were rarely good: Dura fell under Sasanian control in 257 and Nisibis in 259. The Gothic raid could therefore have taken place in 256 or 259. The confusion in the historical record is a direct result of the material catastrophe befalling the east throughout these years.

The situation was a powder keg, waiting to go off. Valerian ignited it and took himself with it, and very nearly the whole eastern empire. The denouement may be simply told. In late spring 260, Valerian marched east with an enormous army. After apparently devastating defeats at Carrhae and Edessa, Valerian and his entire officer corps were taken prisoner and his army surrendered. The captives were taken to Persia and used as slaves in building projects.[27] The western accounts have the merit of giving some scope to the horror the event provoked, but unsurprisingly they seem to have had little precise or accurate knowledge of it (Dodgeon-Lieu 3.3.1). We rely once again upon Sapor:

> (18) In the third contest, when we marched upon Carrhae and Edessa and laid siege to Carrhae and Edessa, Valerian Caesar came against us. (19) And there was with him from the province of Germany; the province of Raetia; the province of Noricum; the province of Dacia; the province of Pannonia; the province of Moesia;

---

27. Though we might wish to know the fate of Valerian himself, accurate information on this score is stunningly unavailable. The source of Victor, Eutropius and the *Historia Augusta* recorded only that Valerian grew old in Persia (Eutropius, 9.7; SHA *Valeriani Duo* 4.2). According to the historian al-Tabari (839–923), as though in prequel to *The Bridge over the River Kwai*, Valerian was commanded by Sapor to use his troops to build the dam of Sostar (Dodgeon-Lieu, Appendix 1, p. 283). Christian sources in late antiquity, angry at the Valerianic persecution, fantasized about the tortures Valerian might have undergone: see, e.g., Lactantius, *De mortibus persecutorum* 5.2–6.

the province of Amastria [correction: Istria]; the province of Hispania; the province of <Lusi>tan<ia?>; (20) the province of Thrace; the province of Bithynia; the province of Asia; the province of Campania [correction: Pamphylia]; the province of Syria [correction: Isauria]; the province of Lycaonia; the province of Galatia; the province of Lycia; the province of Cilicia; the province of Cappadocia; the province of Phrygia; the province of Syria; (21) the province of Phoenice; the province of Iudaea; the province of Arabia; the province of Mauretania; the province of Germany; the province of Lydia; the province of Asia; and the province of Mesopotamia a force of 70,000.

(22) And on the other side of Carrhae and Edessa with Valerian Caesar there was for us a great battle and we defeated Valerian Caesar with our own hands and the others – the praetorian prefect and the senators and the officers, whoever was commanding in that army, all those we seized in our hands and led them to Persia. (23) And the province of Syria and the province of Cilicia and the province of Cappadocia we burned with fire and laid waste and destroyed and conquered.

[Another list of individual cities and territories follows.]

(30) And men from the Roman empire, from among the non-Aryans, we led in captivity; and in our empire, the empire of the Aryans, in Persia and in Parthia and in Assyria and in the other lands and provinces – wherever there are foundations of ourselves and our fathers and our grandfathers and our ancestors – there we settled them. (31) And we sought many other lands and fashioned a great name and performed many acts of courage that we did not inscribe here, beside these [that are inscribed here]. Because of this we ordered this to be inscribed, so that whoever is after us will know our name and courage and this our rule. (*Res Gestae Divi Saporis* 18–23, 30–1 [Greek text])

Sapor also celebrated his capture of Valerian in relief. In a remarkable image from Naqsh-e Rustam, Sapor is depicted on horseback, and so in a position of power and command, facing two Roman emperors: Philip the Arab kneels in submission, while Valerian stands captive, his hands bound (Figure 14). In this single image, the temporal and contextual distance between two events is collapsed to present a single, coherent image of continuing Persian dominance over Rome.

It would be almost impossible to overstate the damage this event worked on Roman prestige in the east, weakened though it already

Figure 14 Relief (6) from Naqsh-e Rustam: Philip the Arab kneels in submission to Sapor, while Valerian stands captive behind, his hands bound (Photograph: Matthew Canepa, reproduced with permission)

was. As defective as the evidence is, it nonetheless seems possible to connect an enormous range of insurrections and upheavals to the arrival of the news, including the revolts of Regalianus and Ingenuus in the Danubian provinces, that of Postumus in Gaul and, more distantly, that of Lucius Mussius Aemilianus, the prefect of Egypt.[28] Ingemar König has also suggested that the election of a new bishop of Rome on July 22 was connected with the arrival of the news: the position had been vacant since the execution of Xystus on August 6, 258, no doubt because no one wanted to make himself so prominent while the Valerianic edict on sacrifice remained in effect.[29] Some of these individuals were no doubt ambitious on their own behalf. Some worked at least for a time to stabilize the regions in which they found themselves. Few struck out against Gallienus, though in time he moved against many of them. Once again one might say that, in

28. Connected to this number are a number of dimly known individuals who seem to have caused further disturbances along the Danube, in Macedonia and in Achaia, as it seems in the aftermath of the defeat of Ingenuus and Regalianus. In the same way, it may be that Mussius Aemilianus did not act until after Macrianus and Quietus had been killed.
29. König, *Die gallischen Usurpatoren*, 27–31.

a moment of desperate need, the political structure of the empire had no means within itself to resolve a crisis of legitimacy.

And yet, it could have gone far worse. The empire of the east was in fact saved. In the short term, this was due to the perseverance and skill of two Roman officials, working loosely together with a local dynast, Odaenathus, lord of Palmyra. In the long run, it was the genius and skill of Odaenathus that sustained the east until such a time as Rome was ready violently to reclaim it.

The situation in 260 was salvaged by Fulvius Macrianus, a financial official in charge of supplies for Valerian's Persian expedition, and one Ballista, a naval officer, whose name is transmitted in some texts as Callistus (and in fact, the evidence does not permit us to say with certainty which form is correct[30]). They appear in the first instance to have worked separately to harass Sapor's columns as the summer progressed. In particular, disasters inflicted on Sapor by Ballista at Sebaste and Corycus (including, if the source of George Syncellus and Zonaras is to be believed, the seizure of his harem[31]) caused Sapor to turn for home, at which point, perhaps in the vicinity of Edessa, he was attacked and successfully thrashed by Odaenathus of Palmyra.

At some point toward the end of summer 260, Macrianus and Ballista conferred and revolted: Macrianus elevated his two sons, Macrianus and Quietus, as co-rulers (we are told he opted not to elevate himself, being lame).[32] In the summer of 261, Macrianus and the elder son set out for the west, leaving Quietus behind with Ballista. The Macriani were defeated by Aureolus in Thrace. We are told by Zonaras that Gallienus then made an overture to Odaenathus: he should deal with Quietus and Ballista, and he might then govern the east on Gallienus' behalf, as *corrector totius orientis*, nominally more or less the position that Julius Priscus had held on behalf of his brother, Philip the Arab. Odaenathus accepted; Quietus and Ballista were apparently slain at Emesa; and the eastern Roman empire passed under Odaenathus' overall guidance for the next six years.

The situation in the east thus came to bear a strong structural resemblance to that in the far west: a regional military crisis had

30. On the name see Potter, *Prophecy*, 344–5.
31. George Syncellus p. 466, ll. 15–23 Mosshammer; Zonaras, 12.23; both passages may be found in Dodgeon-Lieu 3.3.5.
32. They are named as joint Augusti on a papyrus from Oxyrhynchus by September 17, 260 (*POxy.* 3476).

exposed the weakness of the central state; military forces with local attachments acted more or less autonomously to deal with the foreign foe; a government by a local elite emerged. In the west, as we have seen, Postumus ruled in form as a Roman emperor over a purely transalpine empire, without formal relation to the government of Gallienus: the institutions of the two empires possessed parallel, non-overlapping structures, and the lack of mutual recognition in their systems of authority could only be resolved by elimination in war or self-abrogation of one or the other party. In the east, by contrast, Gallienus offered Odaenathus *de facto* rulership over "the entire east" (whatever that meant geographically: certainly Egypt was excluded), by accepting which Odaenathus recognized Gallienus as his nominal overlord and the source of his authority outside Palmyra itself.

This last point bears some clarification. Palmyra was a great and rich city, with a remarkably cosmopolitan culture. Its epigraphy attests the local use of many languages. But its political culture remained linguistically Palmyrene, and many of its political forms were thus distinctly Semitic. This was so despite Odaenathus' own long experience at the (elevated) margins of Roman power: for example, he had evidently received senatorial rank and consular honors already in the 250s, perhaps in reward for some action performed during Sapor's invasion of 252/3.[33] In consequence of his agreement with Gallienus, Odaenathus (and his heirs) had consistently to live a Roman existence – and in that world Odaenathus and his heirs exhibited a bravura virtuosity with the languages of Roman power. In practice, their engagement in this world did not occlude or efface their simultaneous use of a distinctly Palmyrene idiom as well. Hence, each also used the traditional eastern title "King of Kings," predominantly in Palmyrene, but it is attributed too at least once to Odaenathus in Greek.[34]

The traditional nature of Odaenathus' Roman title notwithstanding, the exact nature and extent of the authority he exercised are not clear. So far as one can tell, for example, he respected Gallienus' authority to make appointments. But his control over the military affairs of the east seems to have been nearly absolute, and whatever

---

33. *CISem.* II 3945 = Potter, *Prophecy*, 388–9, transcribing and translating the Greek and Palmyrene texts = Dodgeon-Lieu 4.2.3.
34. This last text is a dedication by the Palmyrene officer and Roman citizen Julius Aurelius Septimius Vorodes: *IGRom.* III 1032 = Potter, *Prophecy*, 385 (without translation) = Dodgeon-Lieu 4.3.4.

his actions in that domain, his relationship with Gallienus apparently remained secure. So, for example, Odaenathus undertook two expeditions against Sapor under his own command, in 262 and 265/6, during the second of which he recovered the former province of Mesopotamia and sacked Ctesiphon.[35] But he also came to the aid of Asia Minor in 267 when it suffered another Gothic raid. Alas, he was murdered in that very year, quite possibly during that expedition.[36] "Some god, I suppose, was angry with the Republic, and would not allow Odaenathus to live with Valerian dead" (SHA *Tyr. Trig.* 15.6).

It was only with the death of Odaenathus that his remarkable, and remarkably elastic, position in relation to the person and station of Gallienus as emperor of Rome had to be clarified and its exceptional nature resolved. For the family of Odaenathus saw themselves as hereditary rulers of a great city, then flourishing more fully than it ever had before. From the perspective of the metropole, on the other hand, Odaenathus was formally no more than an appointed official, exercising power at the pleasure of the emperor. The looming conflict between these perspectives was postponed, however, by the death of Gallienus the very next year. To the final years of Gallienus, and the situation he bequeathed to his successors, we now turn. We will return to Palmyra and the east in 272, when the emperor Aurelian captured the city and its queen.

The death of Gallienus (261–8)

After the death of Macrianus and his sons in fall 261, then, Gallienus found himself in a remarkably (in?)secure situation. In a period of perhaps eighteen months, he had lost direct rule over a dozen and a half provinces containing many millions of people, with a corresponding loss in tax revenue; and the *de facto* defection of numerous legions made a mockery of his status as commander of the army – the essence, one might say, of his position (*Imperator* did, after all, mean "Commander"). It is astonishing that he was not immediately assassinated. That he was not is due in large measure to the loyalty of Aureolus, and no doubt in some measure also to a combination

---

35. Zosimus, 1.39.2; Eutropius, 9.10; SHA *Duo Gallieni* 10.
36. I discount Zosimus' claim that he was killed at Emesa. Among other things, Odaenathus' death in Asia (as related by George Syncellus) is the easiest way to explain the fact – if such it be – that the Gothic invaders were allowed to depart with their booty.

of astonishment in the population at large that the edifice had not collapsed and a widespread inability to imagine a world ordered on other terms.

Gallienus himself appears to have decided that his own survival required not the immediate recovery of greater Rome but the consolidation of the world as he now found it. He was the luckiest of the three regional dynasts in at least one respect: he controlled the wealthy and productive provinces of North Africa, including Egypt. These not only generated enormous revenues and grain, but by virtue of their (relative and absolute) lack of military disturbance, their economies continued to churn along. The major source of social upheaval in those areas – at least, of such social upheaval as can now be easily detected – was still the edict on sacrifice propagated by Valerian and Gallienus in 257, and it was now rescinded (Eusebius, *Hist. eccl.* 7.13, describing Gallienus' action as following immediately upon his father's capture).[37]

Within the truncated empire he now ruled, Gallienus did of course have to deal with further attacks by Goths across the Danubian and Black Sea frontiers: incursions are attested in 262, 266 and 267/8, the last the most serious. In that year, invaders by land besieged Philippopolis in Thrace and raiders by sea caused devastation throughout peninsular Greece, including major damage to Athens, Corinth and Sparta. The reaction of Athens, which included the hasty conscription of a local militia, received a dramatic rehearsal in the history of Dexippus: the city itself was seized, and Dexippus gathered 2,000 men to organize the harassment of the "Skythians" from woods and positions of hiding and strength.[38]

Gallienus appears in these years to have acted as a Roman emperor might in less tumultuous times: he traveled to Athens in 264 to be initiated into the Eleusinian mysteries, and he may have served as honorary archon of the city while there. He was perceived by some, no doubt accurately, as a sympathetic patron of the arts: it was

---

37. It is important to observe that the cancellation of the edict ended the conflict of Christians with the state. The enormously bitter conflict within the Christian community over the status of those who had complied with the edict would, however, continue.

38. Dexippus' account: *FGrH* 100 F 28. The career of Dexippus serves as an aperçu into cultural and intellectual life in third-century Athens, and the nature of Greek resistance to the Goths, in a classic article by Fergus Millar, "P. Herennius Dexippus: The Greek world and the third-century invasions," *JRS* 59 (1969), 12–29 = Millar, *Rome, the Greek World, and the East*, vol. 2: *Government, Society, and Culture in the Roman Empire*, eds Hannah M. Cotton and Guy M. Rogers (Chapel Hill: University of North Carolina Press, 2003), 265–97.

imagined by the philosopher Plotinus and his circle that Gallienus might sponsor the building of a new city in which a genuinely philosophic form of governance would obtain (Porphyry, *Life of Plotinus* 12).

But by the traditionally minded historians of subsequent generations, these years are uniformly described as ones of incomprehensible and criminal sloth. No doubt a nagging problem was the unspeakable sense of embarrassment and weakness caused by the fragmentation of the state and the emperor's evident willingness to tolerate it. Gallienus did finally attack Postumus, ineffectually, in 265, and it may be that the campaign was intended not so much to succeed as to silence criticism.[39] In 267 Aureolus revolted, perhaps disgusted by Gallienus' complacency, but like many emperors, Gallienus could be stirred to action by a domestic revolt if by nothing else. At some point during the revolt, Aureolus recognized Postumus as the legitimate emperor of Rome, no doubt hoping to entice him across the Alps. The appeal did not succeed. Aureolus was defeated in battle and besieged in Milan.

As it happened, Aureolus was not alone in his disaffection. Over the next few months a more comprehensive plot was formed among the military elite – an elite now composed heavily of soldiers recruited from the Danubian provinces (see also p. 150). Illyrians might well have come to dominate the upper echelons of the army in any event, but their success in this period was overdetermined by the total disconnect in these years between the military elites of the Gallic and Gallienic empires, and the functional disconnect between Rome and the east. Their background may be important in another respect, too: it may well be that Gallienus' willingness to abandon the campaign against the Goths in order to confront Aureolus particularly angered the officers of Danubian background. The plot of 268 was successful: as Gallienus continued the siege of Milan, he was enticed from his tent by a false announcement that Aureolus was approaching and killed; his brother Valerian was killed then or soon thereafter (SHA *Duo Gallieni* 14; Eutropius, 9.11.1).

Normally, of course, the assassination of an emperor was treated as a crime, even by his successor: what emperor wishes it known that killing an emperor is occasionally permissible? In the case of

39. It is reported that Gallienus won a major battle and besieged Postumus in an unnamed city, but withdrew when he personally suffered a wound. This is just the sort of focalization on the figure of the ruler that makes much of ancient historical narrative deeply suspicious and, frankly, somewhat unpalatable to a modern historical sensibility.

Gallienus, suggests Aurelius Victor, the anonymity of his assassin was due to just this logic, operating in a sort of inversion: "His death went unpunished, perhaps because of some inability to identity the author of the deed – or because it had occurred to the public good" (Aurelius Victor, 9.33.16–22 at 22). According to the *Historia Augusta*, the first act of the conspirators was a verdict on the past: Gallienus was named a *tyrannus*; the last fourteen years, a mistake.[40]

40. SHA *Duo Gallieni* 15.2.

CHAPTER 8

Government and governmentality

The discussion in Chapter 4 of the grant of universal citizenship, and that in Chapter 6 of the edicts on sacrifice, raised important questions regarding the efficiency and reach of government in the Roman empire. It is the ambition of this chapter to discuss the various means by which the power of the central government was made immanent in daily life. Again, the picture provided is not intended to be comprehensive – there is not scope to discuss all aspects of ancient government, nor is there justification in a volume within a series to discuss any one aspect in its chronological totality. I focus instead on aspects and institutions that exhibit significant change across the third century, whether that change is at some level endogenous to the institution and continuous with earlier trends (as, for example, in the spread of imperial properties and corresponding growth in the administrative reach of the imperial household) or more directly spurred by developments in the political sphere in the third century itself (as might be claimed, to a point, regarding the consequences of the Antonine Constitution).

I shall argue obliquely in this chapter, and more directly in the Conclusion, that the ongoing work of the central state exercised a determinate role in the empire's survival of the third-century crisis. This was so in part because it enabled populations to draw a conceptual distinction between the operation of the depersonalized institutions of the state and the person of the emperor. It further contributed insofar as it shaped expectations about the nature of government writ large. In consequence, regardless of the ultimate ambitions of their rulers, the splinter states in Gaul and Palmyra presented themselves nearly wholly within the paradigm provided by Rome: this enabled them to fill the vacuum created by the withdrawal of Roman power (a withdrawal that they promoted, of course), but it also naturalized the transition back to Roman control in the reign of Aurelian.

When I speak of "the ongoing work of government," I refer to two broad types of activity. The first consists in the functioning of depersonalized institutions: the census, birth and death registrations, courts of law, tax collection, policing and so forth. I describe these as "depersonalized" because they were expected to operate in the same way regardless of the idiosyncratic qualities and capacities of the individuals who staffed them. (We can acquire some sense of these expectations from petitions in which individuals urge one official to compel another to act in accordance with his job description, to use modern terminology: "for it is proper to him to do x" would be an ancient equivalent.[1]) The frustration of this expectation is a common theme in surviving documents from the third century: we will turn to this problem by and by. The second type of activity includes the construction and maintenance of the material forms – specific building types, monumentalized urban cores, roads – wherein those institutions operated and which in their totality rendered Roman power manifest in provincial landscapes.

The full scope of activity embraced by these two categories might usefully be described as the infrastructural elaboration of the Roman state – the means, in personnel, functions and *matériel*, whereby the state penetrated and governed its territory. To speak thus is to invoke a particular form of historical sociology, which might help one to understand aspects of imperial history in themselves (such as the contribution made by institutions to the survival of the central state in our period), and also aid in capturing with appropriate analytic precision points of historical difference between ancient states.[2]

The second term in the title of this chapter, governmentality, refers to a concept developed within a different branch of modern social theory. Within this tradition, associated above all with Michel Foucault, the operation of government is assessed with regard to its power to condition the self-understanding and self-fashioning of persons, in themselves and in their social and economic relations. Foucault introduced the term to isolate and describe a development in relations between state and society in the early modern period. In his view, it was in this period that the state developed a set of practices and likewise a set of conceptual tools that rendered it possible to conceive of government as concerned not with cities or

1. See, e.g., *P.Abinnaeus* 51 l. 17.
2. For an important early statement in this vein of scholarship see Michael Mann, "The autonomous power of the state: Its origins, mechanisms, and results," in John A. Hall, ed., *States in History* (Oxford: Blackwell, 1986), 109–36.

communities, say, but with individuals. Crucially, he argued that conceptions of personhood and practices of self-fashioning in society at large developed in ways homologous with, and responsive to, these new ways of knowing: people began to understand themselves according to the same analytic indices employed by the state in knowing them, as having one or another ethnicity or specific bio-metrics or a particular economic output or what have you.

Foucault himself understood these developments in knowledge systems and conceptions of the self as innovations of the early modern period. In his view, they were dependent upon particular developments in what we might call statistics and the social sciences, and also in the technologies of knowledge and memory production. To put the matter bluntly, a modern state can list its people and (some of) their attributes on the basis of information recorded on state-issued identification cards, even as each person knows herself or himself as such. A polity in which those mutual relations of state to person and person to state are not so fixed, captured and knowable is a very different place. My own use of this conceptual apparatus in the study of a pre-modern society is thus in tension with an important postulate of the theory itself. In so writing, I therefore contest a central empirical claim advanced in the theory's first articulation. Though I acknowledge that fact here, this is not the place to consider the normative implications of such a contestation.

Citizenship, census and social differentiation

As we have seen, the central government is likely to have delegated the actual enforcement of the edicts on sacrifice to local officials. (The power to exact significant punishment, by contrast, was reserved to agents of Rome.) Regardless, the ability of any institu-tion, whether metropolitan or local, to know the population rested in this period on the census. The functioning of the census is not so well attested in the third century as it is earlier, but its basic operation required heads of households to present themselves to supervising magistrates and supply information about themselves, the members of their household, and the habitable and arable property under their possession.[3] As regards the last category,

---

3. That said, the jurist Paul, who served as praetorian prefect under Severus Alexander and so knew intimately all the workings of civilian government, wrote, like Ulpian, a work on the census comprising at least two books. The single extant fragment derives

namely land, we can get a sense of the level of detail required by Roman authorities from an extract of Ulpian's work on the census, written in all likelihood under Caracalla:

> It is provided in the schedule for the census that land should be recorded in the census in this way: the name of the property to which it belongs, and in what civic community and in what district it belongs, its nearest two neighbors; the extent of the land on the property under cultivation over the last ten years, measured in *jugera* (a Roman measure, approximately $^3/_5$ acre); how many vines in its vineyards; how many *jugera* of olives under cultivation and how many trees; how many *jugera* of pasture have been mowed [to produce hay] over the last ten years; how many *jugera* of pastureland there seems to be; likewise, how much of forest. (Ulpian, *De censibus* bk. 3 fr. 22 Lenel = *Dig. 50.15.4.pr.*)

We can likewise glimpse something of the impression made by the central government's administrative apparatus, as well as its appetite for inventory, from the massive use made of the Lucan census in Christian literature for dating the birth of Christ (Luke 2:1). (It was not simply dating that was at issue: in bringing Mary and Joseph to the city where they held *domicilium*, or residence, Rome was held to have played a providential role in the fulfillment of prophecy.) A similar impression is conveyed also by an anecdote of the late fourth century preserved in the Babylonian Talmud:

> The sages said in the name of Rav: If all the seas were ink, all reeds were pens, all skies parchment, and all men scribes, they would be unable to set down the full scope of the Roman government's concerns. And the proof? The verse, said R. Mesharsheya, "Like the heaven for height, and the earth for depth, so is the heart of kings unfathomable" (Prov. 25:3). (Babylonian Talmud Shabbat 11a, excerpted in Sefer Ha-Aggadah 5.93)

The rationality and punctiliousness of Roman government penetrated the consciousness of the sages at a kindred level to that at

---

from book 2, and it preserves a catalog of communities, broken down province by province, that possessed the status of an Italian city (Paul, *De censibus* bk. 2 frag. 42 Lenel = *Dig.* 50.15.8). The fragment is likewise remarkable for recollecting the historical moment when any given community achieved that status. In any event, it surely attests the ongoing relevance of communal status to the work of government. See also *P. Teb.* II 285, a rescript of Gordian III on the registration of births, testifying to an ongoing practice. The extant text was copied several decades later: hence someone thought it useful to retain it.

which it functioned in the commentary tradition on the Gospel of Luke. By the time of the conversation recorded in the Talmud, the actions of Roman government had become so naturalized, the sages' identification with its processes and aims so complete, that reflecting on them caused the rabbis to think of their own scriptures. For the contextual power of the verse quoted by Rabbi Mesharsheya will have depended in part on his and his interlocutors' assenting to the verse that precedes it: "It is the glory of God to conceal the rationale for things, and the glory of kings to honor the things themselves." The associative network behind the conversation of the sages thus sets Jewish God and Roman emperor, world empire and world-embracing knowledge, in mutual relation. In making of the Roman emperor a Solomonic king, the rabbis constructed themselves as Roman subjects.

The Roman census was not narrowly a mechanism for gathering data, nor was it a purely financial instrument. (No census is.) It also served to record rank, and in so doing it defined people's juridical status not simply in relation to the state, along some absolute scale, but also in relation to each other. This was already true in Rome early in the classical period, when the term *census* could be used to refer to a person's legal rank and also to her or his wealth – two of the social aspects of personhood assessed in the procedure and recorded in its results (*OLD* s.v. *census* 2, 3c). A modern might be tempted to describe such usages as metonymic, were it not for the fact that evaluation was an intrinsic and essential component of the Roman census.

Where the third century and in particular provincial life were concerned, across the third century but commencing already in the second, new forms of social differentiation were coming into being in Roman society and, importantly, were confirmed and codified at law. Two very general forms might be distinguished. The first consisted in the elaboration of systems of rank within the governing class, the conjoined equestrian and senatorial classes. What emerges, commencing a decade or so before the period treated by this volume, is a system of titles based lexically on adjectives (usually superlatives): a given individual might be designated *vir egregius* or *vir perfectissimus*, "outstanding man" or "most perfect man," to select but two examples. These naturally affected a tiny number of people, and though they served to distinguish such individuals from the mass of the population, their true function was nothing other than the creation of a unitary governing class. This is not to say that distinctions between equestrian and senatorial rank ceased to have any importance, but the career paths of the upper classes within imperial government, and the system of government at large, had long demanded rationalization, and the titles gave social expression to such logic as was already latent and also shaped its further development.[4]

It might be useful to consider for a moment the pressures that impelled this change, in the service of better understanding of it in its own right and by way of clarifying the second major form of social differentiation that emerged in this period. All societies exhibit forms of social dissonance, meaning a lack of harmony or homology among the varied systems of rank, status and esteem in operation at any given time. The salience and meaning of particular forms of dissonance change across time as the systems of rank and status themselves adapt and evolve. The early Principate famously exacerbated underlying trends in this area as low-ranking members of the imperial household, particularly freedmen, gained enormous social power by virtue of their proximity to the emperor and their control over access to his person. A wide variety of other such loci for dissonance might be mentioned.

Again, early in the Principate emperors had exploited the discrepant social prestige of equestrians and senators by employing or patronizing the former in ways that undermined the latter or, at least, excluded the latter from power. The restriction that only equestrians might govern Egypt is only the most notorious case; a more subtle one would be the encouragement provided by Augustus to equestrian authors to take up forms of intellectual activity previously restricted (so far as we can tell) to senators.[5] Up to a point, such problems had been resolved through the assigning of important tasks within the imperial household to equestrians, on the one hand, and the public display of imperial esteem for the senate at

4. The most obvious future developments were, unsurprisingly, the decline in prestige of some titles (*perfectissimus* is a case in point) and the inflation and invention of others, so that officials described as *perfectissimus* in one century become *clarissimus* ("most illustrious," a title denoting senatorial rank) in the next.
5. On status dissonance generally see Peter Garnsey and Richard Saller, *The Roman Empire: Economy, Society, Culture* (Berkeley: University of California Press, 1987), 118–23. On Augustan patronage of equestrian literary production see Andrew Wallace-Hadrill, "*Mutatio morum*: The idea of a cultural revolution," in T. N. Habinek and A. Schiesaro, eds, *The Roman Cultural Revolution* (Cambridge: Cambridge University Press, 1997), 3–22.

large, on the other.[6] Over the long term, we should also not neglect
the essential role played in their resolution by demography: the
failure of the Roman elite *stricto sensu* to replace itself, coupled with
the influx of first Italian and later provincial aristocracies into the
imperial governing class, destabilized some conventions and expectations even as it contributed to and consolidated others.[7]

That said, equestrians could not linger as second-class citizens for
long, for three reasons above all. First, the technical terms used
to describe ranks within the professional equestrian class, such as
achieved something like stable form in the reign of Commodus,
referred to their salaries – a *ducenarius* received a salary of 200,000
sesterces, and so forth. Their logic was far too nakedly economic to
sustain a system of social prestige. Second, the increasing size of the
equestrian bureaucracy – a function very largely of the enormous
expansion in the emperor's property holdings – brought equestrian
officials into direct and public converse with senators in provincial
landscapes. This produced an ever increasing number of occasions
for status dissonance, when equestrian officials by virtue of representing the emperor, or merely through control of financial affairs,
might well cause a loss of face to a higher-status individual.
This form of status dissonance impeded the proper functioning
of normative social distinctions, of course, but possibly also that of
government. The third and final reason is this: the ultimate barrier
between senators and equestrians – that senators might become
emperors but equestrians could not even be imagined as such – had
now collapsed. This last change postdates the emergence of the new
titulature, but it should be taken as symptomatic of the same broad
currents of change that necessitated the formal expression of this
emergent social reality.

The second form of social differentiation that emerges in the high
empire affected a vastly greater range of the population and had real

6. On the equestrian career in the early and high Principate readers in English might
begin with Fergus Millar, "The equestrian career under the empire," *JRS* 53 (1963), 194–
200 = Millar, *Rome, the Greek World and the East*, vol. 2: *Government, Society, and
Culture in the Roman Empire*, eds Hannah M. Cotton and Guy M. Rogers (Chapel Hill:
University of North Carolina Press, 2003), 151–9. On the place of the Senate in the
second century see pp. 8–9.
7. An historical phenomenon given classic expression in Keith Hopkins, "Elite mobility
in the Roman empire," *Past & Present* 32 (1965), 12–26; cf. Hopkins, *Death and
Renewal* (Cambridge: Cambridge University Press, 1983). The replacement of a more
narrowly Roman aristocracy by an Italian one, and the creation under the Principate of
an imperial governing class, was of course a major theme of the work of Ronald Syme.

importance for social life in the third century. It might be described in one or the other of two ways, by reference to the terms used in normative texts of the period or by reference to the most important consequences that followed upon the emergence of the distinction. Simply put, a distinction emerges at law between "more humble" and "more honorable" people: the more humble were exposed to a range of violent punishments and to distinctive forms of public humiliation that the "more honorable" were spared. The terminology used to describe the ranks is deliberately vague; the binarism commonly used in modern scholarship, *humiliores::honestiores*, "more humble::more honorable," achieves stable form only toward the end of the third century. The imprecision of the language must have been intended to deliver discretion into the hands of local authorities. For example, the jurist Julius Paulus (Paul), who served as legal advisor to prefects and emperors for nearly thirty years from Septimius Severus to Severus Alexander, cited on punishments a number of earlier imperial rescripts, including one by Antoninus Pius:

> In the case of free offenders, you will have them beaten with clubs and relegate them for three years, or if they are *sordidiores*, persons of lower status [literally, "more filthy"], condemn them to public works for the same period. Slaves you will flog with the lash and condemn to the mines.

From these Paul abstracted the following principle: "Generally in such cases as in others, careful assessment is to be made in light of the status of the offender and the gravity of the offense."[8]

Three related aspects of the emergence of this system deserve our attention. First and most importantly, there can be no doubt that the distinction emerged contrapuntally with the gradual evacuation of meaning from the distinction between citizen and alien. That distinction had already faded through attentuation, by virtue of grants of the franchise, well before it was erased by Caracalla. For example, citizens had once been exempt from flogging, an exemption endorsed in a law passed by the emperor Augustus himself and repeated by Ulpian in the reign of Caracalla – though Ulpian himself is concerned most directly with the liability of a magistrate for prosecution if the beating or execution of a citizen on his orders prevented that

8. Paul, *Ad edictum* bk. 54 fr. 678 Lenel = *Dig.* 47.9.4.1 (trans. J. A. C. Thomas), the crucial phrase being *ex personarum condicione et rerum qualitate*. The passage concerns looting, whether of burnt buildings or shipwrecks.

citizen from exercising his right of appeal.[9] Lower-class citizens were explicitly rendered susceptible to beating with rods in a constitution of Septimius Severus and Caracalla from 198, and their ruling was echoed by jurists later in the period.[10] For example, the jurist Callistratus, writing under Severus and Caracalla, observed: "It is not customary that all are beaten with rods, but only those who are free and of more slender means (*tenuiores homines*); more honorable persons are not subject to the rods, a rule expressly laid out in imperial rescripts."[11]

Roman citizens were likewise once exempt from torture, but increasing classes of lower-status individuals were made liable to torture as the third century progressed. For example, the jurist Arcadius Charisius urged toward the close of the third century that the testimony of "a gladiator or similar person" should not be trusted without torture.[12] The ultimate breakdown of the system might be said to be that moment when the question arises, "How should slaves be punished?" and the answer takes the form: "They should be punished following the example of more humble persons." Just this act of assimilation – postulating the free poor as paradigmatic of the lowest of the low, to whom is assimilated the condition of the slave – was performed by the jurist Aemilius Macer, who wrote his book *On criminal proceedings* under Alexander Severus.[13]

The second aspect of this developing system of social and legal differentiation that deserves our attention concerns the linguistic form taken by the distinction. It is almost always expressed in relational terms, for example, by employing comparative adjectives such as *humiliores*, *tenuiores* and *sordidiores*. The purpose of the system in effecting social differentiation could not be made more clear. The utility of penal law in shoring up structures of social prestige is perhaps most clearly affirmed by the indignation aroused, and harsh penalties levied, when a person of lower status committed

---

9. Ulpian, *De officio proconsulis* fr. 2202 Lenel = *Dig.* 48.6.7.
10. *Cod. Iust.* 2.12.5. Like many laws on punishments, the actual text of *Cod. Iust.* 2.12.5 is concerned to specify an exemption, in this case that individuals of the curial class are not susceptible to beating with rods. Those below that class may therefore be so beaten.
11. Callistratus, *De cognitionibus* bk. 6 fr. 45 Lenel = *Dig.* 48.19.28.2; see also *Dig.* 48.19.28.5, where Callistratus again allows himself to speak *generaliter*, to speak in general terms, by abstracting a principle from "imperial constitutions."
12. Arcadius Charisius, *De testibus* liber singularis fr. 4 Lenel = *Dig.* 22.5.21.2.
13. Aemilius Macer, *De publicis iudiciis* bk. 2 fr. 39 Lenel = *Dig.* 48.19.10.*pr.*: *In servorum persona ita observatur, ut exemplo humiliorum puniantur.*

a crime of social injury against a person of more elevated rank. As Ulpian saw it, "because of their ignominy and poverty," such persons had no fear of the standard punishments for insult and so had to be dealt with severely.[14]

The final aspect of this system deserving our attention here is as follows. These classifications applied to persons and certain protections followed upon them, but the protections did not adhere to the person as a modern legal right is imagined to do. They were a consequence of the status, which was fluid. It was always possible for the status of individuals to be revised downward – hence, for protected persons to be made susceptible to beating or torture in public, as well as condemnation to hard labor (unto death). The principle, where it was expressed, was that conviction for certain crimes necessarily entailed a loss of *existimatio*, reputation or social prestige. In consequence of that loss, a person might well cease to be "more honorable" and become "more humble." Though the legal sources discuss numerous hypothetical examples – and imperial rescripts refer to a number of concrete cases – we also witness the working-out of this system in a highly concrete way in North Africa, where a number of bishops were condemned to work the mines for their refusal to obey Valerian's edict on sacrifice.[15] We know of these cases from the correspondence of Cyprian, who received a letter from the bishops in question and himself replied. The interest of the correspondence lies not simply in what it reveals about penal law, but also in the ability of bishops serving such a sentence to correspond with Cyprian, who was himself serving a sentence of internal exile at the time.

Fergus Millar has suggested that the gradual subjection of free citizens to physical coercion in the service of judicial inquiry and punishment amounted to a major revolution in the history of the empire. "Looked at from the point of view of penal principles and practice, the development under the Empire of custodial penalties involving the subjection of free people to beating, fettering, and hard labour represents a radical innovation both in the coercive capacities of the state and in the attitude to individuals."[16] It would be hard to quarrel with this judgment.

14. Ulpian, *De omnibus tribunalibus* bk. 3 fr. 2265 Lenel = *Dig.* 47.10.35.
15. See Cyprian, *Ep.* 76 (to the Christians in the mines, including the immortal claim that Christians, who placed their hope in the wooden cross, have nothing to fear from a wooden club) and 77 (from the Christians in the mines back to Cyprian).
16. Fergus Millar, "Condemnation to hard labour in the Roman Empire, from the Julio-

At the same time, viewed against the long history of class relations in the ancient world, the changes appear less startling: the situation of the poor had always been terribly precarious; there was always a likelihood that a change of material circumstance would induce deprivation, suffering or crushing debt; and debt could always lead to forms of servitude. What is more, the powerful had always retained the *de facto* ability to harm the poor with impunity. It had been the protections offered by the state to ordinary citizens largely against arbitrary or abusive action *by agents of the state* that made Roman citizenship distinctive over against other classes of persons in the classical period. Those protections were now dissolved.

The expansion of the state

Historians of the Roman empire tend to temper their remarks on the efficacy and effects of ancient government with cautions as to its reach. The total number of non-military personnel employed in imperial government under the Principate was inconceivably tiny – smaller, I once observed, than the administrative apparatus of a modest modern university. What is more, within any given province, though a governor might exercise power kindred to that the emperor exercised over the totality of the empire (to adapt a formulation of Ulpian's), the staff available to a governor was extraordinarily limited, and on any understanding would have been spread thin on the ground beyond the imagining of a resident of any modern nation-state.

So described, the empire might seem to offer a poor comparison even to early modern Europe, and what is more, to be a poor candidate for a history of governmentality. Nor, I hasten to add, did the empire in the period of the Principate witness any significant revision or expansion in its understanding of its own pragmatics. On the contrary: in the first two centuries of this era, the primary means available for deepening the penetration of the central state in any given area was alteration in the number of provinces. By this means, the apparatus of the state was occasionally (and usually temporarily) reduplicated across the terrain, but its functioning was emphatically not reconceived.[17]

Claudians to Constantine," *Papers of the British School at Rome* 52 (1984), 123–47 = Millar, *Rome, the Greek World, and the East*, 2:120–50 at 148.
17. For this reason, a map of the empire in the age of Severus – such as appears in this

That said, the third century witnessed the culmination of two long developments that did bring the central government, its agents and concerns, deeper into the ongoing life of local societies. One was, of course, the extension of citizenship. Chapters 3, 4 and 6 have described various consequences of this act, using shifting perspectives from social, legal and religious history. Here two points only bear repetition. First, this change created in provincial populations a self-interested motivation to study the new legal regime that potentially, at least, regulated their affairs. One of the hallmarks of the use of Roman courts even before the Antonine Constitution had been the sense that one or another party to a legal action had turned to Rome because doing so would bring some legal advantage. That situation was now generalized. The second point needing emphasis with regard to the extension of citizenship is that it enabled, even enjoined, further governmental action perhaps unforeseen in the decade of its passage. I refer, of course, to the edicts on sacrifice. At some level, of course, these required no more action on the part of individuals than did the census or registrations of property or birth or death. But for some, clearly, response to the edicts on sacrifice was a political act of a wholly different nature. At the very least, the edicts on sacrifice represented a wholly new occasion, if not an occasion of a new type, when the central state directly identified and addressed individuals (and not communities) and created them as subjects of government.[18]

The second development that implicated the central government more deeply in local and regional life was the closely related processes of an increase in the size and number of imperial properties in provincial landscapes and the development and growth of an administrative apparatus for supervising them. The officials in question were generally termed procurators, from Latin *procurare*, "to exercise care over"; these were uniformly equestrian posts. Within Roman public or constitutional law, one might properly distinguish financial officers who looked after the personal property of the emperor from those who exercised duties of care over

volume (Map 1) – will not be accurate for ages before or after, or even at times for the whole of an emperor's reign, because of administrative changes that yoked Bithynia to Pontus, say. Interested readers should consult the survey of changes in provincial organization provided by John Wilkes in *CAH*[2] XII, Appendix I, pp. 705–13, together with his analysis, pp. 233–52.

18. A modern social theorist would say, "The central state directly *interpellated* them as individuals and so created them as subjects of government."

properties of the state, and both of these from a third category, equestrian procurators who from time to time or even systematically governed select provinces in place of an official of senatorial rank. It is with the first two categories, financial procurators, I am most directly concerned, and in the eyes of locals, the fine distinction between those who superintended imperial and those who super-intended public properties cannot have mattered a great deal.

The gradual increase in their number, which was a direct con-sequence of the increase in quantity and complexity of legal and economic relations between the central state and local players (whether persons or institutions), did have the effect of increasing the presence of imperial administrators on the ground. What is more, whatever their bailiwick and however their powers were originally circumscribed, financial procurators came to exercise all manner of magisterial and jurisdictional functions – to operate, in other words, as a shadow administration to the real one. The major *legal* innovations in this history predate our period: for example, some procurators appear to have been granted jurisdiction (as opposed to having merely exercised it *de facto*) already in the first century AD. That said, the effects of these innovations deserve our attention in this volume for a number of reasons.

First, the pressure impelling procurators to exercise the functions of magistrates came in part from below. That is to say, it was not simply the result of their ambition or rivalry with senatorial governors or legates, or even an outgrowth of their assigned respon-sibilities. It is also clear that procurators were often approached by provincials by virtue of their most basic function, that of represent-ing and embodying Roman officialdom, and were often asked to settle disputes or represent local interests to Roman officials higher in the hierarchy. To that extent, the deeper penetration of the Roman state represented by the elaboration of the functions of procuratorial administrators should be regarded as in part a response to demand from below. Second, the social importance that equestrian procur-ators thus achieved, to the central state and to their contexts of employment – as well as the rivalry, reduplication of function and administrative friction they caused vis-à-vis senatorial officials – were principal impetus behind the development from Commodus on of the new titulature of the governing class discussed above.

The third reason a history of equestrian administration is directly relevant to a history of the third century is that a proper institutional history does not focus solely on developments internal to the institution, but on the effects of those changes and the work of the institution in society at large. In that perspective, the documentation attesting procuratorial involvement in local life explodes in the late second century and assumes a central importance to the actions of government in the third.

As a case study of the dynamics of local administration that is interesting in its own right, but that also gestures toward the topic of the last section of this chapter, let us turn to the inscribed record of a dispute brought before a succession of procurators in Phrygia by two villages, Anossa and Antimacheia, whose public affairs were certainly overshadowed by (and whose territory may have lain wholly inside) a great imperial estate.[19] The dispute stretched from before AD 213 – perhaps 200 – to at least 237. The fragmentary text preserves the records of proceedings before three procurators, as well as two letters seeking to enforce a decision, addressed from a procurator's assistant to the councils of the villages in question. (I term the text fragmentary because the left edge of the stone is broken off: depending on the area of the stone, perhaps 20–5 characters are missing from the left of each line.) With regard to the records of proceedings, the formal aspects of this inscription present a near-perfect match to those employed in the temple inscription from Dmeir (on which see p. 61): that is to say, the protocols – dating formulae, names of the speakers, etc. – are in Latin, while the text of the speeches is in Greek.

The dispute concerns an obligation placed on communities along (Roman) roads, to wit, to supply animals for transport (and care for those animals) for the *cursus publicus*, the official system of transportation that moved messengers but also eligible officials around the empire. It is clear that the obligation placed on the villages is assessed in two units: a distance along the road or roads that pass through their territory (described by reference to milestones: "for those coming from Synnada, from the fifth mile" [l. 5]), and cash, a contribution very likely made in kind but assessed in cash, that was apparently directly proportional to the village's overall tax liability ("according to a proportion of the [tax] liability" [l. 11]). The dispute arises between two villages but the procurator clearly feels the heart of the issue at this moment to be that one village does not

---

19. The inscription was published with enormously helpful but abbreviated commentary by W. H. C. Frend, "A third-century inscription relating to *Angareia* in Phrygia," *JRS* 46 (1956), 46–56. The text is translated in Barbara Levick's superb sourcebook, *The Government of the Roman Empire*, 2nd edition (New York: Routledge, 2000), no. 57.

wish to meet its obligation, and he seeks to discover why the village feels it can no longer provide in the future the contribution it has always made in the past. And on it goes.

A number of aspects of the dispute, the behavior of the principals, and the text deserve our attention. First, the villagers are fully aware that the structure of Roman administration, and the administration's procedures, allowed nearly any decision to be appealed and nearly every question to be re-opened. In the first hearing, the spokesman for the poorer village, one Panas, evidently sensed the conversation turning against him and threatened an appeal over the procurator's head (ll. 11–12). Though the procurator asked a rhetorical question, "What more would you say there than you have said here?" and obviously considered the matter closed, we of course know that the case did in fact continue. It continued both because one party appealed, and because the people of Anossa complained that the people of Antimacheia had not been acting in accord with some aspect of the earlier judgment. That said, the essential points to emerge from the explicit references to both appeals and lower- and higher-ranked officials are that the villagers understood themselves to be engaging a hierarchical bureaucracy and furthermore that they were savvy in manipulating it.[20]

The second aspect of the dispute deserving our attention is precisely enforcement. In this text, the problem is made visible in the request filed by the smaller village at the second stage, in AD 213, for the seconding of a soldier to enforce the decision and protect them from abuse at the hands of the wealthier village.

> Valens said: "The Anosseni ask to receive a *stationarius* [a soldier seconded to police duty]."
> Philokyrios the procurator said: "In order that these decisions be observed, I will give a *stationarius*." (ll. 32–3)

In this case, the weak required protection against predation by the strong, and to that end they turned to Rome, which they evidently regarded as possessing a monopoly upon legitimate – and effective – violence. A number of honorific inscriptions for such soldiers-turned-policemen survive from third-century Asia Minor: they were needed and with some frequency thanked.

---

20. The characterization of Rome's administrative apparatus as hierarchical (and rational, in a Weberian sense) is a major theme of Clifford Ando, *Imperial Ideology and Provincial Loyalty in the Roman Empire* (Berkeley: University of California Press, 2000), which focuses in particular on provincial awareness of this fact.

That said, the ongoing nature of this dispute gestures to an additional problem, more visible elsewhere but latent here, too. The ability of the central state to enforce its decisions was limited, particularly when the criminals were themselves part of the state apparatus. Here one might cite the copies, reproduced in multiple locations over many years, of the order that senators were not to be forced to supply board to passing officials and soldiers, as evidence that even the socially prestigious were regularly victimized (pp. 46–7). But one should also take note of the existence from just this period of numerous appeals to the emperor, inscribed on stone, in which small provincial communities of varying legal condition requested aid against illegal exactions and extortion at the hands of soldiers in particular. These have been read in aggregate as testifying to a break-down in the rule of law in general, and more particularly to the loss of the central state's control over its personnel; and that is a wholly legitimate interpretation of at least one aspect of these texts.[21]

But one might say more. Like the text of the Anosseni, the petitions to the emperor reveal immensely subtle rhetorical tech-nique, and often exhibit formal characteristics intended to make their public display more efficacious. For example, they seek to align their own interest with that of the emperor by urging that their losses effectively count against his income, whether indirectly through a diminution in tax receipts or directly if they themselves work on imperial estates (e.g., Hauken, *Petition*, no. 3, ll. 41–8, from Lydia under either Severus or Philip).[22] At times, like the petitioners to Julius Priscus from the middle Euphrates they cite unnamed laws and earlier decisions, aligning themselves with the rule of law (pp. 88–9); with some frequency, they urge superior officials (includ-ing the emperor) to order subordinate officials to take action (e.g. Hauken, *Petition*, no. 4, from Lydia, probably under Severus).[23] Indeed, they sometimes go farther and demand that the emperor redeem his claim to care that all villages should prosper ("That

21. See esp. Peter Herrmann, *Hilferufe aus römischen Provinzen* (Göttingen: Vanden-hoeck & Ruprecht, 1990), and Tor Hauken, *Petition and Response: An Epigraphic Study of Petititons to Roman Emperors, 181–249* (Bergen: Norwegian Institute at Athens, 1998).
22. Hauken provides a text and translation. The text is reproduced in F. F. Abbott and A. C. Johnson, eds, *Municipal Administration in the Roman Empire* (Princeton: Prince-ton University Press, 1926), no. 226. Abbott and Johnson is one of the great monuments of classical scholarship. A translation may also be found in Levick, *Government*, no. 226.
23. Abbott and Johnson, *Municipal Administration*, no. 143.

in your most happy and everlasting times the villages should be inhabited and prosper, you have on many occasions stated in your rescripts": Hauken, *Petition*, no. 5, ll. 11–15, from Thrace under Gordian III; see also below, p. 227). Indeed, like Caracalla referring to himself, the villagers refer to the province of their residence using a possessive of the emperor, "your Thrace" (Hauken, *Petition*, no. 5, l. 26), subtly asserting that his self-interest overlaps with theirs.[24]

Finally, a number of the inscriptions that include petitions to or responses from the emperor – or both – are bilingual, and preserve in Latin either the formal protocols that indicate imperial authorship (e.g., the first-person notation in Latin "I have signed") or the protocols that indicate the origin of the text or some part thereof in a record of proceedings (e.g., Hauken, *Petition*, nos 5 and 6, from Phrygia under Philip[25]).

In other words, the format of these documents attests a faith, however motivated or strong, in the social efficacy of the procedures of Roman government. A similar faith might be said to inhere in the act of inscription itself, which can only have been undertaken in the hope that the very display of a text would induce obedience to its content. The format of the inscriptions also attests a conviction that others will recognize and esteem Roman documents by virtue of their formal aspects: their use of Latin, their dating formulae and other characteristics specific to particular genres, whether the record of proceedings or the rescript.

Returning to the dispute between Anossa and Antimacheia, a modern reader might well be struck by the very high level of the debate, as well as the high degree of agreement among the participants over what the terms of the debate should be. In the first hearing, everyone knows, and no one contests, the formula that defines the burden for each community. What is at issue are the facts that one should plug into the formula. Here, the procurator's global knowledge of practice past and present plays an essential role. (Reflecting on similar cases that drew the attention of senatorial governors in the first two centuries, one might add that if this case had not come before a procurator with detailed knowledge of administration, then consultation with such an individual would have been necessary in any event.)

---

24. An inordinately famous text: see also Abbott and Johnson, *Municipal Administration*, no. 139 = *HD044445*.

25. Abbott and Johnson, *Municipal Administration*, no. 141 = *MAMA* X 114.

We should likewise observe the very profound sense in which the pragmatics of Roman government shapes the life of these villages and villagers. On the one hand, their relations with each other are mediated by formulae controlled, and justice dispensed, by Roman officials. Even at the level of village-to-village micro-regional relations, the superordinate structures of empire played a role. The same was true at an even more profound level of the legal, economic and cultic ties between villages and cities.

And on the other hand, the lives of the villagers themselves were shaped by, even as their mutual relations revolved around, one of the great material facts of empire, its roads. The road systems of Asia Minor antedated the arrival of Roman power, of course. But it would be nearly impossible to overstate the material and symbolic importance of the roads in uniting the local, regional and imperial in the Roman period. What is more, Roman agents had long recognized this importance on both levels: they devoted enormous resources to building and maintaining roads, and they exploited fully the opportunities afforded by road systems to address their users. In the discursive system so established, roads were a gift of imperial power, and the road system was described as uniting the local, provincial and imperial into a single whole.[26] The Romanness of this ideological apparatus, and even of the conception of physical space that underlay its use, is visible even in this text in the casual use by all parties of the Latin loan-word "mile" in Greek.

The infrastructural elaboration of the state

In assessing the history of government as it affected the great mass of the population across the third century, we require an apparatus that unites an assessment of its practices and pragmatics with an appreciation for its material manifestation. Indeed, one could say much the same of Roman history as a whole and, indeed, of ancient history in general. The closest scholars have come in the past are partial analyses focused on single moments or genres of activity:

26. Perhaps the most remarkable provincial monument to this ideology is the monumental milestone, 15 meters in height, dedicated to Claudius in Lycia: see *SEG* 51, 1832 (in English) and C. P. Jones, "The Claudian monument at Patara," *ZPE* 137 (2001), 161–8. On the impact on provincial mentalities of imperial conceptions of political space see Clifford Ando, "Imperial identities," in Tim Whitmarsh, ed., *Local Knowledge and Microidentities in the Imperial Greek World* (Cambridge: Cambridge University Press, 2010), 17–45.

the administration of justice as a social drama, or the theatrics of diplomatic exchange. Otherwise, even the best studies of the creation of provincial landscapes or the Romanization of urban centers have in general been carried out without due consideration of their role in staging particular administrative processes; *mutatis mutandis*, very fine studies of provincial legal cultures or the administration of the annual loyalty oath have failed to imagine these activities as intensely staged. Where the history of government writ large is concerned, we shall not be able to explain to what degree the Roman empire intervened more intensely in local life or penetrated more deeply than other ancient empires – or why this degree of intervention mattered within the history of subjectivity or culture change, for example – if we proceed without such an apparatus. Comparisons on more isolated axes – Did different empires have similar structures of taxation? How autonomous were regional governors? – are bound to produce trivial results.

It was to this end that I invoked the concept of infrastructural elaboration, embracing as it does both material and institutional manifestations of state power. This volume is not the place to attempt an holistic analysis of this kind. But the problem of assessing the broader functioning of government is relevant to the history of the third century in two respects. First, certain indices suggest a broad failure of government – at least in the administration of justice – over the course of our period, most notably in the paroxysm of external invasion and internal crisis between 235 and 284. Table 1 extracts from Tony Honoré's reconstruction of third-century rescripts the gross number of imperial rescripts assigned to the reigns of emperors between Severus and Carinus.[27] If we relied on these alone – and in any context the numbers are remarkable enough to mean *something* – we should have to posit a systemic collapse of the system for appeals, or of the imperial archives, or of the judicial system, or of government more generally. We should, however, temper any such assessment by weighing the data so generated against the data produced by pursuing some other index of analysis (or multiple ones), and ideally we would do so region by region.

27. Tony Honoré, *Emperors and Lawyers*, 2nd edition (Oxford: Clarendon Press, 1994).

Table 1   *Rescripts by reign, Pertinax to Carinus*

Reign of emperor	Number of imperial rescripts
Pertinax (193, 3 months)	3
Septimius Severus (193–5)	15
Severus and Caracalla (196–7)	13
Severus, Caracalla and Geta (197–211)	196
Caracalla and Geta (211)	9
Caracalla (211–17)	240
Elagabalus (218–22)	2
Elagabalus and Severus Alexander (222)	3
Severus Alexander (222–35)	453
Maximinus (235–8)	3
Pupienus, Balbinus and Gordian III (238)	8
Gordian III (238–44)	269
Philip, alone and with his son Philip (244–9)	81
Decius, alone and with his sons (249–51)	8
Gallus and Volusianus (251–3)	2
Aemilianus (3 months, 253)	0
Valerian and Gallienus (253–60)	80
Gallienus (260–8)	10
Gallic empire	
Postumus (260–9)	0
Marius (269)	0
Victorinus (269–71)	0
Tetricus (271–4)	0
Palmyra	
Odaenathus (260–7)	0
Vaballathus (267–72)	0
Claudius (268–70)	1
Quintillus (September 270)	0
Aurelian (270–5)	7
Tacitus (275–6)	0
Florianus (3 months, 276)	0
Probus (276–82)	4
Carus, Carinus and Numerianus (282–3)	9
Carinus and Numerianus (283–4)	18
Carinus (284–5)	3

The second reason to engage in analysis at this level is that we should very much like to understand how the fragmentation of the empire affected the lives of those who found themselves under the hegemony of Postumus or Odaenathus, on the one hand, and what role continuities or ruptures in the practice of government may have played in the paths taken by those regions in their reincorporation under Aurelian – to say nothing of the broader role that sheer institutional continuity played in the sustaining of provincial and imperial political cultures in the period.

To continue the theme established by our consideration of the dispute between Anossa and Antimacheia, I will focus in a moment on roads. But we should not forget that the construction and maintenance of the material infrastructure of political life (and to a point daily life) was an ongoing concern of the central government and, crucially, was always envisaged as a collaborative project of locality and empire, regardless of who was understood as the primary user of the buildings in question. By the Severan period, of course, many cities were abundantly supplied with public buildings, and the primary duty of governors was to cooperate with local authorities, or nudge those authorities, to see to their upkeep. In a manual produced for provincial governors at some point during the decade after the Antonine Constitution, the jurist and praetorian prefect Ulpian wrote on this topic thus:

> If the governor should come to a famous city or the capital of the province, he should allow the community to praise itself, nor listen ungraciously when the provincials boast to their own credit, and he should allow festivals according to the customs and practice that had obtained in the past. He should conduct a circuit of sacred buildings and public works in order to inspect them – whether the buildings or roofs are in good condition or need some repair, or whether such work, once begun, needs completion, in keeping with the resources of the commonwealth.[28] Moreover, he should take care to assign *curatores* who will take all appropriate care in supervising the work, and he should second military assistance, if there is just cause, to assist the *curatores*. (Ulpian, *De officio proconsulis* bk. 2 fr. 2147 Lenel = *Dig.* 1.16.7.*pr*.1)

The dynamics of the collaboration between imperial and local governments took many forms. The imperial government might supply architectural or engineering expertise, labor and a financial

---

28. The term "commonwealth" here translates *res publica*, which was increasingly used across the second century and beyond to refer to the constituent communities of the imperial polity. The usage is little explored but no doubt is itself an index to broad changes in imperial political culture. For now see Clifford Ando, "Law and the landscape of empire," in Stéphane Benoist and Anne Daguey-Gagey, eds, *Figures d'empire, fragments de mémoire: Pouvoirs, pratiques et discours, images et représentations, et identités sociales et religieuses dans le monde romain impérial. Ier s. av J.-C.–Ve s. ap. J.-C.* (Paris: Presses Universitaires de Septentrion, 2011), 25–47.

subvention (this last often took the form of tax relief). And of course, at times imperial officials might put the brakes on some local initiative, on grounds of excessive cost, and on those occasions no doubt the potential harm to the tax receipts of the central government weighed heavily in the calculus.

In discussing the reign of Philip, I cited the data compiled by Ernst Stein regarding the roadwork performed during his reign. Already in 1918, Stein was able to catalog 100 milestones from fifteen provinces: Africa Proconsularis, Aquitania, Asia, Britannia, Cappadocia, Dalmatia, Gallia Narbonensis, Upper Germany, Mauretania Caesariensis, Upper Moesia, Noricum, Numidia, Lower Pannonia, Upper Pannonia and Sardinia (p. 118). To a point, this focus on roads was idiosyncratic to Philip, and of course the central administration was likely motivated by a concern for the movement of troops and *matériel* for war. That said, milestones exist attesting the attention of virtually all emperors to the roads. More importantly, milestones were read, and roads were used, regardless of any one emperor or administrator's motive in seeing to their repair.[29]

In the event, two comments are called for. First, such data present an important counter-weight to rescripts. Each form of information was naturally subject to hazards of survival, the rescripts in particular being subject to political intervention at moments of archiving and collation. Neither is wholly reliable. Nonetheless, the activity attested by Philip's milestones urges that we not overesteem the seeming drop-off in *per annum* production of rescripts from Gordian's reign to his.

Next, as important as Rome's distinctive conception of the rule of law proved in the construction of the imperial political community, roads and buildings naturally performed their own essential ideological work. Roads were an essential practical and symbolic means for representing the macro-regional and interregional connnectivity that was a hallmark of empire. Together with boundary stones and the cadastration of the countryside, they represented nothing less than the extension of state power into the very landscape of the empire. Likewise, the support of the central administration for

---

29. Though it scarcely need be said, I speak of "the emperor's attention to roads" as a form of shorthand: imperial political discourse naturally assigned a broad agency and oversight to the emperor regarding matters whose particulars are overwhelmingly likely to have escaped his attention completely. The most sustained consideration known to me of the value of milestones for varied forms of historical inquiry is Christian Witschel, "Meilensteine als historische Quelle? Das Beispiel Aquileia," *Chiron* 32 (2002), 325–93.

the urban fabric of its constituent communities demonstrated its commitment to their ongoing vitality, and underscored a shared belief in the contribution made by local social orders to some imperial whole. On a more particular level, the conjoined operation of state institutions within buildings and urban landscapes of a peculiarly Roman form aided in the depersonalization of institutional power that was a hallmark of Roman government, and must have endowed the operation of those institutions with a sense of continuity, however idealized or desperate, that was much wanted in the mid-third century.

The information provided by such evidence is particularly important in the assessment of life in the splinter states in west and east in the reigns of Gallienus and Aurelian. There, naturally, neither the warfare that brought about their reintegration, nor the efforts by Aurelian to delegitimize their governments, were conducive to the survival within the imperial archival tradition of records of their reigns, nor were the codifiers of law in the reigns of Diocletian, Theodosius or Justinian likely to include legal decisions by emperors excluded from the canon.

In fact, the epigraphic record in both west and east testifies strongly to a robust continuance of practice, ideological superstructure and the discursive expression of that structure before, during and after the formation and dissolution of the splinter states. In the reign of Vaballathus, for example, the extension of Palmyrene power into Roman Arabia was inscribed nearly immediately on the road system, in the form of milestones advertising Vaballathus' titulature.

> Lucius Aurelius Septimius Vaballathus, King, Emperor, Leader of the Romans. 15 miles.[30]

A translation cannot convey the very significant fact that Vaballathus inscribed his milestones in Latin, a deep evocation of the Romanness that he sought to project.[31] Likewise, the seizure of

---

30. T. Bauzou, "Deux milliaires inédits de Vaballath en Jordanie du Nord," in Philip Freeman and David Kennedy, eds, *The Defence of the Roman and Byzantine East* (Oxford: British Archaeological Reports, 1986), 1–8. Another series of three stones carries different titulature in a slightly different grammatical form: "To *Imperator* Caesar Lucius Julius Aurelius Septimius Vaballathus Athenodorus, *Persicus maximus, Arabicus maximus, Adiabenicus maximus*, pious, blessed, unconquered Augustus" (*HD033156*).
31. To the Latin of Vaballathus' milestones we might compare the Latin inscription rededicating the temple of Jupiter Ammon at Bostra: it had been rebuilt with silver statues (so the inscription reads) after it had been destroyed "by hostile Palmyrene forces" (*IGLS* XIII.1.9107).

Egypt by Palmyra was initially marked by uncertainty about who held power overall, but the clearest records of this uncertainty at the documentary level are formulaic acknowledgments that the writer did not know who had the power to name the consuls and thereby the year. It was simply not imagined that the system would ever change so radically that the year might not be named by consular dating at all. As it happened, the consolidation of Palmyrene control led rapidly to the appearance of dating formulae and documentary protocols that describe a co-rulership of Aurelian and Vaballathus, each a fully Roman emperor in form and legitimacy.[32] In sum, the infrastructural elaboration of Palmyrene power followed precisely the channels and patterns set out by the Roman state.

The empire of Postumus exhibits a similar pattern. Postumus is named as emperor on milestones throughout his territory – or, one might say, we know, even as contemporaries knew, that the territory was subject to Postumus in part because the road system was the pre-eminent means by which state power was extended through space.[33] Similarly, Postumus is credited on dedicatory inscriptions as having rebuilt and dedicated public buildings – meaning, presumably, that he gave financial support to the rebuilding of public structures – sometimes in the aftermath of enemy attack.

> Imperator Caesar Marcus Cassianus Latinius Postumus, Pious Blessed Unconquered Augustus, *pontifex maximus*, in the tenth (?) year of his tribunician power, consul for the fourth (?) time, father of the fatherland, restored from the very foundation and dedicated these baths, which had been destroyed by fire through the deceit of a public enemy.[34]

As we have seen, it was essential that the emperor be seen to defend the state and, what is more, to choose where necessary to combat enemies of the community instead of enemies of his person. That failing, the emperor should make good harms suffered from their attacks. Hence Postumus' titulature, as well as the claims he advanced about what he did and why he acted, should be understood as deeply continuous with the world from which Gallienus and Aurelian might say he broke away.

But there is more, for the care evidently taken by Postumus'

32. See pp. 210–11 and 226.
33. See for example *HD019696*; *HD013852*; *HD041559*; *HD041560*; *HD007641*; *HD048457*; *RIB* 2255. The list is not exhaustive.
34. *HD052138*, from Gelduba in Lower Germany; see also *RIB* 605.

administration to mark the landscape as his, and to display to soldiers, travelers and merchants that his power extended through their world – the boast, even, that their ability to travel that world was the result of his attention; the collaboration shown between the central state and local authorities in the reconstruction of purely local conveniences of public care: all these things marked the government of Postumus as exercising legitimate social power because and insofar as its energies were directed at acknowledged social goods. The stability of his reign no doubt rested in part on the widespread intelligibility of these actions; and the reincorporation of the Gallic provinces into the Roman state was no doubt eased by the profound continuity these actions reveal.

CHAPTER 9

Reconquest and recidivism, 268–84

The conspiracies that formed against Gallienus were undoubtedly symptomatic of a broad dissatisfaction among the upper echelons of the military. We should beware, however, of attributing too great coherence to them, or too great stability to the government that emerged. The temptation to do so is strong, but it is largely the product of a related desire to see the dominance of officers with origins in the Danubian provinces as itself a coherent movement, rather than the predictable result of convergent but also contingent processes of the age. The mere fact that we can situate individuals in relation to one another within a particular institutional culture – even the strong likelihood that they knew one another – does not in itself justify attributing to some group the status of a faction, let alone the ascription to it of a program. Roman historians of the middle and late Republic will be familiar with the waxing and waning of theories that attributed real historical coherence and stability to political factions around labels like "optimate" and "popularis" or, more pointedly, around friendships and marriage alliances. Prosopography – the study of careers, based (in the Roman case) largely on the information supplied by public monuments – tells us in the first instance about the careers of individuals as people wished them to be known to the general public, and secondarily supplies such information about institutional cultures as career patterns can reveal. All else is conjecture.

The instability of the political situation that issued from the murder of Gallienus is visible on a number of levels: the execution of Aureolus suggests a lack of confidence on the part of the new regime, such as it was. (If it was right and proper to murder Gallienus, then why was it not right and proper for Aureolus to have revolted? He could still have been useful.) The murder of Gallienus' brother, and the rapid murder of Quintillus, brother of Gallienus' successor Claudius II (on which see below, p. 205), suggest a lack of consensus within the conspirators or conspiratorial class over not only the selection but perhaps even the principles by which consensus might be achieved.

A further index of political instability is the posthumous fate of Gallienus and his sons. We have already seen that the *Historia Augusta* declared the first act of the post-Gallienic era to have been the condemnation of Gallienus as an illegitimate ruler, a *tyrannus* (p. 175). Gallienus himself oversaw the posthumous consecration of his sons Valerian II and Saloninus. Whatever the truth of the *Historia Augusta*'s account, the emperor chosen to succeed Gallienus in fall 268, Claudius II, evidently felt the need to consecrate Gallienus, very likely upon his arrival in Rome in winter 268/9.[1] Whether the gesture had a specific audience – specific units of the army, perhaps, or aristocratic adherents whose collaboration or goodwill he sought to buy – or was intended merely as an emphatic statement that emperors *qua* emperors are honorable is not known. A further consequence in any event was to broadcast a message of stability with regard to acts taken by and under the previous regime, and as a related matter of stability with regard to the imperial system more generally. But in the very near future the gesture toward the house of Valerian and Gallienus itself was emphatically repudiated at the local level, and the inscriptions of Gallienus and his sons were defaced across the west (see, e.g., *ILS* 556, 557, 558 with Dessau's notes).

Toward a resolution on the Danube: Claudius II and Quintillus, 268–70

The general chosen by the conspirators to succeed Gallienus was one Marcus Aurelius Claudius. He appears to have pursued an equestrian military career: in all probability, it had been spent on the Danubian frontier. Virtually nothing is known of his life before his accession. In keeping with the demands of biography, the *Historia Augusta* supplies a rich store of facts, virtually none of which can be corroborated. Beyond the medium- or long-term challenge posted by the sundering of the Roman state, the major challenge before him was the extended Danubian frontier and the Goths who sailed

---

1. The testimony regarding the consecration provided by Aurelius Victor, 33.27, would probably have been set aside, the final sentences of chapter 33 being a tissue of ill-founded assertion, except that Gallienus is attested as *divus* on a papyrus the following year (*CPR* I 9, l. 7, to be consulted in revised text *SPP* XX 72) and on an undated dedication from Numidia (*HD020219*).

the Black Sea and Hellespont. This challenge was primary for two reasons above all: first, the truncated empire of Gallienus could not long survive if social order in Asia were significantly compromised. On a political and financial level, that would have spelled ruin. At the same time, mounting major military campaigns on the basis of a shrunken tax base had already stretched the revenues of the central state to the breaking point: under Claudius, the percentage of silver content of the antoninianus shrank into the low single digits.

The second reason that Claudius had to make the Danube his first priority was its importance on a personal level to the upper echelons of the officer corps. Even if we cannot determine the province of origin of Claudius himself, an enormous range of the higher-ranking officers whose origins we can know came from the Danube. (A phenomenal percentage also bears the name Aurelius, identifying them as stemming from families that received Roman citizenship only under Caracalla.[2]) It may well be that the high degree of their disaffection with Gallienus stemmed from his willingness to abandon the Gothic campaign of 267/8 to deal with Aureolus. As we have seen, Roman imperial culture related several exemplary tales of emperors who ostentatiously ignored usurpers, pretenders and the like, in favor of the needs of the state. Gallienus failed that test, and he did so in a fashion that slighted the welfare of the home territory of the officer corps.

The surviving literary sources differ on the question of whether Claudius was present at the culmination of the plot against Gallienus.[3] There is a strong likelihood that he was present for the siege of Aureolus. Likewise, there is a strong likelihood that Claudius traveled from Milan to Rome immediately after the deaths of Gallienus, Valerian and Aureolus, there to arrange the civilian administration and endure the collaborative rituals of legitimation. That said, he took the title Germanicus Maximus in 268, for a victory hard to place in this itinerary (*ILS* 569). However that

2. Notable among these are the praetorian prefect Aurelius Heraclianus, who is credited in sources reliant upon Dexippus with a leading role in the plot against Gallienus (Zosimus, 1.40; Zonaras, 12.25; SHA *Duo Gallieni* 14.1; see also *IGBR* 3.2.1568, a dedication to Heraclianus); his brother, Marcus Aurelius Apollinarius, the governor of Thrace (*IGBR* 3.2.1569; see also *HD*011451, possibly a dedication by Apollinarius from an earlier point in his career); Marcus Aurelius Aurelianus, emperor 270–5; Marcus Aurelius Probus, emperor 276–82; and Marcus Aurelius Carus and his sons, emperors 282–4.
3. Aurelius Victor, 33.28, places him at Ticinum; Zonaras, 12.26, supposes only that he was neither with the army nor in Rome.

victory occurred within this timeline, Claudius departed Rome in early spring 269 for the Danubian frontier.

The situation at the start of 269 was grim. When Gallienus took his army from the front to attack Aureolus, he probably left the general Marcianus behind, with the thankless task of harassing the Goths with depleted forces.[4] Gallienus' rapid departure had therefore left a vacuum, and the Goths appear by early 269 to have been actively besieging both Marcianopolis and Thessalonica, while the parties that had devastated peninsular Greece were still abroad. By blockading the passes over the Haemus and harassing the enemy, Claudius and Marcianus compelled the Gothic groups to combine and forced a set battle near Naïssus. The result was an overwhelming Roman victory: Claudius compelled an agreement that the Goths would remain north of the Danube, an agreement that held for more than a generation.[5]

The sea-faring Goths were naturally not directly affected by the battle of Naïssus, and it is no longer possible to reconstruct in any detail the naval operations of 270. Zosimus reports that the prefect of Egypt, Tenagino Probus, a man of remarkable industry attested in building projects and military operations across North Africa, mounted a campaign against pirates for the emperor Claudius.[6] Given that Probus appears to be attested as successful in a land campaign in Cyrenaica in 269 (AE 1934, 257), the action described by Zosimus can only have taken place in 270. The involvement of the prefect of Egypt in such a campaign would suggest considerable effort and central planning. In the event, the territories of the western Aegean and the lower Danube were largely untroubled from the sea after this year. The final suppression of Gothic raids against Asia Minor, however, would await the reign of Tacitus in 275/6.

The outcome of these campaigns notwithstanding, the restraint shown over the next generation by the populations north of the Danube and along the Ukrainian coast of the Black Sea demands some explanation. It might be, of course, that the losses inflicted

---

4. The *Historia Augusta* makes Marcianus a chief conspirator against Gallienus and places him in Milan, but neither need be true, and neither consent to the conspiracy nor consent to its outcome required his presence in Milan (SHA *Duo Gallieni* 14.1 and 15.2). On Marcianus see *AE* 1975, 770c, an inscription in honor of Marcianus erected by the city of Philippopolis.

5. The most cogent surviving narrative is Zosimus, 1.40.

6. Zosimus, 1.44; see also Zonaras, 12.27. For Probus' other activities see *HD011796*, *HD021192* and *HD024303*.

in 269/70 were materially too significant or too discouraging at the level of morale, and we are not now in a position to prove or disprove these suggestions. Certainly Rome had won such wars of attrition before through sheer fecundity, the ability endlessly to mobilize new units without overly adverse effects on economic output. (This is thematized in the remarkable first book of Appian's *Civil War*.) But we should also consider the possibility that the Goths, Iuthungi and so on were astute observers of the Roman political scene: the chronology is hard to fix, but there is a reasonably strong correlation between spikes in raiding activity and disarray in imperial politics. Raiding for plunder – like the exchange of tribute and subsidy – was an appetite that grew by what it fed upon, and it tended to slow or stop when a coherent military response rendered the activity too dangerous to justify the diminishing profits that renewed Roman strength permitted.

By summer 270, Claudius himself had moved to Sirmium, north and west of Naïssus. What he intended to do from there is not clear: there is a strong temptation to read back from events and policy changes over the next decade and imagine that Claudius was anticipating threats to Italy by the Iuthungi or devising some scheme to retake or release Dacia. But as it happened, a plague struck the region: it may in fact have struck the Goths first, weakening their forces already in 269. By summer 270 it had spread through the Roman army. After a summer of apparent inactivity, Claudius died in September, just shy of the second anniversary of his rule.[7]

We know nothing the negotiations that took place during Claudius' illness, nor, frankly, what decision was reached, how, when and by whom, or how the news was cast abroad. Nonetheless, immediately upon Claudius' death, his younger brother Quintillus – who may have been a lowly procurator in Sardinia as recently as 268 and was stationed in Aquileia in fall 270 – was acclaimed emperor in succession to his brother. Within the terms of imperial politics, the action was entirely intelligible. At virtually the same time, however, the troops in Sirmium acclaimed a wholly different figure, an equestrian cavalry officer named Marcus Aurelius Aurelianus, whose first prominent act had been his participation in the conspiracy against Gallienus (Figure 15).

The willingness of Claudius' own army to rise against his brother

---

7. Plague affecting the Goths: SHA *Claudius* 11.3. The death of Claudius: SHA *Claudius* 12.2; Eutropius, 9.11.2.

Figure 15 Gold medallion from the mint of Rome, bearing the portrait of Aurelian on the obverse and a hopeful, perhaps admonitory message on the reverse: CONCORDIA LEGIONUM, "The harmony of the legions" (Photograph: British Museum, reproduced with permission)

must testify at some level to his brother's insignificance and to the esteem in which it held Claudius. In the event, Aurelian marched on Aquileia, and before any confrontation could take place, Quintillus was dead; whether by murder or suicide is not known. Perhaps the most interesting fact about Quintillus is that, despite an apparent effort by Aurelian to denounce him as having usurped his position, the historical tradition is clear on one thing: he was in fact an emperor, not a tyrant.[8] His rule – over the empire of Aquileia? – lasted seventeen days.

Reunification I: Aurelian and Zenobia (270–2)

The brief reign of Aurelian is notable on three grounds: he defeated Palmyra; he reintegrated the Gallic empire into Rome; and he instituted a massive reform of the coinage. I take these in turn, after an initial remark on Aurelian's first two years in office.

Aurelian confronted two long-term challenges before he could

8. *Epit. de Caes.* 34.5: "His brother Quintillus succeeded him. He was killed after having held power for a few days." See also Eutropius, 9.12: "After him, his brother Quintillus was chosen emperor by agreement of the soldiers, a man of singular moderation and civility, the equal or better of his brother; by consensus of the Senate he was named Augustus. He was killed on the seventeenth day of his reign." Zosimus, 1.47: "After Quintillus, who was the brother of Claudius, was acclaimed emperor, lived a few months and accomplished nothing worthy of remembering, Aurelian ascended the royal throne."

turn his attention to the reunification of the empire. First, Claudius' victory over the Goths had checked one antagonist but had not completely secured the frontier. Aurelian devoted himself to the western front in 270 and 271, along two lines. First, he engaged in sweeping military campaigns, which temporarily subdued the aggressive energies of further populations. His final peace nego- tiations with parties among the Iuthungi received a famous descrip- tion by the historian Dexippus, who describes Aurelian's massive marshaling of troops bearing standards, with himself on a platform: the Iuthungi, Dexippus writes, approached with confidence but were so intimidated by the display that they waited to speak until they had been granted permission.[9] Aurelian's second action in respect to the western frontier was the final surrender of "transdanubian" Dacia (as the *Historia Augusta* names it): all Roman populations that wished to return south of the Danube were encouraged to do so, and a new province (also named Dacia) was carved out there amidst the Moesias, masking somewhat the surrender of territory (SHA *Aurelianus* 39.7). Aurelian took the title Got(h)icus Maximus in the same year, 272: a signal way to retrieve personal victory from territorial loss.

The second long-term challenge confronted by Aurelian was the vulnerability of Italy as it had been revealed by the Germanic invasions of recent years. Beyond various military actions, he addressed this problem principally through the construction at Rome of a massive new wall (Figure 16).[10] (He supported the construction of walls at other Italian cities, too: various Greek cities in Greece and Asia Minor had already taken it upon themselves to rebuild their city walls over the last decade and a half.) Aurelian now turned east.

The murder that claimed the life of Odaenathus of Palmyra also claimed an elder son, Herodianus. But he also left behind a younger son, Vaballathus, not yet 10 years old at his father's death, and his wife, Zenobia, who emerges in literature, art and historical narrative as one of the strongest personalities of the age, for five years at least

9. *Excerpta de legationibus*, Dexippus 1 de Boor (*FGrH* 100 F 24 = Dindorf *HGM* fr. 22).
10. Construction of the wall commenced under Aurelian; it was finished under Probus. See SHA *Aurelianus* 21.9 and 39.2, together with Alaric Watson, *Aurelian and the Third Century* (London: Routledge 1999), 143–52, Filippo Coarelli, *Rome and Environs: An Archaeological Guide* trans. James J. Clauss and Daniel P. Harmon (Berkeley: University of California Press, 2007), 18–27.

Figure 16 A restored section of the wall of Aurelian at Rome, between the Porta San Sebastiano and the Porta Ardeatina (Photograph: Lalupa; source: Wikimedia Commons)

a dominant figure in imperial politics – as good a run as any Roman emperor of the day.[11] The deterioration of the situation in the east turned largely (but not wholly) on the different expectations that Rome and Palmyra held in respect of the position of Odaenathus vis-à-vis the central government. As regards Odaenathus himself, and even Zenobia, we can only conjecture as to their ambitions and motivations on the basis of their actions as reported by others and the (self-)representations provided by titulature recorded on stone. But on that basis, it seems clear that Odaenathus sought no conflict with Gallienus: he made no revision in his claims to public power, nor acted toward other Roman officials or institutions, in ways that overstepped the seemingly underdetermined bailiwick described by the title *corrector totius orientis*.

What also seems fundamentally clear is that neither Gallienus nor any successor understood the position granted Odaenathus as

11. The reconstruction of the extended family of Odaenathus and Zenobia is far more difficult than one might think: see David S. Potter, *Prophecy and History in the Crisis of the Roman Empire: A Historical Commentary on the Thirteenth Sibylline Oracle* (Oxford: Clarendon Press, 1990), 386–8.

hereditary – as an effort to revive some form of client kingship, or to institute a permanent relationship between two royal houses or two sovereign states. Gallienus had rather made the best of things, adapting an existing Roman institution and using the traditional language of Roman public law, in order to co-opt a regional dynast to the service of the central state. But immediately upon the death of Odaenathus, Zenobia (it seems) engineered the succession of Vaballathus to his father's position not only within the Palmyrene royal house but in the east at large. This fact is most clearly stated on a contemporary bilingual Greek–Palmyrene milestone (the Palmyrene text is nearly complete; I underline the portion that survives in Greek and place in brackets language peculiar to the Palmyrene version):

> For the safety and victory of Septimius Vaballathus Athenodorus, illustrious King of Kings, who is also *corrector* of the entire region, son of Septimius Odaenathus, King of Kings; and also on behalf of (the safety) of Septimia [Bath-Zabbai] (Zenobia), (most) illustrious Queen, mother of the King, daughter of Antiochus. Fourteen miles.[12]

It is altogether unclear how Claudius or any successor to Gallienus might have dealt even with Odaenathus, but it seems highly improbable that they would have conceded to a boy and his mother a privilege and a problem they regularly imposed on their own people, namely, the rulership over Romans of one's own incompetent child.

The chronology of relations between Rome, Roman agents in the east, and Palmyra in the reign of Claudius cannot now be reconstructed: it may be, for example, that the praetorian prefect Heraclianus undertook a diplomatic negotiation with, or even a military action against, Vaballathus, in either 268 under orders from Gallienus or 270 under orders from Claudius, but we cannot say for sure.[13] (We are likewise unable to say with certainty why Claudius of all people adopted the title Parthicus Maximus, a title credited to him in a dedication by the colony of Thubursicum in Numidia before his death in 270 [*ILS* 571].) The most probable explanation remains that the mission was planned to restore a Roman order in the east after the death of Odaenathus, though its scope, effectiveness and timing were no doubt affected by the death of Gallienus.

---

12. *CISem.* II 3971; text and translation in Potter, *Prophecy*, 390–1. I have slightly altered the presentation without any revision to the meaning.
13. David S. Potter, *The Roman Empire at Bay, AD 180–395* (London: Routledge, 2004), 266–7.

On the Palmyrene side, Zenobia took two actions on behalf of her son and city that would have provoked Roman action regardless. First, she began to innovate with his titulature, laying claim to ever more grandiose powers: she named Vaballathus "king, emperor and *dux Romanorum*, leader of the Romans," and the like, and advertised these on coins.[14] (Odaenathus had not presumed to mint coins at all.) This change went hand in hand with a shift in the dating of Vaballathus' reign, backdating its start so that he suddenly appeared to have been ruling since 267. Though documents generated from areas under Palmyrene control still respect Aurelian's primacy by naming him first in dating formulae, the result of the new chronology is that Aurelian is described as coming to power three years after Vaballathus, who is thus made the senior colleague.[15]

Zenobia's second and more serious act was the direct assertion of control over Arabia and Egypt, provoking the armed resistance of the governors of both regions. These events raise the questions of whether the governors' resistance was due to their unwillingness to recognize Vaballathus or whether they would likewise have resisted any similar arrogation of power on the part of Odaenathus, but no answer to either question can now be advanced. In the case of Egypt, Palmyrene forces succeeded in displacing and killing the dynamic prefect Tenagino Probus. According to John Malalas, whose chronicle displays a particular emphasis on the history of Antioch and the east, the governor of Arabia was also killed when he resisted Palmyra's advance. Palmyrene aggression and control over Arabia are confirmed by the inscribed record of repair to a local temple and milestones in the territory announcing the sovereignty of Vaballathus.[16] The die was now cast.

14. On the coinage of Vaballathus see C. Gallazzi, "La titolatura di Vaballato come riflesso della politica di Palmira," *Numismatica e Antichità Classiche* 4 (1975), 249–65. See also Michael Peachin, *Roman Imperial Titulature and Chronology, A.D. 235–284* (Amsterdam: Gieben, 1990), 45; Fergus Millar, *The Roman Near East, 31 BC–AD 337* (Cambridge, MA: Harvard University Press, 1993), 172.
15. On the papyrological evidence for the change in Vaballathus' regnal year, see Dominic Rathbone, "The dates of the recognition in Egypt of the emperors from Caracalla to Diocletianus," *ZPE* 62 (1986), 101–31 at 123–4 and J. Rea, *POxy.* vol. 40, pp. 15–30.
16. John Malalas describes Zenobia as attacking Arabia and killing its governor (Malalas 12.29), and Palmyrene *de facto* and *de jure* control over Arabia is confirmed by milestones in the name of Vaballathus: T. Bauzou, "Deux milliaires inédits de Vaballath en Jordanie du Nord," in Philip Freeman and David Kennedy, eds, *The Defence of the Roman and Byzantine East* (Oxford: British Archaeological Reports, 1986), 1–8, together with Benjamin Isaac, *The Limits of Empire: The Roman Army in the East* (Oxford:

Aurelian's arrival in the east generated a number of tales that survive in the tradition largely dissociated from any grand narrative, bits of local lore that passed into biography as revealing something about Aurelian without any demand for coherence in history. Other tales from the same period clearly testify to anxieties aroused by the efforts of Zenobia to fortify the position of Palmyra in anticipation of Aurelian's attack. The overall importance of this material surely lies in two trends clearly visible throughout: first, local communities feared the consequences of taking sides, even as the nature of (civil) war forced them to do so; and second, once the question of hegemony was settled, the passage of the east from Palmyrene back to Roman domination occurred largely without incident. This latter is an issue to which we shall return in the Conclusion.

Although Zenobia had sought to extend her influence into Asia Minor, her forces did not engage Aurelian until he arrived in Syria: two set battles took place in rapid succession, first near Antioch and later near Emesa, as Aurelian advanced toward Palmyra.[17] At this point, resistance largely collapsed. Aurelian was forced to besiege Palmyra, but Zenobia herself was captured fleeing the city during the siege, very likely after having lost a debate over how or whether to continue resistance. After the city capitulated, Aurelian withdrew back toward Europe. In typical Roman fashion, spectacular punishment was administered locally: the leaders of the city were executed after a trial in Emesa, while Zenobia was retained to march in Aurelian's triumph at Rome. But before that triumph could be staged, there was apparently a further uprising in the winter or early spring, very likely desperate resistance to whatever financial penalties Aurelian had imposed: Aurelian returned and ordered the destruction of the city.[18] He then toured the east, displaying himself

Clarendon Press, 1990), 222–3, esp. n. 22, citing unpublished milestones from Judaea. Temple repair: *IGLS* XIII.1.1907, on which see Chapter 8 n. 31. Tenagino Probus was dead by autumn, as Palmyrene control over Egypt (with the notional approval of Aurelian) is attested by a papyrus from Oxyrhynchus by the second week of December 270 (*POxy.* 2921). For a chronology of politics in Egypt in this period see Gerald Kruecher, "Die Regierungszeit Aurelians und die griechischen Papyri aus Ägypten," *Archiv für Papyrusforschung* 44 (1998), 255–74; a more general chronology is available in Rathbone, "Dates of the recognition" and Rea, *POxy.* vol. 40, pp. 15–30. On Arabian perceptions of and apprehensions about Palmyrene power in this period see G. W. Bowersock, *Roman Arabia* (Cambridge, MA: Harvard University Press, 1983), 131–7.
17. Zosimus, 1.50–3, provides a narrative. The specification by the *Historia Augusta* of Daphne as the site of the first battle may be correct, but urban growth had rendered Daphne by this time a suburb of Antioch (SHA *Aurelianus* 25.1).
18. SHA *Aurelianus* 31; Ernest Will, "Le sac de Palmyre," in R. Chevallier, ed.,

as a symbol of Roman order restored, before turning west once again.

Reunification II: Aurelian and the empire of Gaul (272–4)

The destabilization of Palmyra's hegemony was in part consequent upon the insufficiency of its system of succession. Though we cannot know for certain who urged its assertions of control over Asia, Arabia or Egypt, it is hard not to see Palmyra's expansionism as motivated, at least in part, by Zenobia's need to shore up the credibility of its child ruler. Those efforts then played no small role in determining the nature and severity of Aurelian's response.

If Palmyra's brief history instantiated one form of the self-subversion inherent in imperial politics, the devolution of the Gallic empire instantiated another (or more than one). As we have seen, Postumus was murdered by his troops in 269 when he refused to allow them to sack Moguntiacum (p. 162). They had attacked Moguntiacum because it had housed – perhaps even supported – an attempted usurpation against Postumus by one Ulpius Cornelius Laelianus. (As we have repeatedly observed, civilian populations had little choice but to support the nearest regime, which does not mean they were not often punished for having done so – a double indignity, since "support" was often extracted at great cost.) But the Gallic empire had no more established depersonalized means for securing the succession and achieving a social consensus than had Rome, and the death of Postumus, who had seemingly enjoyed considerable consensual support, initiated a contest that the Gallic empire could little afford. For quite apart from the enormous cost in lives and resources entailed by a civil conflict and the door such conflicts left open for outside invasion, the Gallic empire, like the Palmyrene hegemony, cohered less well – had a weaker grasp upon its regional components – than it needed. Hence internal conflict exacted a double cost from the Gallic empire: civil war deprived the government of its legitimacy, while the use of force in regional control only encouraged other regions to break away. And in the cases of both Palmyra and Gaul, the border states had a choice.

So it was that two candidates emerged after the death of Postumus, each needing to eliminate the other: Marcus Aurelius

Mélanges d'archéologie et d'histoire offerts à André Piganiol (Paris: SEVPEN, 1966), 1409–16.

Marius, an officer on location when Postumus died, and Marcus Piavonius Victorinus, praetorian prefect to Postumus, whose career in the army stretched back at least to 265 (*ILS* 563). Victorinus was successful against Marius, but in the meantime, or very soon thereafter, the Spanish provinces declared their loyalty to the emperor Claudius.[19] The Gallic empire was no use to them if it became no better than Rome. Around this time, Claudius ordered a trial of Victorinus' strength that was itself ineffective but may have helped to provoke an apostasy from Gaul to Rome on the part of Augustodunum. Alas for Augustodunum, 270 was, as we have seen, a year of laxity and torpor on the part of Claudius, and in an act of appalling moral and political failure, he sent no aid to Augustodunum. After a siege reported at seven months, the city fell to Victorinus.[20]

The fall of Augustodunum may nonetheless have had one lasting effect. The length of the siege apparently advertised a level of weakness or distraction on Victorinus' part that his grip on the throne could scarcely afford. He was himself murdered not long thereafter, at Cologne in spring 271.[21] He was succeeded by one Gaius Esuvius Tetricus, whose name advertised a Gallic origin but who is described even in this period as "a senator of the Roman people and governor in Gaul."[22] Though Tetricus tried, as most emperors did, to secure his position by founding a dynasty – he named his son Caesar, perhaps in 273 (Aurelius Victor, *Caes.* 33.14) – he had not the strength to face Aurelian, nor the will to die fighting. When Aurelian approached in 274, Tetricus managed to negotiate his own surrender while sacrificing his army to the need of Rome and Aurelian for blood and closure. He led his army into an impossible position on the so-called Catalaunian plan where it was utterly destroyed, while he himself gave up without a struggle (Eutropius, 9.13.1; Aurelius Victor, *Caes.* 35.4; Zosimus, 1.61.2).

Aurelian then returned to Rome to hold a spectacular double triumph, the first imperial triumph in the city in many years and

19. J. F. Drinkwater, *The Gallic Empire: Separatism and Continuity in the North-Western Provinces of the Roman Empire*, AD 260–274 (Stuttgart: Steiner, 1987), 120.
20. The event lingered long in local memory, being discussed by two orators when speaking before the emperor and cited still by Ausonius two generations later: see Eumenius, *Pan. Lat.* V(9).4.1; Anonymous, *Pan. Lat.* VIII(5).4; Ausonius, *Parentalia* 4.6–10.
21. SHA *Tyr. Trig.* 6.3 and 7.2; Eutropius, 9.9.3; Aurelius Victor, *Caes.* 33.12.
22. SHA *Tyr. Trig.* 24.1; see also Eutropius, 9.10, who specifies Tetricus' province as Aquitania; *Epit. de Caes.* 35.7.

one long remembered. Those longing for a return to some former condition of strength and security must have found Aurelian's victories deeply satisfying. Zenobia, Tetricus and his son all marched in captivity; Zenobia in particular rapidly came to serve as an exemplum of defeat.[23] Though their followers had been massacred, each survived to a distinguished old age: Zenobia married a Roman senator and bore more children, while Tetricus became *corrector* to the Italian region of Lucania and he and his son entered the Senate.[24]

Aurelian and the reform of the coinage

The territorial integrity of the greater Roman empire now restored and his triumph celebrated, Aurelian advertised himself to have restored the world: the title *restitutor orbis* is added to his titulature in fall 274. He now undertook an astonishing act of currency reform, whose effects are as clear as its motivations are obscure.[25] To understand what Aurelian did and why it had the effect it had, let us return to the problems of imperial finances as they have been outlined thus far.

Roman coinage had its heyday early in the Julio-Claudian period, when the gold and silver coinage was astonishingly pure; the size of the coins was remarkably consistent; and the coins appear to have traded, bronze for silver and silver for gold, at official values. Between the end of the Julio-Claudian period and the accession of Aurelian, three trends are visible in economic life of relevance here. First, the precious metal content of the silver coin was reduced, at first intermittently and slowly, and later rapidly, regularly and precipitously. By the reign of Claudius, it vacillated between 1.5 and 3 percent. Second, the size of the gold coins shrank, and the size of both the silver and gold coinage became less regular. (They were, *inter alia*, simply less well made than they had been earlier.) Third,

23. Eutropius, 9.13.2; Jerome, *Chron. sub anno* 274; Festus, 24; SHA *Tyr. Trig.* 30.24–7; SHA *Aurelianus* 33.2–34.3; Zosimus, 1.59; Zonaras, 12.27.
24. Zenobia in Rome: SHA *Tyr. Trig.* 27.2; *ILS* 1202; Antonio Baldini, "Discendenti a Roma da Zenobia?" *ZPE* 30 (1978), 145–9. Tetricus: Aurelius Victor, *Caes.* 35.5; Eutropius, 9.13.2.
25. For a large-scale history of currency in this period see Elio Lo Cascio, "Teoria e politica monetaria a Roma tra III e IV d.C.," in Andrea Giardina, ed., *Società romana e impero tardo antico*, 4 vols. (Rome: Laterza, 1986), 1:535–57, 779–801, including an insightful reading of Paul, though Lo Cascio fairly regularly employs an erroneous reference for the passage (see n. 28 below). For general treatments of Aurelian's reform Watson, *Aurelian*, 125–42, and Potter, *Empire at Bay*, 273–4.

prices rose, not consistently but in fits and starts. (A fourth change, which affected the articulation of the system but not its functioning, was the introduction of a new coin, the antoninianus [p. 108].)

As I observed earlier, at one time it was presumed that prices rose *because* of the debasement of the coinage: people somehow knew, it was supposed, that the silver content had diminished and therefore they valued it less – traded it against gold at a lesser value than the official rate, and esteemed it less as a commodity. But the gradual accumulation of evidence for prices, along with the exploitation of more sophisticated means of averaging, has revealed rates of inflation in the second and third centuries to have moved largely independently of the silver content of the coin. Inflation and debasement did not co-vary.[26] Likewise, although there is some evidence that silver coin traded against gold at higher than the official rate, those data are not so robust as to permit generalization; and again, the evidence suggests that the rate at which silver traded against gold was not determined by the precious metal content of the coins.

As a final observation, the acceptance of coin – its use as legal tender – served as a metaphor for the legitimacy and efficacy of certain ritual acts, and in those contexts what was taken to be determinative of the acceptability of coin was the face inscribed on it, not its metallurgical purity.[27] There is therefore some reason to believe that Rome had backed into having a more-or-less token coinage (in which the value of the object is determined by a social consensus of whatever kind, independent of the value of the material from which it is made), without having any understanding of that fact, or any language with which to describe it.[28]

26. Dominic Rathbone, "Monetisation, not price-inflation, in third-century AD Egypt?" in C. E. King and D. G. Wigg, eds, *Coin Finds and Coin Use in the Roman World: The Thirteenth Oxford Symposium on Coinage and Monetary History 25–27.3.1993* (Berlin: Gebr. Mann, 1996), 321–39.

27. Clifford Ando, *Imperial Ideology and Provincial Loyalty in the Roman Empire* (Berkeley: University of California Press, 2000), 215–28. These texts should be read in conjunction with Dominic Rathbone's interpretation of *POxy.* 1411, the edict of a prefect in 262 ordering people to accept coins bearing the emperor's portrait: Rathbone ("Monetisation") identifies the problem as residing in people's reluctance to use coins bearing the portraits of the usurpers Macrianus and Quietus (or, perhaps one should say, emperors who were rendered usurpers by failure). Popular hesitation thus arose from concerns over the legitimacy of the tender, not specifically from some concern over its precious metal content.

28. The only text to suggest otherwise is not a reflection on debasement as such but on money, by the jurist Paul, who describes money as a "material, whose stable and public value supported commerce by overcoming the difficulties of [barter-exchange]." Paul

Aurelian intervened on two levels. First, he is often described as having reacted against the debasement of the coinage – and he did in fact do that – but in truth, he raised the purity of the silver coin only to 5 percent, and he marked the coins with numbers to indicate this fact (XX.I or XXI, meaning 1/20). Second, he purified and enlarged the standard gold coin. (The limited nature of his action with regard to the silver coinage undoubtedly stems in large measure from the fact that Aurelian was in no better position than his predecessors to solve the chronic shortfall in the supply of silver.) He then demanded that people exchange their old coin for new. This process of exchange in turn demanded the opening of new mints, to distribute the capacity to institute the reform.[29]

The result was runaway inflation, both in the immediate aftermath of his act and for the next quarter century. Indeed, it was so severe that by the fourth century – and more and more going forward – the gold coinage replaced the silver in government circles, effecting a separation between the statal and public economies, on the one hand, and also sharpening a social differentiation between classes, those with access to gold coin (often through salaries) on one side, and all others on the other.

The most likely explanation is simply that the primary effect of Aurelian's ostentation was to draw attention to the debased status of the coinage. Indeed, the enormous spike in inflation offers further proof, if any were needed, that debasement in itself was not a simple or exclusive cause of inflation in earlier years, and, concomitantly, that popular knowledge of the silver content was far less precise than earlier generations of scholars imagined.

As regards Aurelian's motivation, we reside strictly in the realm of conjecture, but the very limited nature of his so-called reforms makes it difficult to credit him with any ambition at the level of monetary policy. (That the reforms had important economic *effects* is a matter wholly separable from the question of intent.) The act was, rather,

had identified those difficulties principally as consisting in finding a partner to barter who wanted what you had and who simultaneously had something you wanted. This "material," Paul continues, being given a specific form by the state (meaning, it was struck by a mint), "showed its utility and title not from its substance as such but from its quantity, nor are the things exchanged one for the other still called wares, but one is called the price" (Paul, *Ad edictum* bk. 33 fr. 502 Lenel = *Dig.* 18.1.1.*pr.*). The distinction between money as a chunk of precious metal – hence a "ware" (*merx*) – and money as token, as price (a *pretium*), is as close as one gets to a modern theory of money in antiquity.

29. Watson, *Aurelian*, 132–6.

nearly wholly symbolic: there were now to be standards, and the standards were to be enforced. In that perspective, one can do no better than cite David Potter's insightful suggestion that Aurelian intended nothing more (and nothing less) than the replacement of coins bearing the portraits of earlier emperors with others bearing his. That these would advertise an economically meaningless but morally severe sense of rigor is wholly in keeping with Aurelian's claim to have renewed the world.[30]

The empire of the sun

The final months of Aurelian in Rome are credited with a whirlwind of activity. Some of it was directed strictly at the populace of the capital: for example, we are told that he added quantities of pork to the food distribution there. We are likewise told that he conducted a systematic review of government accounts and cracked down severely on extortion and judicial improprieties. Oversight of the food supply and a passion for good governance are among the most conventional characteristics of good emperors. Of course, this does not mean that Aurelian did not take such measures, and their existence within the discourse of rulership perhaps makes it all the more likely that he would have done so. But we should be wary. The long arc of the conventional narrative of the third century makes the reign of Gallienus its nadir, and that logic has long demanded that Aurelian and his successors be described as earnest and good, even if they achieved nothing.

Much is made in modern scholarship of Aurelian's religiosity. He felt a special devotion to a particular instantiation of the sun god, Sol Invictus, the Unconquered Sun. Sol had been worshipped at Rome for centuries under several names. In a wholly traditional act, Aurelian identified the guise of the sun that had aided him as distinct from those already worshipped at Rome. Or perhaps one might say, he insisted that his special relationship with the sun should receive articulation in cult distinct from consideration given in cult to other relationships between persons (or the populace) and Sol. (For what it's worth, Aurelian seems to have received this aid from Sol Invictus in his battle against Zenobia at Emesa, and the Sol he worshipped was none other than Elagabal under a Latin name and with Roman rites [SHA *Aurelianus* 25.6].) To this end, Aurelian built a massive

---

30. Potter, *Empire at Bay*, 273.

new temple to Sol Invictus at Rome and celebrated the god on coins. Naturally, the building of temples to gods in consequence of the receipt of aid in battle was a wholly traditional act, and Aurelian's interest in Sol receives exactly one sentence of commentary in each ancient narrative of his reign that bothers to mention it, where it is universally observed only that he built an expensive temple.[31]

That temple was dedicated on December 25, 274. The historical curiosity that the temple of Sol Invictus celebrated its anniversary on Christmas has, needless to say, attracted a great deal of attention from syncretists, to be set alongside late ancient imagery of Christ as charioteer in the reconstruction of some grand history of a so-called solar theology. This is all humbug.

Aurelian was killed the next year, 275, at a minor staging post called Caenophurium on the road just west of Byzantium. It seems to have been a fundamentally irrational act by a low-level administrator, perhaps fearful that his own illegalities were about to be discovered. Not only is this the story put forth in all extant narratives, but it seems clear enough that no plan, nor even any private ambition, was then mature enough to impel a rapid succession.[32]

Waiting for Diocles (275–84)

With the conference of Aurelian with the Iuthungi in 272, we arrived at the last fragment of the histories of Dexippus. Although select sources of late antiquity clearly preserve local traditions of some accuracy regarding specific events – the sack of Augustodunum by Victorinus recalled in a later panegyric (p. 213); the attention paid by John Malalas to the history of Antioch (p. 210) – on the whole the years between 272 and 284 are nearly unknowable outside the sort of bare-bones rehearsal of accessions and deaths reported in the Latin breviary tradition of the later fourth century. Drawing on the data provided by Tony Honoré, I have occasionally cited the production of imperial rescripts as an index of the vitality of government in any given emperor's reign. (I have essayed a more robust framework for assessing such vitality in Chapter 8, Table 1.) In

---

31. Eutropius, 9.15.1; Aurelius Victor, *Caes.* 35.7; SHA *Aurelianus* 35.3.
32. Aurelius Victor, *Caes.* 35.8; Eutropius, 9.15.2; *Epit. de Caes.* 35.8; SHA *Aurelianus* 36.

summary, the figures for emperors within the canon from 260–84 are remarkably low: Gallienus as sole ruler 10; Claudius 1; Aurelian 7; Probus 4; Carus, Carinus and Numerianus 9; Carinus and Numerianus 18; Carinus 3. By way of comparison, Gordian III, who ruled just a few months longer than Probus, is credited with 269 private rescripts. We cannot now say how reliably these figures track the actual production of rescripts in each reign, but the numbers are striking nonetheless. These reigns are poorly attested – they are poorly known – in part because, one senses, they were hanging on by their fingertips.

Conventional narratives of the reign of Aurelian cast it as a turning point, during which the empire turned a corner and from fragmentation and chaos began to rise again to stability and strength. But nothing about the reigns of Tacitus or Florianus (hint: they are not present in the list above), or indeed any of their successors, suggests that Aurelian's considerable military successes had restored charisma to his office, in such a way that successors to Aurelian were protected by the aura of office from disgruntled underlings raising rebellions on the pettiest of grounds. Likewise, one is often told that Aurelian's coinage reform should be considered a testimonial to the solvency of the central government in the aftermath of reunification and the recovery of its greater tax base. That may just be so, but the extraordinary inflation that continued for nearly a quarter century thereafter makes it hard to credit Aurelian in this domain, either.

That said, there can be little doubt that the reunification of the empire contributed in the long run to the restoration of the social order and economic stability in the Mediterranean at large. But that achievement was by and large the work of the next generation. (It was aided, too, by the long peace on the eastern frontier that followed on the last campaign of Sapor: the successors to Sapor, Hormizd I [272–3], Vahran I [273–6] and Vahran II [276–93] undertook virtually no aggression toward Rome. As the shortness of their reigns suggests, the death of Sapor introduced a period of political instability in the Sasanian empire.)

The death of Aurelian issued in a period of some confusion: no plan had evidently been made for the succession, and the event was unexpected enough that no factions rapidly emerged. The situation was taken by the *Historia Augusta* as an opportunity to offer an indictment of the age as a whole. Supposing (falsely) that six months passed without an emperor, the text proclaims:

> What concord prevailed among the soldiers! How great was the peace for the people! How weighty was the authority of the Senate! No *tyrannus*, no usurper emerged, while the world was governed by the collaborative judgment of Senate, army and people. (SHA *Tacitus* 2.2)

The suggestions that the empire was better off without an emperor – or at least the sort of emperor it had recently had – and that without an emperor to kill, there was no point in seizing power, are biting observations on the nature of third-century politics. They are also astute. The Conclusion will take up much the same theme, namely, the role played by the institutions of government in the survival of the third-century crisis.

That said, the recourse of the army to the apparently retired general and senator Marcus Claudius Tacitus must reflect a consensus among the leading generals, as well as many individual decisions on their part not to instigate their own acclamation. Viewed in those terms, it bears structural comparison with the nomination of relatively junior officers as emperor by a general staff apparently unwilling to elevate one of its own members (on this pattern see p. 115).

Tacitus may in fact have been in Italy when chosen in late fall 275, and so may have entered into office as consul on January 1, 276 in the city of Rome. But he soon left for the east. The Greek tradition credits Tacitus with decisive action against the still problematic raids by Black Sea Goths, and indeed the raids of 276 were the last serious attacks of their kind.[33] Aurelius Victor, by contrast, credits him only with executing by torture the murderers of Aurelian, while Eutropius, who seems to feel pressure to admire Tacitus, offers the concessive that he was unable to achieve anything because he was murdered in the sixth month of his reign (Aurelius Victor, *Caes.* 36; Eutropius, 9.16). In a sort of historical doublet to the triad Claudius–Quintillus–Aurelian, Tacitus' praetorian prefect Marcus Annius Florianus, who appears also to have been Tacitus' brother, was acclaimed by the army in Asia. But Florianus had no sooner started for Rome and the west than he learned of the simultaneous acclamation of Marcus Aurelius Probus, a commander on the eastern front. Florianus moved to come to grips with Probus but was killed by his own soldiers before fighting began. To adopt the perspective of the *Historia Augusta*, Florianus reigned – he minted

---

33. Zosimus, 1.63.1; Zonaras, 12.28; see also SHA *Tacitus* 12.2.

coins, and inscriptions survive that display his titles – but his sole actions in the sixty or eighty or possibly eighty-eight days that he was emperor were to march west, then east, then die.[34]

The reign of Probus presents a series of contrasts: on the one hand, he was constantly on the move. The vast array of military campaigns with which he is reliably credited can only be accommodated to his six-year reign by supposing that he marched nearly the whole time he was not fighting. On the other, he was also confronted with a remarkably high number of usurpers and, it seems, bouts of severe local unrest.[35] On a personal level, the high number of usurpers, not least in contrast with Aurelian, suggests a level of restiveness in the higher officer corps that in earlier reigns we have associated with imperial indolence. Probus was not lazy, but it may be that he was very bad at his job.

More seriously, the reign of Probus suggests in an overwhelming way that the fundamental problems of the third-century empire had not been solved. The Goths excepted, the borders remained remarkably porous and Italy in danger. We are told, for example, that Probus rushed west after his accession because "all the Gauls had been in upheaval after the death of Postumus and, after the death of Aurelian, they were seized by the Germans" (SHA *Probus* 13.5; see also Aurelius Victor, *Caes.* 37.3). It might be, of course, that the death of Aurelian is employed here simply as a chronological marker, but we have already observed that Rome's enemies on the Rhine and Danube frontiers seem consistently to have exploited instability within the empire to their advantage. Hence, the ongoing failure of imperial politics continued immediately upon Aurelian's death to induce military aggression, which can only have weakened the political system further.

Military aggression weakened the system in numerous ways. The trouble in Gaul awaited action from Probus because Tacitus had evidently not delegated global authority over the front to a general with sufficient resources to handle it. Tacitus was no fool and wanted no rival. The fact that only Philip and Priscus and Valerian and Gallienus had proved capable of overseeing two fronts at once without the one killing the other (I bracket the question whether

34. Sixty days: SHA *Tacitus* 14.2. Eighty days: Eutropius, 9.16. 88 days: the Codex Calendar of 354 (*Chron. min.* 1:148).
35. Dietmar Kienast, *Römische Kaisertabelle: Grundzüge einer römischen Kaiser-chronologie* (Darmstadt: Wissenschaftliche Buchgesellschaft, 1990) s.v. Probus lists a conservative three *Gegenkaisern*, but other local figures might be named.

they did their jobs *well*) exposes the fatal consequences of the empire's continued reliance on dynastic succession. But imperial incapacity or neglect is precisely what had generated the various forms of local self-help that characterized the long reign of Gallienus, whether in Gaul, Palmyra or even Athens. In the long run, the central government did not want local militias of any kind, let alone ones led by some self-declared *dux Romanorum*.

Probus himself had no solution for these problems. He achieved enough in the west to name himself Gothicus in 277 and Gothicus Maximus and Germanicus Maximus in 279, and upon his return to Rome in 281 he celebrated a triumph. But when in 282 he marched east he was killed at Sirmium: the Latin tradition preserves no knowledge of the circumstances and supposes a random act of violence on the part of the soldiery, while the Greek insists that the act had been planned by his praetorian prefect, Marcus Aurelius Carus, a Narbonensian Gaul.[36]

Carus tried to solve the problem of political stability using the tried-and-failed method of elevating his sons, Carinus and Numerianus, of whom Carinus was the elder, perhaps in his early thirties, while Numerianus was closer to thirty. There is little evidence that Carus was recognized by the Senate, nor that the Senate was asked its opinion. Carinus was sent west to deal with the inevitable irruption of Germans that Probus' death had occasioned, while Carus and Numerianus went east, there to mount a campaign against Sasanian Persia.[37] They could offer the justification that Rome needed finally to avenge the capture of Valerian. In addition, for once Rome could exploit the internal weakness of an enemy, rather than have its own weakness exploited by others.

As it happens, while on campaign in late summer 283, Carus suffered the finest imperial death of the third century, even now at its gloaming: he was struck by lightning. (Or, to adopt the language of Eutropius [9.18.1], "he was killed by the force of a divine thunderbolt.") Whatever the truth of the matter, the death of Numerianus

36. Aurelius Victor, *Caes.* 37.3–4; Eutropius, 9.17.3; *Epit. de Caes.* 37.4; SHA *Probus* 21.1–4. By contrast, see Zosimus, 1.71.4–5 and Zonaras, 12.29: Carus is acclaimed by the legions of Raetia and Noricum and Probus is slain by his own soldiers when they learn the news.

37. Aurelius Victor, *Caes.* 38.1–2: "Therefore Carus, who then held power as praetorian prefect, was clothed in the imperial garb, with his sons Carinus and Numerian as Caesars. And because, the death of Probus becoming known, some barbarians had seized the occasion to attack, the elder son was sent to strengthen Gaul, while Carus took Numerian as his companion straight to Mesopotamia."

nearly outdid that of his father: he was murdered by his uncle-in-law and praetorian prefect Aper, who then lacked the courage or power base to elevate himself. He therefore put it about that Numerianus had a disease of the eye and could not be exposed to the light of day. It was only the stench of Numerianus' decaying body that exposed the lie. Aper was immediately killed.[38] The local officer corps chose as emperor a junior member of its number, a Danubian named Gaius Valerius Diocles, whose earlier career is, stunningly, virtually entirely unknown. Upon his acclamation in November 284, Diocles took office under a new name, Marcus Aurelius Gaius Valerius Diocletianus. He had no intention of being the new Probus or new Aurelian, thank you very much. And a new era began.

We cannot close the curtain on the third century without disposing of Carinus, who appears, frankly, to have been no worse than many a third-century emperor. He mounted campaigns in the north in 283 and 284 and took the titles Germanicus Maximus and Britannicus Maximus (*ILS* 608). He faced three usurpers. One sought to exploit the death of Carinus' father, Carus: this was Marcus Aurelius Julianus, who minted coins at Siscium before being killed in Illyricum. The second was Carinus' own praetorian prefect Sabinus Julianus, who was simply fed up with Carinus but acted after the death of Numerianus. The third, of course, was Diocletian. Carinus successfully suppressed the first Julianus in 283 and the second Julianus in 284/5. He was betrayed to Diocletian by his own next praetorian prefect, Tiberius Claudius Aurelius Aristobulus. At least when the last of the third-century emperors died, no one else's blood was shed for him, nor, it is likely, any tears.

---

38. SHA *Carus* 12; Aurelius Victor, *Caes.* 38.6–8; Eutropius, 9.18.2.

CHAPTER 10

Conclusion

The power of arguments over the nature and importance of the third-century crisis derives in part from *a priori* interpretive choices made by their advocates. Those who deny the existence or importance of the crisis discount imperial politics in favor of social and economic life; they favor material over textual evidence; they privilege regional over macro-regional assessment. At the same time, they deny importance to the broader connectivity often deemed a hallmark of empire and likewise decline to credit state institutions with the capacity deeply to affect local life. In some form, these are all interpretive positions with important advocates in contemporary scholarship. In strong form, none seems to me tenable.

This book has staked out a different argument. The upheaval in politics that followed the murder of Commodus set patterns of conduct that worked profound damage in nearly every province of the empire. On the most superficial level, Septimius Severus and his peers substantially weakened the conventional structures of legitimation that had protected emperors in office, and no alternative method for the construction of a social consensus emerged. The result was cycles of violence that exposed fatal weaknesses in the political system.

That violence, and its effects in domestic politics, substantially exacerbated the harm suffered by the state in foreign wars. Weak emperors could little afford to elevate competent generals to overarching commands along entire fronts, while aggression along those fronts was undoubtedly heightened in proportion as Rome's enemies perceived emperors as weak and the empire as distracted. Furthermore, in the case of Sasanian Persia the course of third-century history might well have looked very different had Severus not attacked the Parthian empire in a war of choice in the 190s, disturbing a long-standing *modus vivendi* – a situation exacerbated by Philip's apparent repudiation of the treaty he himself had negotiated, an act almost undoubtedly to be attributed to fear of the domestic consequences of having negotiated so one-sided a treaty in the first place.

At the level of economics, we can neither quantify nor adequately map the economic and social harm worked by the civil wars alone, bracketing foreign invasion, but the aggregate effects of both were enormous. Massive loss of life could only be addressed by intensive recruiting, which must have affected the labor supply in ways that diminished both agricultural productivity and the capacity of local labor markets to support infrastructural repair. What is more, such energy as existed within local economies was often distracted by the terror occasioned by invasion: in the east, huge outlays were directed toward rebuilding city walls; in the west, many city walls were rebuilt, too, but often populations removed themselves to more easily defended hilltop positions. In the process, some regions of agricultural production were abandoned. In respect of both numbers and settlement patterns, the demography of the third century displays signs of retrenchment and retreat.

Likewise in the domain of monetary policy. The state clearly faced huge shortfalls in bullion already in the Severan period, which it met through a combination of heightened extraction and debasement of the coinage. But political upheaval and crises in foreign affairs raced far ahead of the system's capacity to address these challenges: new armies acclaiming new emperors wanted ever larger donatives, while newly aggressive enemies wanted tribute. In consequence massive transfer payments flowed from center to periphery and from civilian to statal coffers, well beyond the speed of circulation's ability to return the money to those who would soon need to pay it again. The economic situation can only have been made worse by the fragmentation of the imperial polity, which was itself an effect of political and military upheaval.

This is to say nothing of the problems in trade that must have resulted from doubts about legitimacy of the currency itself. As the *Historia Augusta* observed, every would-be emperor had to mint coins. But the politics of public memory must have made people reluctant to accept coins bearing the portrait of failed usurpers or those of the emperors of Gaul post-reintegration, for that matter. What was to prevent the government from repudiating such coin as legal tender? Risk increased. Prices rose.

That said, in very significant respects, the political culture of the empire remained unitary. The coins of the usurpers evoked in precise and deliberate fashion the designs, legends and denominations of the imperial coinage. The contest among candidates was merely over one's place in the system, not over the nature of the system itself.

What is more, all those actual and would-be emperors spent their money on similar things – when, that is, they had any to spend. They subvented public works and local institutions; they sought to sustain the public accommodations central to Roman urbanism; and they advertised their status as Roman emperors in doing so.

More importantly, continuity in the ideology of imperial government as it was advertised from above was matched by expectations of continuity, indeed, demands for it from below. We might distinguish three manifestations of this. First, purely local institutions continued to coordinate their actions with each other and in space and time by reference to the functioning of imperial government, even when it was not obviously functioning at all. The most clear-cut example of this derives from Egyptian texts in fall 270, when Palmyra was asserting control over Egypt even as Aurelian sought to succeed Claudius in central Europe. The Romans had dated by consuls, and the consuls were named by the emperor. The marking of time and the keeping of historical memory were thus explicitly political acts. How should one name the year, if the rulership of Egypt were in doubt?

The common answer, revealed above all by papyri from Oxyrhynchus but not only from there, was to employ some such phrase as "Under the consuls of the present year."[1] In other words, the coordination of local and imperial continued in spite of an awareness of the deep uncertainty then obtaining in the domain of geopolitics. A confidence in the Romanness of the world outside and above the local abided. To these texts we might compare others that continue to name Valerian as partner to Gallienus long after his capture by Sapor.[2] These are of two sorts: rescripts from the imperial archives redacted into the late antique law codes and a contemporary papyrus. The nature of the error thus differs from the first sort to the second, but certainly the papyrus is likely to attest an unreflective moment of confidence in institutional continuity, beside which the idiosyncratic identity of the emperor(s) was epiphenomenal.

---

1. See J. R. Rea, *POxy.* vol. 40, pp. 16 and 20, together with *POxy.* 2906ii, 2907i and 2907ii. See also Dominic Rathbone, "The dates of the recognition in Egypt of the emperors from Caracalla to Diocletianus," *ZPE* 62 (1986), 101–31 at 123.
2. Ingemar König, *Die gallischen Usurpatoren von Postumus bis Tetricus* (Munich: Beck, 1981), 25.

A second form taken by demands from below for continuity in governance consists of those petitions that ask imperial officials or the emperor himself to abide by long-standing principles, whether of law or politics. For example, the heart of the claim made upon Julius Priscus by the villagers of the middle Euphrates was as follows (see also pp. 89 and 115–16):

> Since, therefore, the case has not thus far obtained resolution, and our fellow villagers are trying to expel us from the lands on which we reside and to force the issue before judgment, and *since the divine constitutions, which you more than all others know and venerate, ordain that those finding themselves in possession of goods should remain so until judgment*, for this reason we have fled to you and we ask you to command by your subscription that Claudius Ariston, *vir egregius*, procurator in the area of Appadana, who superintends the diocese, should preserve everything unharmed and should forbid the use of force before your blessed visit to the region when, obtaining our desire, we will be able to render Your Fortune our eternal thanks. (*P.Euphrates* 1, ll. 10–16)

The villagers from Thrace who petitioned Gordian III for aid against illegal exactions employed a similar move, reminding that emperor that he "had on many occasions stated in [his] rescripts" "that in your most happy and everlasting times the villages should be inhabited and prosper" (see p. 192). Neither party cited – perhaps neither needed to cite – the "divine constitutions" or the many rescripts pertinent to their claim. Support for the rule of law and purely local flourishing lay at the heart of imperial rhetoric and had done so for two centuries. It hardly mattered whether Gordian or Philip had themselves made such claims: they were called upon to redeem them, as emanating from the office they now occupied.

The papyrus from the middle Euphrates makes explicit a further point, namely, that the principled claims regarding the nature of government that emanated from the top were expected by those below to permeate the workings of government as a whole. We have already seen that Alexander Severus offered just this assurance to the empire at the outset of his reign (for the context see p. 70):

> For neither my own welfare nor anything else will be a concern for me except to increase the empire through love of humankind and doing good, in order that my own conduct might stand as an example of the greatest moderation for the governors of the provinces and the procurators sent out by me, whom I dispatch after a most rigorous examination. Let the governors of the provinces

learn more and more with how great zeal they should look after the provinces over which they are appointed, when it is possible for them all to see the emperor conducting the duties of kingship with so much orderliness and wisdom and self-control. (Oliver, no. 275)

But this expectation – this hope, that Alexander would indeed set an example and enjoin good conduct on his subordinates – was also implicit in practice. The erection of an inscription displaying an edict or rescript amounted to an endorsement, however contingent, limited, and self-interested, of the mechanism that had produced the ruling it contained. It likewise expressed the wish and perhaps the expectation that viewers of the inscription – whether civilians, soldiers or officials – would abide by its normative force.

Often crucial to the local erection of imperial texts was the mimicking of their form: inscriptions in the east might use Latin protocols or dating formulae; texts repeat some form of direct address to a subordinate, who was of course not the primary audience for the inscribed version; they quote verbatim phrases announcing that the text is an extract or authenticated copy, when the inscription is that once removed; or they repeat language in the first person appropriate to a signature, though the signature was naturally not reproduced in the transfer to stone.[3] Where Roman government itself was concerned, this was, of course, a response to a deep problem at the level of practice, namely the couching of officialdom in modes of deportment and display that signaled its authority and removal from the everyday. We may acquire some appreciation for the deep association achieved between Roman authority and its symbols from the *Acts* of Pionius. There, when the local magistrate is urged by the crowd to punish those who refuse to sacrifice, he responds: "But the *fasces* do not precede us, such that we have the power [to punish]" (*Acta Pionii* 10.4). The text does more than gesture to the fact that Roman magisterial authority was symbolized by its own distinctive apparatus – authority that arrogated to itself sole power to inflict capital punishment. Through its diction ("precede us"), it also alludes to the ceremonial form by which *fasces* were known: special attendants, lictors, carried the *fasces* in procession before any magistrate holding power of command.

The trappings of Roman power and the conduct of Roman officialdom thus came to occupy an archetypal position in the high

3. See pp. 46, 61, 189 and 192.

imperial imaginary. This was so in religious life, where one finds
around the third-century empire small statuettes of local gods
dressed in military uniforms or carrying military standards.[4] It was
also true in religious discourse, where the titles and hierarchical
structure of Roman officialdom become a dominant source of
imagery for describing the rule of god in heaven.[5] And it was true in
the organization and conduct of non-statal institutions. We have
already seen that the form of Christian martyr acts, in mimicking
that of official records of proceedings, effectively endorsed the
authority of the Roman state in the recording and preservation of
memory. To this we might add the profound influence of the Roman
Senate, in its rules and procedures, upon the conduct of official
bodies around the empire, not least the councils of the Christian
church.[6]

All this was true despite the ebb and flow and regional variation
in the popularity of particular emperors. Apart from the efforts
made at the center to control public and popular memory of earlier
reigns, the haphazard nature of the evidence for the erasure of names
– and likewise for honors to those officially consecrated – strongly
suggests that local feeling played an important role in the construction of posthumous esteem. But the existence of discrepant local
memories of specific emperors – and the role of personality in popular memory – should not distract us from the overriding historical
importance of statal institutions in shaping expectations of government and the political and social imaginary of provincial populations. The empire's weathering of the third-century crisis – the very
form taken by the splinter states and oppositional movements in the
period – testifies to the sustaining power in a period of crisis of the
achievements of peace and ambitions of government.

4. Mikhail Rostovtzeff, "*Vexillum* and Victory," *JRS* 32 (1942), 92–106; Ernst
Kantorowicz, "Gods in uniform," *Proceedings of the American Philosophical Society*
105 (1961), 368–93 = Kantorowicz, *Selected Studies* (Locust Valley, NY: Augustin,
1965), 7–24, a lovely volume with fresh plates; Geza Alföldy, "Die Krise des Imperium
Romanum und die Religion Roms," in Werner Eck, ed., *Religion und Gesellschaft in der
römischen Kaiserzeit: Kolloquium zu Ehren von Friedrich Vittinghoff* (Cologne: Bohlau,
1989), 53–102 at 81 and 92.
5. Clifford Ando, *Religion et gouvernement dans l'empire romain* (Paris: École des
Hautes Études en Sciences Sociales, 2013), chapter 1.
6. Pierre Batiffol, "Le règlement des premiers conciles africains et le règlement du sénat
romain," *Bulletin d'Ancienne Littérature et d'Archéologie Chrétiennes* 3 (1913), 3–19;
Francis Dvornik, "The authority of the state in the oecumenical councils," *Christian East*
14 (1934), 95–108.

Emperors and usurpers

The list below is neither as complete nor as precise as one might wish.[1] It is incomplete because the category of usurper is necessarily elastic. Appearances to one side, it is imprecise because our data are often faulty, and where they are not faulty, they are often fictive. (For example, Caracalla advertised the anniversary of his reign on a date other than the one on which he was first elevated.) Where possible, I have listed the dates on which individuals were elevated to the rank of Augustus, though I have listed some Caesars who died before their elevation to formal co-rule.

Pertinax	193
Didius Julianus	193
Septimius Severus	193–211
Pescennius Niger	193–4
Clodius Albinus	193–7
Caracalla	198–217
Geta	209–11
Macrinus	217–18
Diadumenianus	218
Elagabalus	218–22
Seleucus	?
Uranius	?
Gellius Maximus	?
Verus	?
Severus Alexander	222–35
L. Seius Sallustius	225(?)–7(?)
Taurinus	?
Ovinius Camillus	?
Maximinus Thrax	235–8
C. Petronius Magnus	235
(Titus) Quartinus	235
Gordian I	238

1. This table is reproduced from Olivier Hekster, *Rome and its Empire*, AD *193–284* (Edinburgh: Edinburgh University Press, 2008), 155–6, with minor modifications.

Gordian II	238
Balbinus	238
Pupienus	238
Gordian III	238–44
Sabinianus	240
Philip the Arab	244–9
Pacatianus	248
Jotapianus	249–?
Silbannacus[2]	?
Sponsianus[3]	?
Decius	249–51
L. (?) Priscus	250
Julius Valens Licinianus	250
Herennius Decius	251
Hostilianus	251
Trebonianus Gallus	251–3
Volusianus	251–3
Uranius Antoninus[4]	253
Aemilianus	253
Valerian	253–60
Gallienus	253–68
Valerianus Iunior (Caesar)	257–8
Saloninus	260
Ingenuus	260
P. C(ornelius?) Regalianus	260 (?)
Macrianus	260–1
Quietus	260–1
Piso	261
Valens	261
L. Mussius Aemilianus	261–2
Aureolous	?–268
Claudius II Gothicus	268–70
Quintillus	270
Aurelian	270–5
Domitian	271
Urbanus	271/2
Septimius	271/2

2. Silbannacus is known solely from coinage and cannot be assigned to the reign of Philip with confidence.
3. Sponsianus is likewise known solely from coinage and cannot be assigned to the reign of Philip with confidence.
4. Although Uranius Antoninus employed imperial titulature, there is no evidence he intended to compete for imperial rule or to establish an autonomous polity based at Emesa.

Tacitus	275–6
Florianus	276
Probus	276–82
Bonosus	280
Proculus	280–1
Carus	282–3
Carinus	283–5
Numerianus	283–4
Diocletian	284–305
Gallic empire	**(260–74)**
Postumus	260–9
Laelianus	269
Marius	269
Victorinus	269–71
Tetricus	271–4
Tetricus II (Caesar)	273–4
Faustinus	273
Palmyra	**(260?–72)**
Septimius Odaenathus[5]	260–7
Vaballathus	267–72
Zenobia	267–72
Antiochus	272

5. Odaenathus did not proclaim himself emperor.

Chronology

Political/Military	Religious/Cultural	Events elsewhere
192 (December 31) Accession of Pertinax		
193 (March 28) Death of Pertinax; accession of Julianus (April 9) Accession of Septimius Severus (c. April 19) Accession of Pescennius Niger Severus appoints Clodius Albinus Caesar (June 1) Deposition of Julianus		
194 Severus defeats Pescennius Niger; conducts first Parthian campaign		
195 Severus appoints Caracalla Caesar; Clodius Albinus declares himself Augustus (late 195) Fall of Byzantium		
197 Severus defeats Clodius Albinus	197 Tertullian's Apology	
197–8 Caracalla named *Imperator destinatus*, later Augustus		198 Severus captures Ctesiphon
197–202 Severus and Caracalla campaign in the East		
199–201 Severus in Egypt		
203–4 Severus in Africa	203 Arch of Septimius Severus dedicated in Rome; Perpetua and Felicitas martyred in Carthage	

Political/Military	Religious/Cultural	Events elsewhere
205 Consulship of Caracalla and Geta; execution of Plautianus		
208 Severus, Caracalla and Geta depart Italy for Britain		208 Accession of Ardashir in Persia
211 (February 4) Death of Severus (February) Death of Geta; Caracalla sole emperor	211 The jurist Papinian murdered at Caracalla's instigation	208–14 Parthian succession contested between Vologaeses V and Artabanus V
212 The Antonine Constitution		
213 Caracalla campaigns in Germany		
215 Massacre at Alexandria		
216 Hearing in Antioch over tax status of temple at Dmeir		
217 (April 8) Death of Caracalla Accession of Macrinus		
218 (May 16) Accession of Elagabalus (June) Death of Macrinus		
220 Consulship of Elagabalus and Comazon		
221 Severus Alexander named Caesar		
222 (March) Death of Elagabalus and accession of Severus Alexander Ulpian assumes office of *Praefectus Annonae* and then Praetorian Prefect		
223 Death of Ulpian		
		224 Artabanus V defeated by Ardashir
	225–30 The Ludovisi battle-sarcophagus	226 Ardashir declared King of Kings of Persia

Political/Military	Religious/Cultural	Events elsewhere
229 Consulship of Severus Alexander and Cassius Dio		
		230 Ardashir attacks Nisibis, then Cappadocia and Syria
232 Alexander campaigns against Ardashir	232 Origen moves to Caesarea; birth of Porphyry	
234 Alexander campaigns in Germany; Maximinus acclaimed		
235 Alexander and his mother are murdered; Senate confirms accession of Maximinus; Maximinus defeats the Alemanni; elevates his son to Caesar		235–8 Ardashir campaigns annually against Rome
236–7 Maximinus campaigns against the Sarmatians and Dacians		236 Sasanians capture Nisibis and Carrhae
238 Gordian I and II acclaimed in Carthage; Pupienus, Balbinus and Gordian III acclaimed at Rome; death of Maximinus; accession of the Gordiani, followed by accession of Pupienus and Balbinus, followed (July 9) by accession of Gordian III		
238–41 Tullius Menophilus campaigns in Moesia	240–5 The Achilles-sarcophagus	240 Ardashir takes Hatra, dies in April; accession of Sapor; Sapor attacks Mesopotamia
241 Timesitheus appointed praetorian prefect		
242–4 Rome campaigns against Sapor, with Gordian in charge from 243	242 (March 20) Mani begins preaching Manichaeism	
244 Death of Gordian III; accession of Philip the Arab		244 Sapor defeats Rome and compels humiliating treaty

Political/Military	Religious/Cultural	Events elsewhere
245/6 Philip campaigns along the Danube		
	247–8 Dionysius is bishop of Alexandria	
248 Roman millennium (April 21)	248 Origen pens *Contra Celsum*; Cyprian becomes bishop of Carthage	
248/9 Usurpations of Jotapianus and Pacatianus		
249 Death of Philip the Arab at Beroea; accession of Decius	249/50 Edict enjoining universal sacrifice	
	250 Birth of Iamblichus	
251 Death of Decius; accession of Gallus	251 Cyprian pens *De lapsis* and *De catholicae ecclesiae unitate*	
252 Massive rupture of Danubian border; Goths sail the Hellespont and attack Asia Minor		252 Sapor drives Tiridates from the throne in Armenia; attacks Roman empire, devastating Syria; rise of Uranius Antoninus at Emesa
253 Aemilianus acclaimed in Moesia; Gallus moves against him; Valerian moves toward Italy; death of Gallus; death of Aemilianus; Valerian acclaimed and appoints Gallienus Augustus	253 Death of Origen	
256 Goths sail the Hellespont		
257 Gallienus headquartered on the Rhine	257 Valerian launches new persecution of Christians	257 Sapor captures Dura
258 Gallienus defeats the Alemanni near Milan	258 (September 14) Martyrdom of Cyprian	
		259 Sapor captures Nisibis

Political/Military	Religious/Cultural	Events elsewhere
260 Valerian defeated and captured by Sapor; Macrianus and Quietus acclaimed; Postumus proclaimed emperor in Gaul	260 Dionysius I is bishop of Rome; Gallienus ends the persecution of Christians	260 Sapor captures Valerian and moves at will through Syria, Cilicia and Cappadocia; Odaenathus of Palmyra rises against Sapor and assumes military leadership of eastern frontier as *corrector totius orientis*
261 Macrianus and Quietus defeated by Aureolus		
262 Odaenathus defeats Persians	262 Arch of Gallienus dedicated	262 Odaenathus campaigns against Sapor
	264 Gallienus initiated into Eleusinian mysteries at Athens	
		265/6 Odaenathus campaigns against Sapor, recovers Mesopotamia and sacks Ctesiphon
267 Aureolus revolts, besieged at Milan		267 Death of Odaenathus; Zenobia assumes rule of Palmyra in name of Vaballathus
267/8 Gothic invasion reaches Athens; defense organized by Dexippus		
268 Death of Gallienus during siege at Milan; accession of Claudius		
269 Death of Postumus in Gaul; accession and death of Marius in Gaul; accession of Victorinus in Gaul		
270 Coordinated campaign against sea-faring Goths; death of Claudius; accession of Aurelian	270 Death of Plotinus	270 Zenobia declares Palmyrene sovereignty over Arabia and Egypt; Vaballathus assumes Roman imperial titles

Political/Military	Religious/Cultural	Events elsewhere
270/1 Aurelian campaigns along the Danube; compels Iuthungi to parlay; surrenders transdanubian Dacia		
271 Death of Victorinus; accession of Tetricus in Gaul	271 Construction of new walls for Rome commences	
272 Aurelian defeats Zenobia		272 Death of Sapor; accession of Hormizd I
		273 Death of Hormizd I; accession of Vahran I
274 Aurelian defeats Tetricus; holds double triumph at Rome; coinage reform enacted	274 Aurelian builds temple to Sol Invictus	
275 Aurelian murdered; accession of Tacitus		
276 Death of Tacitus; Florianus acclaimed, marches, is murdered; Probus acclaimed		276 Death of Vahran I; accession of Vahram II
277 Probus campaigns against the Goths		
279 Probus campaigns against Goths again		
281 Probus celebrates a triumph at Rome		
282 Probus murdered; accession of Carus, who names his sons Carinus and Numerianus Caesars		
283 Carus struck by lightning		283 Vahram II makes peace with Rome
284 Numerianus murdered; Diocles acclaimed; assumes rule under name Diocletian		
285 Carinus murdered		

Guide to further reading

Sources

Historians of the third century are, alas, not well served by the primary providers of material in translation: Cassius Dio, Herodian and the *Historia Augusta* are all available in wholly reliable editions from the Loeb Classical Library, but the late antique sources generally are not. The histories of Eutropius and Aurelius Victor are available in translation with problematic commentary by H. W. Bird in the series "Translated Texts for Historians," but I know of no modern translation of the *Epitome de Caesaribus* into English. Likewise, there have been at least two translations of Zosimus into English, of which the modern version by Ronald T. Ridley is both rare and not wholly reliable. Those who can should instead consult the superb French edition by François Paschoud. Thomas Banchich and Eugene Lane have done historians a very great service by translating the portion of Zonaras' *History* covering the years 222–395. Jordanes has been translated multiple times: the so-called Princeton translation by Charles Christopher Mierow has been reprinted by several presses and, being out of copyright, can also be downloaded for free. Finally, those who find the Thirteenth Sibylline Oracle baffling will benefit from the superb scholarly apparatus in David Potter's edition; those who want a translation only, with very limited notes, can also consult the translation by J. J. Collins in J. H. Charlesworth, ed., *The Old Testament Pseudepigrapha* (Garden City, NY: Doubleday, 1983–5), pp. 453–68.

Christian texts of the third century are in general abundantly and well translated. A considerable percentage of surviving literary material – outside Origen – can be found in the series *Ante-Nicene Fathers*, edited by Alexander Roberts and James Donaldson, now out of copyright and available online from multiple sites. That said, the English translations of Cyprian's correspondence and the *Octavius* of Minucius Felix are particularly well served by the superb editions of Graeme Clarke. The *Apology* of Tertullian and the *Ecclesiastical History* of Eusebius are also available in Loeb editions.

The martyr acts constitute a special case. The edition and translation by Herbert Musurillo holds a near monopoly in the Anglophone world; it is, alas, deeply unreliable. Those who can should consult the collective edition produced under the leadership of A. A. R. Bastiaensen, who likewise edited and translated the *Life of Cyprian*, both works being published by the Fondazione Lorenzo Valla. There is likewise a superb translation and commentary on the *Acts* of Pionius in French by Louis Robert, a text published posthumously thanks to Glen Bowersock and Christopher Jones.

I know of no complete translation of the *Res Gestae* of Sapor into English, but several sections are translated in Michael Dodgeon and Samuel Lieu's wide-ranging sourcebook, *The Roman Eastern Frontier and the Persian Wars*. Their coverage is superb and the translations strike me as fine; the presentation and scholarly apparatus is, alas, not wholly user-friendly.

The bulk of the legal material derives from two sources: the collection of jurisprudential literature edited into a sourcebook under Justinian, known as the *Digest*; and the collection of imperial rescripts known as the *Code*. The *Digest* was translated into English by multiple hands and published under the editorial guidance of Alan Watson: it is on the whole extremely well done, though a small number of the translators are conspicuously less reliable than the rest. The *Code* has long been available in a baroque but not hugely misleading translation privately published by S. P. Scott. Bruce Frier of the University of Michigan is now editing a second modern English translation, to be published by Cambridge University Press, which, if accurate and appropriately priced, could have a transformative effect on the teaching of Roman history.

There exist a number of sourcebooks translating documentary material (or at least, primarily documentary material). James H. Oliver, *Greek Constitutions of Early Roman Emperors from Inscriptions and Papyri*, is not complete, nor was it brought up to date after his death; it is nonetheless an invaluable resource. Likewise, the collection of legal material translated by Allan Chester Johnson, P. R. Coleman-Norton and Frank Bourne, *Ancient Roman Statutes* (Austin: University of Texas Press, 1961), is wholly without peer and deserves a far wider audience than it seems to have received. Barbara Levick's *The Government of the Roman Empire* (London: Routledge, 2000) is superbly well done, though it not surprisingly concentrates on material from the Flavian and Antonine periods. Of the many sourcebooks on ancient religion, allow me simply to mention three: Mary Beard, John North and Simon Price, *Religions of Rome*, volume 2; Ramsay MacMullen and Eugene Lane, *Paganism and Christianity, 100–425 C.E.* (Minneapolis: Fortress Press, 1992); and J. Stevenson, *A New Eusebius: Documents illustrating the History of the Church to AD 337*, revised by W. H. C. Frend (London: SPCK, 1987).

Finally, Olivier Hekster has produced a wonderful sourcebook on the third century, *Rome and its Empire, AD 193–284*, also published by Edinburgh University Press, which includes supremely clear introductory essays.

Secondary material

In addition to his commentary on the thirteenth Sibylline Oracle, David Potter has also supplied the most rigorous and detailed narrative of the third century now available in English, *Empire at Bay*. Given the absence of serious alternatives in English, let me here draw attention to two fine works in French: Jean-Michel Carrié and Aline Rousselle's *L'empire romain en mutation des Sévères à Constantin 192–337* (Paris: Seuil, 1999) and Michel Christol's *L'empire romain du IIIe siècle: Histoire politique* (Paris: Éditions Errance, 1997).

A related genre of modern study, the imperial biography, also fails in the third century, for obvious reasons. That said, the three such studies that do exist in English are very useful: A. R. Birley's *Septimius Severus: The African Emperor*, Lukas de Blois's *The Policy of the Emperor Gallienus* (Leiden: Brill, 1976), and Alaric Watson's *Aurelian and the Third Century*.

Several superb regional histories offer extensive reflection on the third-century empire, especially Fergus Millar's *The Roman Near East, 31 BC–AD 337* and Stephen Mitchell's *Anatolia: Land, Men, and Gods in Asia Minor* (Oxford: Clarendon Press, 1993). For the west, nothing in English can compare to Christian Witschel's splendid *Krise, Rezession, Stagnation?*, but Anglophone readers can at least consult Witschel's summary, "Re-evaluating the Roman west in the 3rd c. A.D.," which offers a thorough bibliography.

The third century has been poorly served by the rash of handbooks, companions and reference works published in recent years. Many of these are of course excellent, and present reliable, detailed surveys of the urban economy or the Greek city, or trade, or the history of the family. But almost none of these treat the third century as a period or concentrate on third-century evidence. An important and delightful exception is Amy Richlin's "Sexuality in the Roman empire," in David Potter, ed., *A Companion to the Roman Empire* (Oxford: Blackwell, 2006); readers will also profit from Andrew Wilson's "Urban development in the Severan empire," in Simon Swain, Stephen Harrison and Jaś Elsner, *Severan Culture* (Cambridge: Cambridge University Press, 2007).

Finally, in this field as in many others, contemporary historians operate in terrain first charted in modern terms by Fergus Millar. So as not to clutter this page, I omit the details of their first publication and cite only the titles of the most relevant papers in volumes 2 and 3 of *Rome, the Greek World and the East*: "Condemnation to hard labour in the Roman empire, from the Julio-Claudians to Constantine"; "The equestrian career under the empire"; "P. Herennius Dexippus: The Greek world and the third-century invasions"; "The imperial cult and the persecutions"; "Italy and the Roman empire: Augustus to Constantine"; "The Greek east and Roman law"; "Paul of Samosata, Zenobia, and Aurelian"; and "Looking east from the classical world."

Works cited

Abbott, F. F., and A. C. Johnson, eds. 1926. *Municipal Administration in the Roman Empire*. Princeton: Princeton University Press.

Alföldy, Geza. 1989. "Die Krise des Imperium Romanum und die Religion Roms." In Werner Eck, ed., *Religion und Gesellschaft in der römischen Kaiserzeit: Kolloquium zu Ehren von Friedrich Vittinghoff*. Cologne: Bohlau, 53–102.

Ando, Clifford. 2000. *Imperial Ideology and Provincial Loyalty in the Roman Empire*. Berkeley: University of California Press.

Ando, Clifford. 2006. "The administration of the provinces." In David S. Potter, ed., *A Companion to the Roman Empire*. Oxford: Blackwell, 177–92.

Ando, Clifford. 2007. "Exporting Roman religion." In Jörg Rüpke, ed., *A Companion to Roman Religion*. Oxford: Blackwell, 429–45.

Ando, Clifford. 2008. "Aliens, ambassadors and the integrity of the empire." *Law & History Review* 26, 491–519.

Ando, Clifford. 2008. *The Matter of the Gods*. Berkeley: University of California Press.

Ando, Clifford. 2010. "From Republic to empire." In Michael Peachin, ed., *Oxford Handbook of Social Relations in the Roman World*. Oxford: Oxford University Press, 37–66.

Ando, Clifford. 2010. "Imperial identities." In Tim Whitmarsh, ed., *Local Knowledge and Microidentities in the Imperial Greek World*. Cambridge: Cambridge University Press, 17–45.

Ando, Clifford. 2011. "Law and the landscape of empire." In Stéphane Benoist and Anne Daguey-Gagey, eds, *Figures d'empire, fragments de mémoire: Pouvoirs, pratiques et discours, images et représentations, et identités sociales et religieuses dans le monde romain impérial. Ier s. av J.-C.–Ve s. ap. J.-C*. Paris: Presses Universitaires de Septentrion, 25–47.

Ando, Clifford. 2011. *Law, Language and Empire in the Roman Tradition*. Philadelphia: University of Pennsylvania Press.

Ando, Clifford. 2012. "Three revolutions in government." In Lucian Reinfandt, Stephan Prochazka and Sven Tost, eds, *Official Epistolography and the Languages of Power*. Vienna: Verlag der Österreichischen Akademie der Wissenschaften.

Ando, Clifford. 2012."Pluralisme juridique et l'intégration de l'empire." In Stéphane Benoist, Ségolène Demougin and Gerda de Kleijn, eds, *Impact of Empire X*. Leiden: Brill.

Ando, Clifford. 2013. *Religion et gouvernement dans l'empire romain*. Paris: École des Hautes Études en Sciences Sociales.

Ando, Clifford, and Jörg Rüpke, eds. 2006. *Religion and Law in Classical and Christian Rome*. Stuttgart: Steiner.

Baharal, D. 1996. *Victory of Propaganda. The Dynastic Aspect of the Imperial Propaganda of the Severi: The Literary and Archaeological Evidence, A.D. 193–225*. Oxford: Tempus Reparatum.

Baldini, Antonio. 1978. "Discendenti a Roma da Zenobia?" *ZPE* 30, 145–9.

Barfield, Thomas J. 2001. "The shadow empires: Imperial state formation along the Chinese–Nomad frontier." In S. Alcock, T. N. D'Altroy, K. D. Morrison and C. M. Sinopoli, eds, *Empires: Perspectives from Archaeology and History*. Cambridge: Cambridge University Press, 10–41.

Bastiaensen, A. A. R., ed. 1975. *Vita di Cipriano, Vita di Ambrogio, Vita di Agostino*. Milan: Fondazione Lorenzo Valla.

Bastiaensen, A. A. R., ed. 1987. *Atti e passioni dei martiri*. Milan: Fondazione Lorenzo Valla.

Batiffol, Pierre. 1913. "Le règlement des premiers conciles africains et le règlement du sénat romain." *Bulletin d'Ancienne Littérature et d'Archéologie Chrétiennes* 3, 3–19.

Bauzou, T. 1986. "Deux milliaires inédits de Vaballath en Jordanie du Nord." In Philip Freeman and David Kennedy, eds, *The Defence of the Roman and Byzantine East*. Oxford: British Archaeological Reports, 1–8.

Beard, Mary, John North and Simon Price. 1998. *Religions of Rome*, vol. 2. Cambridge: Cambridge University Press.

Belayche, Nicole. 2007. "Les immigrés orientaux à Rome et en Campanie: Fidélité aux *patria* et intégration sociale." In André Laronde and Jean Leclant, eds, *La Méditerranée d'une rive à l'autre: Culture classique et cultures périphériques*. Paris: Diffusion de Boccard, 243–60.

Belayche, Nicole, and Simon C. Mimouni, eds. 2003. *Les communautés religieuses dans le monde gréco-romain: Essais de définition*. Turnhout: Brepols.

Bendlin, A. 2000. "Looking beyond the civic compromise: Religious pluralism in late republican Rome." In Edward Bispham and Christopher Smith, eds, *Religion in Archaic and Republican Rome and Italy*. Edinburgh: Edinburgh University Press, 115–35.

Benjamin, A., and A. E. Raubitschek. 1959. "Arae Augusti." *Hesperia* 28, 65–85.

Birks, P., A. Rodger and J. S. Richardson. 1984. "Further aspects of the

Tabula Contrebiensis." *JRS* 74, 45–73.

Birley, A. R. 1988. *The African Emperor: Septimius Severus.* 2nd edition. London: Batsford.

Birley, Eric. 1978. "The religion of the Roman army, 1895–1977." *ANRW* 2.16.2, 1506–41.

Bowersock, G. W. 1983. *Roman Arabia.* Cambridge, MA: Harvard University Press.

Boyarin, Daniel. 2004. *Border Lines: The Partition of Judaeo-Christianity.* Philadelphia: University of Pennsylvania Press.

Brunt, Peter. 1977. "*Lex de imperio Vespasiani.*" *JRS* 67, 95–116.

Bruun, Christer. 2007. "The Antonine plague and the 'third-century crisis.'" In Olivier Hekster, Gerda de Kleijn and Daniëlle Slootjes, eds, *Crises and the Roman Empire.* Leiden: Brill, 201–17.

Bureth, P. 1964. *Les titulatures impériales dans les papyrus, les ostraca, et les inscriptions d'Égypte: 30 a.C.–284 p.C.* Brussels: Fondation Égyptologique Reine Élisabeth.

Burton, Graham P. 1975. "Proconsuls, assizes and the administration of justice under the empire." *JRS* 65, 92–106.

Campbell, J. B. 1984. *The Emperor and the Roman Army, 31 B.C.–A.D. 235.* Oxford: Clarendon Press.

Canepa, Matthew. 2009. *The Two Eyes of the Earth: Art and Ritual of Kingship Between Rome and Sasanian Iran.* Berkeley: University of California Press.

Canepa, Matthew. 2010. "Technologies of memory in early Sasanian Iran: Achaemenid sites and Sasanian identity." *American Journal of Archaeology* 114, 563–96.

Chaniotis, Angelos. 2010. "Megatheism: The search for the almighty god and the competition of cults." In Stephen Mitchell and Peter van Nuffelen, eds, *One God: Pagan Monotheism in the Roman Empire.* Cambridge: Cambridge University Press, 112–40.

Clarke, Graeme. 2005. "Third-century Christianity." *CAH²* XII, 589–671.

Coarelli, Filippo. 2007. *Rome and Environs: An Archaeological Guide,* trans. James J. Clauss and Daniel P. Harmon. Berkeley: University of California Press.

Compatangelo-Soussignan, R., and Christian-Georges Schwentzel, eds. 2007. *Étrangers dans la cité romaine. "Habiter une autre patrie": Des incolae de la République aux peuples fédérés du bas-empire.* Rennes: Presses Universitaires de Rennes.

Coriat, Jean-Pierre. 1997. *Le prince législateur: La technique législative des Sévères et les méthodes de création du droit impérial à la fin du Principat.* Rome: École Française de Rome.

Cotton, Hannah, Walter Cockle and Fergus Millar. 1995. "The papyrology of the Roman Near East: A survey." *JRS* 95, 214–35.

Cracco Ruggini, Lellia. 1980. "Nuclei immigrati e forze indigene in tre grandi centri commerciali dell'impero." In J. H. D'Arms and E. C. Kopf, eds, *The Seaborne Commerce of Ancient Rome*. Memoirs of the American Academy in Rome, 36. Rome: American Academy at Rome, 55–76.

de Blois, Lukas, ed. 2001. *Administration, Prosopography and Appointment Policies in the Roman Empire: Proceedings of the First Workshop of the International Network Impact of Empire (Roman Empire, 27 B.C.–A.D. 406), Leiden, June 28–July 1, 2000*. Amsterdam: Gieben.

Dietz, K. 1980. *Senatus contra principem: Untersuchungen zur senatorischen Opposition gegen Kaiser Maximinus Thrax*. Munich: Beck.

Dodgeon, M. H., and S. N. C. Lieu, eds. 1991. *The Roman Eastern Frontier and the Persian Wars*. London: Routledge.

Drew-Bear, Thomas, W. Eck and P. Herrmann. 1977. "*Sacrae Litterae*." *Chiron* 7, 355–83.

Drinkwater, J. F. 1987. *The Gallic Empire: Separatism and Continuity in the North-Western Provinces of the Roman Empire*, AD 260–274. Stuttgart: Steiner.

Dvornik, Francis. 1934. "The authority of the state in the oecumenical councils." *Christian East* 14, 95–108.

Edmondson, Jonathan. 1989. "Mining in the later Roman empire and beyond: Continuity or disruption?" *JRS* 79, 84–102.

Elsner, Jaś. 2012. "Sacrifice in late Roman art." In Chris Faraone and Fred Naiden, eds, *Greek and Roman Animal Sacrifice: Ancient Victims, Modern Observers*. Cambridge: Cambridge University Press.

Feissel, D., and J. Gascou. 1995. "Documents d'archives romains inédits du Moyen Euphrate (IIIe s. après J.C.)." *Journal des Savants* 1995, 65–119; (with J. Teixidor) 1997, 3–57; and 2000, 157–208.

Fink, R. O., A. S. Hoey and W. F. Snyder. 1940. "The *Feriale Duranum*." *YClS* 7, 1–222.

Fournier, Julien. 2010. *Entre tutelle romaine et autonomie civique: L'administration judiciaire dans les provinces hellénophones de l'empire romain. 129 av. J.-C.-235 apr. J.-C.*. Athens: École Française d'Athènes.

Frend, W. H. C. 1956. "A third-century inscription relating to *Angareia* in Phrygia." *JRS* 46, 46–56.

Frend, W. H. C. 1965. *Martyrdom and Persecution in the Early Church: A Study of a Conflict from the Maccabees to Donatus*. Oxford: Blackwell.

Gallazzi, C. 1975. "La titolatura di Vaballato come riflesso della politica di Palmira." *Numismatica e Antichità Classiche* 4, 249–65.

Gardner, Iain, and Samuel N. C. Lieu, eds. 2004. *Manichaean Texts from the Roman Empire*. Cambridge: Cambridge University Press.

Gardner, Jane F. 2001. "Making citizens: The operation of the *lex Irnitana*." In Lukas de Blois, ed., *Administration, Prosopography and Appointment Policies in the Roman Empire: Proceedings of the First Workshop of the International Network Impact of Empire (Roman*

Empire, 27 B.C.–A.D. *406), Leiden, June 28–July 1, 2000.* Amsterdam: Gieben, 215–29.

Garnsey, Peter, and Richard Saller, 1987. *The Roman Empire: Economy, Society, Culture.* Berkeley: University of California Press.

Gerhardt, Thomas. 2006. "Zur Geschichte des Krisenbegriffs." In Klaus-Peter Johne, Thomas Gerhardt and Udo Hartmann, eds, *Deleto paene imperio Romano: Transformationsprozesse des Römischen Reiches im 3. Jahrhundert und ihre Rezeption in der Neuzeit.* Stuttgart: Steiner, 381–410.

Giardina, Andrea. 2006. "Préface." In Marie-Henriette Quet, ed., *La crise de l'empire romain de Marc Aurèle à Constantin.* Paris: PUPS, 11–18.

Giardina, Andrea. 2007. "The crisis of the third century." In Walter Scheidel, Ian Morris and Richard Saller, eds, *The Cambridge Economic History of the Greco-Roman World.* Cambridge: Cambridge University Press, 757–64.

Gibbon, Edward. 1994. *The History of the Decline and Fall of the Roman Empire,* ed. David Womersley. 3 volumes. London: Allen Lane.

Gilliam, J. F. 1965. "Dura rosters and the 'Constitutio Antoniniana'." *Historia* 14, 74–92.

Guey, J. 1961. "Deniers (d'or) et denier d'or (de compte) anciens." *Syria* 38, 261–74.

Hanslik, R. 1958. "Vibius. 58." *RE* VIII.A.2, cols 1984–94.

Hasebroek, J. 1921. *Untersuchungen zur Geschichte des Kaisers Septimius Severus.* Heidelberg: C. Winter.

Hauken, Tor. 1998. *Petition and Response: An Epigraphic Study of Petitions to Roman Emperors, 181–249.* Bergen: Norwegian Institute at Athens.

Haynes, Ian P. 1997. "Religion in the Roman army: Unifying aspects and regional trends." In Hubert Cancik and Jörg Rüpke, eds, *Römische Reichsreligion und Provinzialreligion.* Tübingen: Mohr Siebeck, 113–26.

Heather, Peter, and John Matthews. 1991. *The Goths in the Fourth Century.* Liverpool: Liverpool University Press.

Hekster, Olivier. 2008. *Rome and its Empire,* AD *193–284.* Edinburgh: Edinburgh University Press.

Hekster, Olivier, Gerda de Kleijn and Daniëlle Slootjes, eds. 2007. *Crises and the Roman Empire.* Leiden: Brill.

Helgeland, J. 1978. "Roman army religion." *ANRW* 2.16.2, 1470–505.

Henze, W. 1896. "Aureolus." *RE* II.2, cols 2545–6.

Herrmann, Peter. 1972. "Überlegungen zur Datierung der Constitutio Antoniniana." *Chiron* 2, 519–30.

Herrmann, Peter. 1975. "Eine Kaiserurkunde der Zeit Marc Aurels aus Milet." *MDAI(I)* 25, 149–66.

Herrmann, Peter. 1990. *Hilferufe aus römischen Provinzen.* Göttingen: Vandenhoeck & Ruprecht.

Honoré, Tony. 1994. *Emperors and Lawyers*. 2nd edition. Oxford: Clarendon Press.

Hopkins, Keith. 1965. "Elite mobility in the Roman empire." *Past & Present* 32, 12–26.

Hopkins, Keith. 1983. *Death and Renewal*. Cambridge: Cambridge University Press.

Hörig, Monika, and Elmar Schwertheim, eds. 1987. *Corpus cultus Iovis Dolicheni (CCID)*. Leiden: Brill.

Isaac, Benjamin. 1990. *The Limits of Empire: The Roman Army in the East*. Oxford: Clarendon Press.

Johne, Klaus-Peter, Thomas Gerhardt and Udo Hartmann, eds. 2006. *Deleto paene imperio Romano: Transformationsprozesse des Römischen Reiches im 3. Jahrhundert und ihre Rezeption in der Neuzeit*. Stuttgart: Steiner.

Jones, C. P. 1984. "The *Sacrae Litterae* of 204: Two colonial copies." *Chiron* 14, 93–9.

Jones, C. P. 2001. "The Claudian monument at Patara." *ZPE* 137, 161–8.

Jongman, Wim. 2007. "Gibbon was right: The decline and fall of the Roman economy." In Olivier Hekster, Gerda de Kleijn and Daniëlle Slootjes, eds, *Crises and the Roman Empire*. Leiden: Brill, 183–99.

Kaizer, Ted. 2009. "Language and religion in Dura-Europos." In Hannah Cotton, Robert G. Hoyland, Jonathan J. Price and David J. Wasserstein, eds, *From Hellenism to Islam: Cultural and Linguistic Change in the Roman Near East*. Cambridge: Cambridge University Press, 235–53.

Kaizer, Ted. 2009. "Patterns of worship in Dura-Europos: A case study of religious life in the classical Levant outside the main cult centres." In C. Bonnet, V. Pirenne-Delforge and D. Praet, eds, *Les religions orientales dans le monde grec et romain cent ans après Cumont, 1906–2006: Bilan historique et historiographique*. Brussels: Belgisch Historisch Instituut te Rome, 153–72.

Kantor, Georgy. Forthcoming. *Roman and Local Law in Asia Minor, 133 BC–AD 212*. Oxford: Oxford University Press.

Kantorowicz, Ernst. 1961. "Gods in uniform." *Proceedings of the American Philosophical Society* 105, 368–93 = Kantorowicz, 1965. *Selected Studies*. Locust Valley, NY: Augustin, 7–24.

Kienast, Dietmar. 1990. *Römische Kaisertabelle: Grundzüge einer römischen Kaiserchronologie*. Darmstadt: Wissenschaftliche Buchgesellschaft.

Kneissl, P. 1969. *Die Siegestitulatur der römischen Kaiser*. Göttingen: Vandenhoeck & Ruprecht.

Knipfing, John R. 1923. "The *libelli* of the Decian persecution." *Harvard Theological Review* 16, 345–90.

König, Ingemar. 1981. *Die gallischen Usurpatoren von Postumus bis Tetricus*. Munich: Beck.

Krisch, Nico. 2010. *Beyond Constitutionalism: The Pluralist Structure of*

Postnational Law. New York: Oxford University Press.

Kruecher, Gerald. 1998. "Die Regierungszeit Aurelians und die griechischen Papyri aus Ägypten." *Archiv für Papyrusforschung* 44, 255–74.

Levick, Barbara, 2000. *The Government of the Roman Empire*, 2nd edition. New York: Routledge.

Liebeschuetz, Wolf. 2007. "Was there a crisis of the third century?" In Olivier Hekster, Gerda de Kleijn and Daniëlle Slootjes, eds, *Crises and the Roman Empire*. Leiden: Brill, 11–20.

Lo Cascio, Elio, 1986. "Teoria e politica monetaria a Roma tra III e IV d.C." In Andrea Giardina, ed., *Società romana e impero tardo antico*, 4 vols. Rome: Laterza.

Lörincz, B. 1979. "C. Gabinius Barbarus Pompeianus, Statthalter von Moesia Superior." *ZPE* 33, 157–60.

MacMullen, Ramsay. 1984. "The legion as a society." *Historia* 33, 440–56, reprinted in MacMullen, 1990. *Changes in the Roman Empire*. Princeton: Princeton University Press, 225–35.

MacMullen, Ramsay. 1993. "The unromanized in Rome." In Shaye J. D. Cohen and Ernest S. Frerichs, eds, *Diasporas in Antiquity*. Brown Judaic Studies, 288. Atlanta: Scholars Press, 47–64.

Mann, Michael. 1986. "The autonomous power of the state: Its origins, mechanisms, and results." In John A. Hall, ed., *States in History*. Oxford: Blackwell, 109–36.

Mattingly, Harold. 1950. "The imperial '*vota*'." *Proceedings of the British Academy* 36, 155–95.

Millar, Fergus. 1962. "The date of the Constitutio Antoniniana." *Journal of Egyptian Archaeology* 48, 124–31.

Millar, Fergus. 1963. "The equestrian career under the empire." *JRS* 53, 194–200 = Millar, 2003. *Rome, the Greek World and the East*, vol. 2: *Government, Society, and Culture in the Roman Empire*, eds Hannah M. Cotton and Guy M. Rogers. Chapel Hill: University of North Carolina Press, 151–9.

Millar, Fergus. 1964. *A Study of Cassius Dio*. Oxford: Clarendon Press.

Millar, Fergus. 1967. "Emperors at work." *JRS* 57, 9–19 = Millar, 2003. *Rome, the Greek World, and the East*, vol. 2: *Government, Society, and Culture in the Roman Empire*, eds Hannah M. Cotton and Guy M. Rogers. Chapel Hill: University of North Carolina Press, 3–22.

Millar, Fergus. 1969. "P. Herennius Dexippus: The Greek world and the third-century invasions." *JRS* 59, 12–29 = Millar, 2003. *Rome, the Greek World, and the East*, vol. 2: *Government, Society, and Culture in the Roman Empire*, eds Hannah M. Cotton and Guy M. Rogers. Chapel Hill: University of North Carolina Press, 265–97.

Millar, Fergus. 1984. "Condemnation to hard labour in the Roman empire, from the Julio-Claudians to Constantine." *Papers of the British School at Rome* 52, 123–47 = Millar, 2003. *Rome, the Greek World, and the East*, vol. 2: *Government, Society, and Culture in the Roman Empire*, eds Hannah M. Cotton and Guy M. Rogers. Chapel Hill: University of North Carolina Press, 120–5.0

Millar, Fergus. 1992 [1977]. *The Emperor in the Roman World*. 2nd edition. Ithaca: Cornell University Press.

Millar, Fergus. 1993. *The Roman Near East, 31 BC–AD 337*. Cambridge, MA: Harvard University Press.

Millar, Fergus. 1999. "The Greek east and Roman law: The dossier of M. Cn. Licinius Rufinus." *JRS* 89, 90–108 = Millar, 2003. *Rome, the Greek World, and the East*, vol. 2: *Government, Society, and Culture in the Roman Empire*, eds Hannah M. Cotton and Guy M. Rogers. Chapel Hill: University of North Carolina Press, 435–64.

Millar, Fergus. 2002. *Rome, the Greek World, and the East*, vol. 1: *The Roman Republic and the Augustan Revolution*, eds Hannah M. Cotton and Guy M. Rogers. Chapel Hill: University of North Carolina Press.

Millar, Fergus. 2003. *Rome, the Greek World, and the East*, vol. 2: *Government, Society, and Culture in the Roman Empire*, eds Hannah M. Cotton and Guy M. Rogers. Chapel Hill: University of North Carolina Press.

Millar, Fergus. 2006. *Rome, the Greek World, and the East*, vol. 3: *The Greek world, the Jews, and the East*, eds Hannah M. Cotton and Guy M. Rogers. Chapel Hill: University of North Carolina Press.

Mitteis, Ludwig. 1891. *Reichsrecht und Volksrecht in den östlichen Provinzen des römischen Kaiserreichs*. Leipzig: Teubner.

Nappo, Dario. 2007. "The impact of the third century crisis on the international trade with the east." In Olivier Hekster, Gerda de Kleijn and Daniëlle Slootjes, eds, *Crises and the Roman Empire*. Leiden: Brill, 233–44.

Nongbri, B. 2008. "Dislodging 'embedded' religion: A brief note on a scholarly trope." *Numen* 55, 440–60.

Oliver, James H. 1979. "Greek applications for Roman trials." *American Journal of Philology* 100, 543–58.

Parsons, P. J. 1967. "Philippus Arabs and Egypt." *JRS* 57, 134–41.

Peachin, Michael. 1989. "Once more A.D. 238." *Athenaeum* 77, 594–604.

Peachin, Michael. 1990. *Roman Imperial Titulature and Chronology, A.D. 235–284*. Amsterdam: Gieben.

Peachin, Michael. 1996. *Iudex vice Caesaris: Deputy Emperors and the Administration of Justice during the Principate*. Stuttgart: Steiner.

Pekáry, Thomas. 1961. "Le tribut aux Perses et les finances de Philippe l'Arab." *Syria* 38, 275–83.

Pighi, G. B. 1941. *De ludis saecularibus populi Romani Quiritium libri sex*. Milan: Società Editrice Vita e Pensiero, 1941; 2nd edn Amsterdam: P. Schippers, 1965.

Pollard, Nigel. 1996. "The Roman army as 'total institution' in the Near East? Dura-Europos as a case study." In David Kennedy, ed., *The Roman*

Army in the East. Ann Arbor: Journal of Roman Archaeology, 211–27.

Potter, David S. 1990. *Prophecy and History in the Crisis of the Roman Empire: A Historical Commentary on the Thirteenth Sibylline Oracle*. Oxford: Clarendon Press.

Potter, David S. 2004. *The Roman Empire at Bay, AD 180–395*. London: Routledge.

Raggi, Andrea. 2004. "The epigraphic dossier of Seleucus of Rhosus: A revised edition." *ZPE* 147, 123–38 = *SEG* 54, 1625.

Rathbone, Dominic. 1986. "The dates of the recognition in Egypt of the emperors from Caracalla to Diocletianus." *ZPE* 62, 101–31.

Rathbone, Dominic. 1996. "Monetisation, not price-inflation, in third-century AD Egypt?" In C. E. King and D. G. Wigg, eds, *Coin Finds and Coin Use in the Roman World: The Thirteenth Oxford Symposium on Coinage and Monetary History 25–27.3.1993*. Berlin: Gebr. Mann, 321–39.

Reynolds, J. 1982. *Aphrodisias and Rome*. London: Society for the Promotion of Roman Studies.

Richardson, J. S. 1983. "The *Tabula Contrebiensis*: Roman law in Spain in the early first century B.C." *JRS* 73, 33–41.

Robert, Louis. 1970. "Deux concours grecs à Rome." *CR Acad. Inscr.* 1970, 7–27 at 13–17 = Robert, 2007. *Choix d'écrits*. Paris: Les Belles Lettres, 247–66.

Robert, Louis. 1994. *Le martyre de Pionios prêtre de Smyrne*. Revised and completed by G. W. Bowersock and C. P. Jones. Washington, DC: Dumbarton Oaks.

Rostovtzeff, Mikhail. 1942. "*Vexillum* and Victory." *JRS* 32, 92–106.

Roussel, P., and F. de Visscher. 1942/3. "Les inscriptions du temple de Dmeir." *Syria* 23, 173–200.

Rubin, Zvi. 1975. "Dio, Herodian, and Severus' second Parthian war." *Chiron* 5, 419–41.

Rubin, Zvi. 1980. *Civil-War Propaganda and Historiography*. Brussels: Revue d'Études Latines.

Rüpke, Jörg. 2006. "Religion in the *lex Ursonensis*." In C. Ando and J. Rüpke, eds, *Religion and Law in Classical and Christian Rome*. Stuttgart: Steiner, 34–46.

Sartre, Maurice. 2001. *D'Alexandre à Zénobie: Histoire du Levant antique, IVe siècle av. J.-C. – IIIe siècle ap. J.-C.* Paris: Fayard.

Šašel, J. 1983. "Dolichenus-Heiligtum in Praetorium Latobicorum: Caracalla, Caesar, *imperator destinatus*." *ZPE* 50, 203–8.

Sasse, C. 1962. "Literaturübersicht zur C.A." *Journal of Juristic Papyrology* 14, 109–49.

Scheid, John. 1985. "Numa et Jupiter ou les dieux citoyens de Rome." *Archives de Sciences Sociales des Religions* 59, 41–53.

Scheid, John. 1999. "Aspects religieux de la municipalisation: Quelques réflexions générales." In M. Dondin-Payre and M.-T. Raepsaet-Charlier, eds, *Cités, municipes, colonies: Les processus de municipalisation en Gaule et en Germanie sous le haut empire romain*. Paris: Publications de la Sorbonne, 381–423.

Scheid, John. 2001. *Religion et piété à Rome*. 2nd edition. Paris: Albin Michel.

Shaw, Brent. 1986. "Autonomy and tribute: Mountain and plain in Mauretania Tingitana." In P. Baduel, ed., *Desert et montagne: Hommage à Jean Dresch. Revue de l'Occident Musulman et de la Méditerranée* 41–2, 66–89.

Sherwin-White, A. N. 1973. *The Roman Citizenship*. 2nd edition. Oxford: Clarendon Press.

Sizgorich, Thomas N. 2009. *Violence and Belief in Late Antiquity: Militant Devotion in Christianity and Islam*. Philadelphia: University of Pennsylvania Press.

Stein, Ernst. 1918. "Iulius. 386. Philippus." *RE* X.1, cols 755–70.

Stoll, Oliver. 2007. "The religions of the armies." In Paul Erdkamp, ed., *A Companion to the Roman Army*. Oxford: Blackwell, 451–76.

Stolte, Bernard H. 2001. "The impact of Roman law in Egypt and the Near East in the third century A.D.: The documentary evidence." In Lukas de Blois, ed., *Administration, Prosopography and Appointment Policies in the Roman Empire: Proceedings of the First Workshop of the International Network Impact of Empire (Roman Empire, 27 B.C.–A.D. 406), Leiden, June 28–July 1, 2000*. Amsterdam: Gieben, 167–79.

Swan, Peter Michael. 2004. *The Augustan Succession: An Historical Commentary on Cassius Dio's Roman History, books 55–56. 9 B.C.–A.D. 14*. New York: Oxford University Press.

Talbert, R. J. A. 1984. *The Senate of Imperial Rome*. Princeton: Princeton University Press.

Verboven, K. 2011. "Resident aliens and translocal merchant *collegia* in the Roman empire." In Olivier Hekster and Ted Kaizer, eds, *Frontiers in the Roman World*. Leiden: Brill, 335–48.

Walker, D. R. 1978. *The Metrology of the Roman Silver Coinage*, vol. 3. Oxford: British Archaeological Reports.

Wallace-Hadrill, Andrew. 1997. "*Mutatio morum*: The idea of a cultural revolution." In T. N. Habinek and A. Schiesaro, eds, *The Roman Cultural Revolution*. Cambridge: Cambridge University Press, 3–22.

Watson, Alan, ed. 1985. *The Digest of Justinian*. Philadelphia: University of Pennsylvania Press.

Watson, Alaric. 1999. *Aurelian and the Third Century*. London: Routledge.

Welles, C. Bradford. 1969. "The gods of Dura-Europos." In R. Stiehl and H. E. Stier, eds, *Beiträge zur alten Geschichte und deren Nachleben: Festschrift für Fritz Altheim*, vol. 2. Berlin: De Gruyter, 50–65.

Will, Ernest, 1966. "Le sac de Palmyre." In R. Chevallier, ed., *Mélanges d'archéologie et d'histoire offerts à André Piganiol.* Paris: SEVPEN, 1409–16.

Witschel, Christian. 1999. *Krise, Rezession, Stagnation? Der Westen des römischen Reiches im 3. Jahrhundert n. Chr.* Frankfurt: Marthe Clauss.

Witschel, Christian. 2002. "Meilensteine als historische Quelle? Das Beispiel Aquileia." *Chiron* 32, 325–93.

Witschel, Christian. 2004. "Re-evaluating the Roman west in the 3rd c. A.D." *Journal of Roman Archaeology* 17, 251–81.

Witschel, Christian. 2006. "Zur Situation im römischen Afrika während des 3. Jahrhunderts." In Klaus-Peter Johne, Thomas Gerhardt and Udo Hartmann, eds, *Deleto paene imperio Romano: Transformationsprozesse des Römischen Reiches im 3. Jahrhundert und ihre Rezeption in der Neuzeit.* Stuttgart: Steiner, 145–221.

Woolf, Greg. 2011. *Tales of the Barbarians: Ethnography and Empire in the Roman West.* Oxford: Blackwell.

Index